The Life and Times of Abū Tammām

Letter from the General Editor

The Library of Arabic Literature makes available Arabic editions and English translations of significant works of Arabic literature, with an emphasis on the seventh to nineteenth centuries. The Library of Arabic Literature thus includes texts from the pre-Islamic era to the cusp of the modern period, and encompasses a wide range of genres, including poetry, poetics, fiction, religion, philosophy, law, science, travel writing, history, and historiography.

Books in the series are edited and translated by internationally recognized scholars. They are published as hardcovers in parallel-text format with Arabic and English on facing pages, as English-only paperbacks, and as downloadable Arabic editions. For some texts, the series also publishes separate scholarly editions with full critical apparatus.

The Library encourages scholars to produce authoritative Arabic editions, accompanied by modern, lucid English translations, with the ultimate goal of introducing Arabic's rich literary heritage to a general audience of readers as well as to scholars and students.

The Library of Arabic Literature is supported by a grant from the New York University Abu Dhabi Institute and is published by NYU Press.

Philip F. Kennedy
General Editor, Library of Arabic Literature

About this Paperback

This paperback edition differs in a few respects from its dual-language hardcover predecessor. Because of the compact trim size the pagination has changed, but paragraph numbering has been retained to facilitate cross-referencing with the hardcover. Material that referred to the Arabic edition has been updated to reflect the English-only format, and other material has been corrected and updated where appropriate. For information about the Arabic edition on which this English translation is based and about how the LAL Arabic text was established, readers are referred to the hardcover.

The Life and Times of Abū Tammām

by

Abū Bakr Muḥammad ibn Yaḥyā l-Ṣūlī

preceded by

Al-Ṣūlī's Epistle to Abū l-Layth Muzāḥim ibn Fātik

translated by
Beatrice Gruendler

foreword by
Terence Cave

volume editors
James E. Montgomery
Tahera Qutbuddin

NEW YORK UNIVERSITY PRESS
New York

NEW YORK UNIVERSITY PRESS
New York

Library of Congress Cataloging-in-Publication Data
Names: Suli, Muhammad ibn Yahya, –approximately 947 author. | Gruendler, Beatrice, 1964– translator. | Montgomery, James E. (James Edward), 1962– editor. | Qutbuddin, Tahera editor. | Suli, Muhammad ibn Yahya, –approximately 947. Risalat Abi Bakr al-Suli ilba Muzahim ibn Fatik. English.
Title: The life and times of Abu Tammam : preceded by Al-Suli's Epistle to Abu l-Layth Muzaim ibn Fatik / by Abu Bakr Muhammad ibn Yahya al-Suli ; translated by Beatrice Gruendler ; volume editors, James E. Montgomery, Tahera Qutbuddin.
Other titles: Akhbar Abi Tammam. English
Description: New York : New York University Press, 2018. | Includes bibliographical references and index.
Identifiers: LCCN 2018012793 (print) | LCCN 2018018833 (ebook) | ISBN 9781479874699 (e-book) | ISBN 9781479897933 (e-book) | ISBN 9781479868025 (pbk. : alk. paper)
Subjects: LCSH: Abu Tammam Habib ibn Aws al-Ta.i, active 808-842. | Poets, Arab—750-1258—Biography.
Classification: LCC PJ7701.6.T35 (ebook) | LCC PJ7701.6.T35 Z813 2018 (print) | DCC 892.7/134 [B] —dc23
LC record available at https://lccn.loc.gov/2018012793

New York University Press books are printed on acid-free paper, and their binding materials are chosen for strength and durability.

Series design and composition by Nicole Hayward
Typeset in Adobe Text

Manufactured in the United States of America

10 9 8 7 6 5 4 3 2 1

To my parents
Wilfried and Lilo Gründler
with love

Contents

Abbreviations

D	Abū Tammām, *Dīwān*, edited by M. ʿAzzām, 4 vols., Cairo 1951–65
GAS	Sezgin, *Geschichte des arabischen Schrifttums*
EI2	*The Encyclopaedia of Islam*, new [second] edition
EI3	*The Encyclopaedia of Islam*, third edition
EAL	Meisami and Starkey, *Encyclopedia of Arabic Literature*
v., vv.	verse(s)
var.	variant
WKAS	Ullmann, *Wörterbuch der klassischen arabischen Sprache*, 2 vols., Wiesbaden, 1970–2000
ا	al-Ṣūlī, *Akhbār Abī Tammām*, Istanbul Fatih 3900
ع	al-Ṣūlī, *Akhbār Abī Tammām*, edited by K. ʿAsākir, M. ʿAzzām and N. al-Hindī, Cairo, 1937
ه	emendations in ع made by N. al-Hindī
عس	emendations in ع made by K. ʿAsākir

Foreword

TERENCE CAVE

> "Rhymes and great deeds last forever
> like a string when fitted with a center pearl." (§60)

In 223/838, the armies of the Abbasid caliphate, led by the Caliph al-Muʿtaṣim himself, carried out a devastating retaliatory attack on the Byzantine Empire, laying siege to the key city of Amorium, sacking it, and slaughtering large numbers of its inhabitants. The victory, which marked a significant realignment in the balance of power between the Muslim and the Christian worlds in the East, was celebrated by Abū Tammām at the peak of his career in his most famous ode (for an abridged version, see §§61.2–3; also §§20.2–5). It was written down, copied, memorized, and widely read among the cultural elite, and brought Abū Tammām immediate financial rewards from the caliph as well as fame. Abū Bakr al-Ṣūlī's compilation, *The Life and Times of Abū Tammām*, provides us with abundant insights into this and other similar episodes.

At the other end of the Mediterranean, just sixty years earlier, another memorable battle was waged between Christians and Muslims. In 161/778, the rearguard of Charlemagne's expeditionary force was ambushed and destroyed at Roncesvaux in the Pyrenees as they were returning northwards. What is now known as the *Song of Roland*, written down some 300 years later, represents this disaster as an episode in a long-term struggle between the Christian forces of Charlemagne and his Muslim adversaries. In fact, it seems that Charlemagne had done a deal with the Abbasid dynasty in Spain to quell the Umayyads, whose army had earlier ventured north as far as Tours, while the ambush at Roncesvaux was executed by Basque forces, angry at Charlemagne's pre-emptive destruction of the city walls of their capital Pamplona. Throughout the whole of this period, the Carolingian dynasty traded with the Abbasid caliphate and sponsored reciprocal diplomatic visits, receiving handsome presents from (among others) al-Muʿtaṣim. The conquest of Amorium was indeed welcomed by the Carolingians since it weakened the political outreach of the Eastern Church and the threat it posed to their own imperial ambitions.

The culture of the Carolingian court is often celebrated as a high-water mark in earlier medieval history. Charlemagne promoted an intensive program of copying and compilation which ensured the transmission of the extant writings of classical (primarily Latin) antiquity, carried out by scribes who for the most part belonged to religious orders. Charlemagne himself couldn't write, and probably couldn't read either, and nearly everything written down in this period was in Latin, the lingua franca of the linguistically diverse regions and kingdoms of Europe. The first extant document written in the European vernaculars was the Oaths of Strasbourg of 842, when Abū Tammām was still alive. The native cultures of Europe were handed down orally until the rise of vernacular writing as a cultural instrument in the eleventh century, as the example of the *Song of Roland* shows.

The Life and Times of Abū Tammām, compiled nearly a century after the death of the poet himself, bears retrospective witness to a culture where the habits of oral composition—live performance, improvisation, memorization, authentication by personal witness—are still deeply ingrained. At the same time, it shows that culture at work preserving valued texts in written form. So we find copying and collection here too, facilitated by new technologies of paper-making; the agents in this process of transmission were not clerics, however, but members of a literate class who also participated in the day-to-day administration of the social and political world. And what was thereby made available for posterity was not a canonized set of texts imported from an alien culture, written in a language that had already become remote from the vernacular, but the rich repertory of classical Arabic poetry stretching unbroken from the pre-Islamic Bedouin poets to the fourth/tenth-century world of Abū Bakr al-Ṣūlī and beyond. Although Abū Tammām himself is the "pearl on the string" of al-Ṣūlī's masterwork, the whole tradition, with its historical phases and its contrasting styles, its cohorts of sponsors and scholars, its debates and controversies, comes into remarkably clear focus in his graphically documented account.

Before moving from this broad comparative perspective to Abū Tammām's life and work as a poet, one other key point needs to be made. Poetry, together with everything that it represents—memorialization, cultural intelligence, linguistic precision, communicative flair, presence of mind, transmission of experience—is central to this culture in ways and to an extent that are perhaps hard to fathom for our instrumentalized, functionalized world. It is overwhelmingly clear, even on the sole testimony of this book, that poetry *mattered* to society at large, not only to poets and a few cultivated patrons, but across a spectrum that included government officials and administrators, merchants, servants, slaves. It is a currency, representing an imaginative capital that depends on constant reassessment and recalibration. It is inextricably enmeshed with the personal politics of those in power and their clients. Its value both as a practice and as a conserved treasure ("Rhymes and great deeds last forever") is absolutely taken for granted. No one in that era thinks of arguing that the aesthetic sphere is, or should be, disjoined from the public sphere. No one would have believed that poetry was somehow merely showy language, a game of commerce and elitist rivalry. The value that poetry had as a medium of communication could only have been derived from the sense of authenticity that it delivered. Hence, again, the chains of testimonials, the eye-witness records, the scenes of friction between the patrons and their clients, or between rival clients, and the long-remembered moments of consummate performance: together, they constitute an extraordinary demonstration of the binding power of poetry in the human ecology.

• • •

> ... poetry pours from men's minds:
> when one group of clouds departs, another follows. (§69.3)

Although Abū Bakr al-Ṣūlī's "life" of Abū Tammām is not a biographical narrative, it contains many biographical episodes, chosen for their relevance to the compiler's purpose, and hence presented in an order which is thematic rather than chronological. After the introductory epistle, the book opens with an extended section bearing witness to the poet's superiority, then moves on to episodes detailing his dealings with a number of leading contemporary figures. It is only in the final sections of the compilation that we find some fragments of biography proper—remarks about Abū Tammām's physical appearance and voice (§156: "he spoke smoothly and eloquently like the Bedouin"), the somewhat uncertain date of his birth, the mediocre poetry of his brother and his son, and his apparently quite sudden death at the age of around forty; the lamentations that ensued, endorsing his eminent place in the canon of Arabic poetry, are transcribed in a concluding section. The celebration of his brilliance as a poet and the disparagement of those who take a different view thus remains the central thread of the whole work; a good deal of this encomiastic strategy is in fact already outlined in the lengthy "Epistle to Abū l-Layth Muzāhim ibn Fātik" which serves as a general preface and an advertisement for al-Ṣūlī's own work as compiler and editor.

As Beatrice Gruendler's Introduction indicates, a key issue which emerges repeatedly in al-Ṣūlī's account of Abū Tammām's merits is the question of what in the European Renaissance is called "imitation" (*imitatio*, the recycling of materials from earlier writers).

No one in either culture expected poets to be uncompromisingly "original." The tradition within which they worked supplied genres, poetic forms, themes, and modes of treatment. Recognition of familiar tropes, techniques, and themes was precisely the objective of the intensive activity of memorizing, repetition, reworking, and editorial documentation to which this book bears witness. What was constantly recalibrated and renegotiated was, on the one hand, the borderline between plagiarism, literary theft, and authentic imitation, and on the other, the acceptability or otherwise of unexpected departures from the norm.

These debates are never, in this work at least, general and theoretical. They are particular, focusing on the agency and credit of individuals. Theories of "the death of the author" and "intertextuality" would have seemed strange and perverse to the actors in this culture; so would the post-Romantic or modernist notion of "originality." In a typical scene of performance, the Abbasid poet ʿUmārah ibn ʿAqīl, famed for the purity of his language, recites one of his own poems to his friends and receives their unqualified praise (§50.1): "We never heard a poem better than this one rhyming in *R*. God favor you, ʿUmārah!" The poet counters by citing an *R* poem by Abū Tammām which, he says, has "blown away any poem in its style." One of those present knows it by heart and recites extracts from it, interspersed with comments on its merits: "How brilliant, by God," said ʿUmārah, "he found what had been lost to other poets, as if it had been set aside for him." This extraordinary remark takes for granted that poetic materials and poetic language form an existing reservoir; the "finding" that ʿUmārah refers to (again like the *inventio* of Renaissance poetics and rhetoric) is an authentic innovation within the spectrum of what is poetically possible and legitimate.

In scenes of performance such as this, or in the account of Abū Tammām's recitation of his Amorium ode, a great deal will be lost to a reader unfamiliar with the techniques of classical Arabic poetry (the *R*-rhyme, for example), or indeed with the Arabic language itself. Yet the thrill of the performance as such is still palpable, even in translation, together with the passionate commitment of the audiences and commentators. And as one reads and re-reads these consummate artifacts produced by one of the most vibrant and exhilarating cultures of the known world, something begins to emerge: the poetry begins to come alive, despite the strangeness of its diction and the loss of essential contexts. There are memories here of the wanderings and lifestyle of the Bedouin tribes, their poets (the "ancients"), and their ready wit (§49.1). There is a potent blend of cultural and ethical values—generosity, wealth, power, violence, revenge. There are sudden turns of phrase that deliver a momentary insight into the possible relations in this culture between belief and counter-belief: "Wisdom is the believer's lost camel. Retrieve your lost camel, even from the polytheists" (§199). There are personal rivalries in the pursuit of the highest fees and the most exquisite phrasings. There is praise and insult, desire both heterosexual and homosexual. There is the flavor of date wine (§§91.1–5), the texture of fabrics, and how it felt to wear them (§§92.1–5):

We were dressed in the garb of summer
  by a generous man whose own garb is noble and heroic deeds.
A Sābirī gown and a tunic
  like eggshells or snakeskin,
Like a shimmering mirage in its beauty
  but unlike its false promise.
Finest linen, trembling in the wind
  by unknown Fate's heeded command,
Fluttering, as if it were ever
  the heart of a man in love or the innards of a man in fear.
Hugging the body,
  It seems part of your ribs and elbows. (§92.2)

In these ways, the poems and their settings afford moments of intense communication, the transmission of experience and values across cultural borders. There is indeed a real sense in which Abū Bakr al-Ṣūlī's book inserts us, as readers from another world, into the chains of personal memory and testimony by means of which the author authenticates his materials and advertises their enduring value. Listen, for example, to this sequence from the section entitled "Abu Tammām as a Source":

> We cite Aḥmad, citing Aḥmad, citing Abū Tammām, who cites ʿAmr ibn Hāshim al-Sarawī as follows:
>
> We were talking at Muḥammad ibn ʿAmr al-Awzāʿī's place [. . .]. A Bedouin from the tribe of ʿUlaym ibn Janāb was present but did not say a word. "You have rightly been called the most taciturn of Bedouins," we said to him. "Will you not talk to the group?"
>
> "One man profits from his ear," the Bedouin replied. "The others profit from their tongue."
>
> "My goodness, how brilliant!" al-Awzāʿī exclaimed.
>
> We cite Aḥmad, who cites Aḥmad, who cites Abū Tammām as follows:
>
> One man said to another, "How beautiful your speech is!"
>
> "You make it so by listening so beautifully." (§§152–3)

Let us then, in conclusion, counterbalance the triumphalist theme of Abū Tammām's Amorium ode and prolong the theme of listening by invoking the poem that begins "Sleepless night of Abrashahr." On a visit to the city of Abrashahr, Abū Tammām is said to have fallen for "a singer with a beautiful voice who sang in Persian." He spent the night listening to her, even though he couldn't understand her words:

> [. . .] She played her strings, sorrowful and yearning;
> had they been able, her listeners would have given their life for her.
> I did not understand what she meant, but it set my heart on fire,
> for I understood her sorrow.

All night long I was like a blind man, broken-hearted,
In love with beauties he cannot see. (§§100.1–6)

Reading the poem in English in the twenty-first century is like falling in love with the ghost of her song as embodied in Abū Tammām's memory of it. He would surely have been pleased to know that both voices, hers and his, had survived close to twelve centuries of cultural conflict, change, and mutually beneficial exchange, crossing unexpected borders on the way.

Terence Cave
St. Johns College, Oxford

Acknowledgments

The author owes a debt of gratitude to the many people who helped see this volume into print, first of all to the general editor of the Library of Arabic Literature, Philip Kennedy, and the executive editors, Shawkat Toorawa and James Montgomery, for accepting this work in their series, and furthermore to my outside referees, Julia Bray and the late Wolfhart Heinrichs, for their encouraging comments and constructive criticism. It is my great regret that my Doktorvater could not see the completion of the book, to which his example as a scholar contributed so much. My style editor, David Brennan, has been a valiant support and inexhaustible source of ideas in my initial struggle to find modern English voices for al-Ṣūlī and Abū Tammām and his contemporaries. My first project editor, Tahera Qutbuddin, with her precise eye, suggested many improvements in content and form. Hugh Kennedy, Everett Rowson, and Letizia Osti generously helped me resolve puzzles in the text; my MA student Hatim Alzahrani commented on parts of the translation; Chip Rossetti kept reminding me gently but firmly that timeless scholarship has deadlines; and Gemma Juan-Simó assisted with logistical matters. I am grateful to my copy editor Allison Brown for her unfailing precision, to the digital production manager Stuart Brown for his artful Arabic typesetting, and to my Bachelor students at Freie Universität Berlin for their enthusiastic reception of a preprint draft. My special thanks go to my second project editor, James Montgomery, who chaperoned the book through its final stages and spared no effort in revising every detail from substance to style: his copious comments were always on the mark.

To the staff of the Süleymaniye Library I say thank you for making the unicum manuscript available to me, and to Bilal Orfali for providing me with a digital copy. I thank the professional staff of Widener Library, Harvard University, for making its excellent collection available to me for research on questions that arose during the process of translation. I also owe much to those scholars who first identified this important work, Khalīl ʿAsākir, Muḥammad ʿAzzām, and Naẓīr al-Islam al-Hindī; their careful edition left me few things to correct.

I could not have accomplished this (or any prior) book without the loving support of my parents, Lilo and Wilfried Gründler, even though for nearly three decades my work took me away from them to another continent. I complete this, having returned to their side of the Atlantic. And as literature is about life, Normand Mainville ensured that I did not forget and kept me in good spirits throughout the entire process.

Any errors that remain are mine alone.

Beatrice Gruendler
Berlin, June 2015

Introduction

> She longed to read *Ulysses*, and when Virginia [Woolf] produced it for her, Katherine [Mansfield] began by ridiculing it, and then suddenly said: "But theres something in this." This scene, Virginia thought, remembering it almost at the end of her life just after Joyce's death, "should figure I suppose in the history of literature."[1]

The Life and Times of Abū Tammām (*Akhbār Abī Tammām*) by Abū Bakr al-Ṣūlī, more than any other book, illustrates the role of poetry in premodern Islamic society. Composed over ten centuries ago, it brings together two salient personalities of cultural history from one of the most dynamic periods of Arabic poetry. This is the first English translation of the work.[2]

Abū Tammām

Abū Tammām (d. 231/845 or 232/846) is one of the most celebrated poets in the Arabic language. He ranks alongside Abū Nuwās (d. ca. 198/813), famed wine poet and hedonist, and al-Mutanabbī (d. 354/965), self-declared prophet and supreme panegyrist. Yet Abū Tammām is virtually unknown in the West. This is largely because his poetic style is very difficult, resulting in a dearth of translations of his verse. Furthermore, Abū Tammām excelled in the composition of the panegyric, a genre that does not sit well with current sensibilities and expectations about the nature and purpose of poetry. Still, classical Arabic poetry, including the panegyric as a major genre, was understood to be a powerful and prestigious form of communication, and a specific audience response was the declared goal of much of this poetry. The present book aims to remedy the dearth of translations and the obscurity of genre and poet by making many passages of Abū Tammām's odes available in English and by presenting these excerpts within their performance context, showing how these poems "worked"—that is to say, why they were written, which issues they treated, and how their audience reacted to them.

At first glance Abū Tammām[3] seems an unlikely candidate for a poetic career. Born in the Syrian countryside, and of Greek Christian background (his father owned a wine shop in Damascus), he engaged in menial occupations until he eventually took up the study of poetry. His success was slow in coming. His first patrons were local Syrian dignitaries whom he lampooned when his praise poems did not yield the desired result—payment. Panegyrics constituted the main source of income for a professional poet, though some deemed (the threat of) lampoons a more effective tool.

Abū Tammām's next patrons were generals in the army of Caliph al-Ma'mūn (r. 197–218/813–33). They became long-standing supporters and were the recipients of many of Abū Tammām's odes throughout their lives. Abū Tammām's career reached its peak under Caliph al-Muʿtaṣim (r. 218–27/833–42). The poet celebrated al-Muʿtaṣim's reign in famous odes, such as those on the conquest of the Byzantine border fortress Amorium, on the quelling of the Bābak revolt, and on the execution of General Afshīn for high treason.

Another group of patrons comprised regional rulers, some from as far away as Khurasan (northeast Iran), where Abū Tammām traveled to present them his odes. Government scribes and high-ranking civil servants also patronized the poet. In the last year of his life, Abū Tammām was appointed head of the postal service in Mosul through the good offices of one such patron. When Abū Tammām died, his loss was mourned by this patron and by many fellow poets.

Unlike many poets of the time, Abū Tammām did not serve an apprenticeship with any other poet, but studied his predecessors' work in book form (§65.2, §86.3). From such books he also compiled a number of anthologies, among them, *The Book on Bravery* (*Kitāb al-Ḥamāsah*). Abū Tammām is said to have put this book together in a patron's library when he was snowed in during his travels.

Abū Tammām's poetry captured the atmosphere of his time. In it he promoted and developed an avant-garde aesthetic that mirrored the intellectual and artistic flourishing of the day. It also reflected the greater cultural openness of the Abbasid dynasty, which programmatically imported foreign science and offered non-Arabs far greater opportunities for professional and social advancement than had previously been the case under the Umayyads (41–132/661–750). The Abbasid elite took pains to acquire and demonstrate their erudition. In Baghdad, grammarians and poets were important cultural forces. Poets no longer hailed solely from Arab tribes, nor did they need to follow the standards of linguistic purity generally held to be the preserve of the Bedouin. They now came from many backgrounds, especially Persian and Byzantine, and created new genres that reflected contemporary material and intellectual life. Baghdadi sophistication came to compete with the cultural ideal of Bedouin purity of language. Abū Tammām forcefully promoted a new avant-garde aesthetic that introduced more craftsmanship and rhetorical finesse into poetry. His verse most obviously displays the features of what came to be known as the "New Style" (*badīʿ*). Even his critics recognized that he had invented an impressive array of poetic motifs.

Abū Tammām relied greatly on his own ingenuity in introducing what some thought were incongruous elements into his particular brand of the New Style. He created logical twists, paradoxes, and antitheses, and specialized in the personification of abstract concepts. But he merged these with an archaic Bedouin lexicon and older poetic motifs. As a result, his poetry sounded very different from what had come before. It echoed the tradition but gave it a new feel, so much so that it shocked. It quickly became both wildly controversial and wildly popular. Some found it daring. Others deemed it strange. Abū Tammām was the talk of his time; whether one liked his verse or not, one had to be prepared to discuss it (§10.1). Al-Ṣūlī says as much himself, referring to Abū Tammām and other modern poets: "Their poetry is also more suited to its time and people employ it more in their gatherings, writings, pithy sayings, and petitions" (§11.2).

One social group that figures prominently in al-Ṣūlī's book is the scribes, who are ubiquitous as financial supporters and artistic partisans of Abū Tammām. In the far-flung lands of the Abbasid caliphate, these highly educated clerks became the mainstay of government. They came from many different backgrounds, and not all of them were Muslims, but their skills, sorely needed to run the empire, outweighed factors such as religious persuasion or ethnic provenance. In fact, non-Arabs (mostly Persians and Aramaic-speakers) flourished in administrative service. They swiftly climbed the social ladder, and some established veritable dynasties. Financially secure in their government employment, and enjoying the social status that came with their wealth, they were in a stronger position than were the poets and scholars on whom rulers called at their whim. These scribes acted as sponsors of poets, as go-betweens who secured stipends and rewards for them, and as amateur critics of poetry. Their profession necessitated training in sundry subjects of elite culture beyond basic competence in the Arabic language and script; some scribes even tried their hand at poetry themselves. The difference, however, was that they were not dependent on poetry as a source of income. Thus they judged it according to their taste and were open to new fashions, a liberty that the philologists could not afford, because their authority hinged on their expertise in the ancient corpus.

The tumultuous state of Abū Tammām's reception is conveyed in the fresh and refreshingly opinionated voice of Abū Bakr Muḥammad ibn Yaḥyā l-Ṣūlī (d. 335/946 or 336/947). He was writing a century after the events he records, but matters were not yet completely settled, though the debate had shifted from the Ancients (*awāʾil*) versus the Moderns (*muḥdathūn*) to the pitting of individual modern poets against one another. In introducing and commenting on Abū Tammām's life and poetry, al-Ṣūlī laid the groundwork for a tradition of serious poetic criticism of Abū Tammām's work. Al-Ṣūlī's contemporary al-Āmidī (d. 371/981–82), in his book *Weighing Up the Merits of Abū Tammām and His Disciple al-Buḥturī* (*al-Muwāzanah bayn shiʿr Abī Tammām wa-l-Buḥturī*), champions the latter. Some half a century later al-Marzubānī (d. 384/994), in his *Embroidered Book* (*al-Muwashshaḥ*), collects Abū Tammām's poetic shortcomings.[4] Al-Āmidī also includes in his book the record of a long debate between supporters of the two poets. A shorter debate is cited by al-Ḥuṣrī (d. 413/1022) in his *Flowering of the Literary Arts* (*Zahr al-ādāb*).[5]

Al-Ṣūlī

Abū Bakr al-Ṣūlī[6] was a man steeped in the culture of his time, positioned through descent and education at the very top of society, and gifted with an aesthetic perception that enabled him to compose nuanced portraits of literary life both of the earlier third/ninth century and his own day. His Turkish ancestor Ṣūl had governed the region of Jurjān southwest of the Caspian Sea and adopted Islam under the general Yazīd ibn al-Muhallab (d. 102/720). Subsequent family members were mostly officials in the chancery, with the exception of al-Ṣūlī's uncle Ibrāhīm ibn al-ʿAbbās (d. 243/857 or later), who excelled both as a poet and a secretary.

Al-Ṣūlī studied with the leading scholars of his day, including the philologists Abū Dāwūd al-Sijistānī, Thaʿlab, and al-Mubarrad, and he quotes many additional authorities in his works. His student al-Tanūkhī (d. 383/994) became a celebrated *adab* author in his own right, and eminent luminaries like al-Marzubānī and Abū l-Faraj al-Iṣbahānī (d. 356/967) quoted al-Ṣūlī extensively.

The bulk of al-Ṣūlī's life was devoted to serving several caliphs as companion, helping them to while away their idle hours with erudite and entertaining conversation, and as tutor of their sons. It was his chess playing that first earned him the attention of Caliph al-Muktafī (r. 289–95/902–8). Thereafter al-Muqtadir (r. 295–317/908–29) entrusted him the care of his two sons, one of whom, when he became Caliph al-Rāḍī in 322/934, gave al-Ṣūlī a privileged position at court. With al-Muttaqī (r. 329–33/940–44) al-Ṣūlī's fortunes waned. In search of new patrons, he made his way to the Turkish commander and future regent Bajkam (d. 329/941) in Mosul before retiring to Basra, where he died in 335/946–47.

The composition of *The Life and Times of Abū Tammām* probably dates to the last two decades of al-Ṣūlī's life. The addressee of its introductory epistle, Muzāḥim ibn Fātik, remains strangely obscure.[7] No contemporary source mentions him, but al-Ṣūlī tells us that the composition of *The Life and Times of Abū Tammām* took place during a period of disgrace (§2.4), which means that it probably happened during al-Ṣūlī's temporary absence from court under al-Qāhir (r. 320–22/932–34), or after his final departure from it under al-Muttaqī. The eulogies al-Ṣūlī appended to the names of the two grammarians al-Mubarrad and Thaʿlab (§4.1), who died in 286/899 and 291/904 respectively, provide a *post quem* for the epistle. Muzāḥim may thus have been a military man of minor importance but with literary interests, whose favor al-Ṣūlī sought when his star was fading. The dedicatory epistle may be a petition for sponsorship and patronage.

Al-Ṣūlī lived at a time when literary scholarship about an earlier oral tradition had become primarily a written exercise, though it did not sacrifice person-to-person teaching and transmission. During the previous century, the standardization of the Arabic language (*ʿarabiyyah*) and the introduction of papermaking from Central Asia had supported a flourishing book culture. Oral transmission continued to alternate with the use of written sources and is preserved in the introductory chains of transmission (*isnād*). Thus a text's journey from memorization to oral transmission to written transcript, sometimes over as long a period as three centuries, was carefully documented, transmitter after transmitter. Al-Ṣūlī owned a large library,[8] but claimed to have studied all his books with relevant authorities.

The books of this era, however, show the history of their inception in their structure—and they differ from the continuous text we expect of books today. The main ingredient of early Arabic prose was short texts, or *akhbār* (sg. *khabar*), which had been transmitted from as early as the sixth century AD. In fact, the large body of orally transmitted literature accelerated the process of book composition and was one of the conditions for the cultural revolution that led to the emergence of the Arabic book; the oral texts in circulation needed to be collected, sorted, and presented on the page. There were two main terms for the production of a book. One kind, the redacting of oral matter, was referred to as *taṣnīf*. The composing of a text from scratch was known as *ta'līf*. Compiling required its own set of skills—the sources still needed to be cited—but disciplines differed in the level of strictness in evaluating the reliability of the transmitters: those of literature and history were not given the same scrutiny as those of Hadith, which served as a basis of religious ritual and law. Authors wrote in this way because they wanted to authenticate their materials; thus, the lines of transmitters are akin to modern footnotes, except that they come at the beginning of an account in reverse chronological order, from the most recent to the earliest—"headnotes" so to speak. In the fourth/tenth century, writing from scratch would come to dominate, and chains of transmitters lost their original function, becoming instead a literary device authors played with or something they invented outright.

Compilation does not make for fluid reading—like a snapshot, each piece captures one situation from a specific angle and together with the others creates a kaleidoscope. While a compiler basically arranged preexisting texts, compiling was no less scholarly or creative than composing anew. Individual compilers differed in their degree of intervention in their material. It could be minimal, simply arranging snippets of text into thematic chapters, or it could be more extensive, clustering variant retellings of the same event, commenting on their differences and relative authenticity, and integrating them into a new overall narrative. Al-Ṣūlī is an "interfering" compiler who leaves his readers in no doubt about his interpretation of the material he collected. And because many of his texts were contemporary with his subject, Abū Tammām, they strengthened al-Ṣūlī's case of showing the poet's acclaim historically.

Al-Ṣūlī's own writings, many of which are extant, treat history and poetry.[9] His *Book of Folios* (*Kitāb al-Awrāq*) chronicles literary aspects of the court during the reigns of caliphs he knew personally, and *The Scribe's Vademecum* (*Adab al-kuttāb*) imparts technical advice and epistolary etiquette to secretaries. But al-Ṣūlī's main concern was modern poetry. He collected the work of nearly every major Abbasid poet and of numerous minor ones, and his list of edited *dīwāns*[10] reads like a who's who of early Abbasid literature. But al-Ṣūlī also treated poetry in its social context, as he deemed audience appreciation important in a proper evaluation of the art of the word. To this end he collected narratives about poets' verses recited in public, their occasions of delivery, and their critical reception. His book on Abū Tammām is a fine demonstration of this. A similar work on al-Buḥturī does not survive as an independent book but has been reassembled from its quotations in the sources by the scholar Ṣāliḥ al-Ashtar.[11]

The Life and Times of Abū Tammām

The Life and Times of Abū Tammām takes readers to the heart of classical Arabic literary and court culture. It showcases the vibrancy of the life of poetry in the third/ninth century. We meet the patrons who rewarded poetry with generous sums of money, robes of honor, and paid positions.[12] Al-Ṣūlī includes chapters on select patrons who supported Abū Tammām as a testimony to the poet's success. According to some contemporaries, during Abū Tammām's lifetime no other poet "could earn a single dirham" (§58). This support of the elite was both material and verbal (§§66.1–2, §§69.1–4). Rulers, generals, and high officials made the novel style not only acceptable but turned it into the ruling fashion for panegyrics in their honor. The patrons formed one important audience group. Al-Ṣūlī also throws light on the social classes that made it possible for the elite patrons to sponsor poets. He describes the day-to-day dealings between individual poets, and between poets and their intermediaries, who connected them to the corridors of power. He thus paints a lively picture of literary life in the capital, Baghdad, and in the palatine city of Samarra.

What is more, *The Life and Times of Abū Tammām* offers unique insight into the formative phase of Arabic poetic criticism. The book lies at the crossroads of various cultural, literary, and intellectual developments. As a compilation, it reveals two stages in the eventful process of the reception of Abū Tammām and his poetry, the first stage represented by the *akhbār*, and the second by the activity of the compiler. The first stage, the layer of the *akhbār*, charts practical criticism from the poet's time: different groups of critics (and fans) are featured and their agendas are evident.[13] The high Arabic language was still being codified in grammar books, and poetry was a principal source. This central role of poetry as a cultural commodity and the importance of its professional stakeholders, the philologists, worked against making Abū Tammām's innovation uniformly welcome. What some relished and paid highly for, others found objectionable, disliked, or did not understand.[14]

Abū Tammām's sophisticated intellectual style was of particular appeal to the scribes, who had a professional mastery of classical Arabic. Their appreciation of his poetry was something the caliphs did not necessarily share. When he was asked, "Did al-Muʿtaṣim understand anything of your poetry?" (§167), the poet's answer was ambiguous. What was true for caliphs also applied to philologists and transmitters, who occasionally conceded their befuddlement at Abū Tammām's verse. In response to one scholar's question, "Why don't you compose poetry that can be understood?" Abū Tammām answered impatiently, “Why can’t you understand the poetry that is composed?” (§42.1).

Abū Tammām thus heralded a crucial phase of growth in the study of Arabic as a language and of literary criticism: much of the debate surrounding the poet can be explained as a turf war between the recently established discipline of language and the competing fledgling discipline of poetics. Al-Ṣūlī, by collecting sources contemporary with Abū Tammām, shows those ideas in ferment, cast into a vivid tableau. This layer of the compilation thus presents the words of others, the contemporaries of Abū Tammām.

The second stage, the layer of the compiler’s craft, presents the arguments of the author-collector al-Ṣūlī himself, as well as his extensive commentary on several of the accounts he cites. He speaks in his own voice as an expert arbiter, and as one who defends the separation of poetics and philology. Al-Ṣūlī lived a century after his protagonist, when personal attack had matured into scholarly debate, and the contested ideas were being reformulated with greater precision. The material al-Ṣūlī provides is unusually concise, accessible, and concrete. He highlights the significance of the new type of poetic criticism, which claimed the status of scholarship, while considering features other than the purely linguistic.

Despite his clear preference for, and defense of, the contemporary poetic style, al-Ṣūlī was an even-handed arbiter between ancient and modern poets. His ire was directed at those critics of the Moderns whom he deemed incompetent and dishonest (§§9–10 and §69.6). Being a poet and an expert on poetic motifs, he well knew the indebtedness of the Moderns to their predecessors. The same is true of his subject Abū Tammām, who excerpted and reused ancient poetry, even though he boasted of his own additions: “The ancient poet has left so much for the modern!” (§109).

Thanks to the efforts of al-Ṣūlī, Abū Tammām was enshrined as one of the classics in al-Qāḍī l-Jurjānī’s (d. 392/1002) *Mediation between al-Mutanabbī and His Opponents* (*al-Wasāṭah bayn al-Mutanabbī wa-khuṣūmihi*), composed when the next genius of Arabic poetry, al-Mutanabbī, had become the major bone of contention. The great theorist ʿAbd al-Qāhir al-Jurjānī (d. 471/1078 or 474/1081) defined metaphor and imagery through a heavy reliance on both Abū Tammām's and al-Mutanabbī's verses. The subsequent fifth/eleventh and sixth/twelfth centuries saw a wealth of commentaries on both Abū Tammām's *Dīwān* and his *Ḥamāsah* anthology.

Contents

The Life and Times of Abū Tammām opens with an introductory epistle, addressed to one Muzāḥim ibn Fātik, about whom almost nothing is known.[15] The opening (§§2.1–4) recapitulates the conversation between al-Ṣūlī and Muzāḥim that prompted the commission to compose *The Life and Times* and edit the *Collected Poems* of Abū Tammām. Al-Ṣūlī then (in §§3–5.2) makes an unfavorable comparison between over-ambitious and pretentious contemporary literary scholarship and the integrity of the previous generation. He next explains (in §§6.1–8) how badly he has suffered at the hands of contemporary scholars. But the favor of the patron and his brothers encourages al-Ṣūlī to continue with the commission. In §§9.1–18, he describes how Abū Tammām was and continues to be faulted by one group of scholars, experts on ancient poetry, who deliberately avoided his poetry and modern poetry generally.[16] In his rebuttal al-Ṣūlī shows how the Moderns improved upon the motifs of the Ancients.[17] Al-Ṣūlī next identifies the second kind of critic of Abū Tammām: would-be litterateurs (§§19.1–26.3). He describes how this group criticizes Abū Tammām as a means of self-promotion. Al-Ṣūlī rebuts the criticism of one particular metaphor and lambasts the ignorance of critics in general and sets Abū Tammām's borrowing alongside his inventiveness. The epistle ends (§§27–28) with the plan of the book, which is also intended as a corrective to the circulation of corrupt variants of verses by Abū Tammām. Al-Ṣulī intimates that his new and superior edition will supersede any other extant versions of Abū Tammām's poems, in the same way as al-Ṣūlī's edition of Abū Nuwās's collected poems had done (§27).

The epistle is followed by a long chapter on the status of Abū Tammām as recorded in instances of practical criticism, and then by chapters that describe Abū Tammām's dealings with illustrious patrons. A judge, two generals, two high officials, two governors, and a prince represent elite support and establish the wide acclaim the poet received. The treatise concludes with shorter chapters on negative criticism and the end of the poet's life. *The Life and Times of Abū Tammām* was in fact originally intended as a preface to the edition of Abū Tammām's *Collected Poems* (§28).[18]

In the first and longest chapter, "The Superiority of Abū Tammām," and a later shorter chapter, "Criticisms of Abū Tammām," al-Ṣūlī assembles competing opinions about the poet. To the philologists, who claimed poetry as their scholarly province, Abū Tammām's verse posed a particular challenge. Al-Ṣulī records testimonies by the philologists Thaʿlab (§4.6, §§10.1–2) and al-Mubarrad (§4.6, §51.1–3, §91.2, §95.2) in which they either reserved judgment or begrudgingly acknowledged Abū Tammām's merit. Other philologists remained puzzled and undecided, such as Ibn al-Aʿrābī (§123), Abū Ḥātim al-Sijistānī (§124), and Muḥammad al-Tawwazī (§125).

Fellow poets were divided. Diʿbil al-Khuzāʿī even denied Abū Tammām the title of poet, excluding him from his book on poets and referring to him as an orator instead (§§122.1–2). Ibn al-Muʿtazz halfheartedly defended Abū Tammām's rhetorical figures by claiming older precedents for them, notably in the Qur'an, admitting his innovation not in kind but in degree. Many other poets, such as ʿUmārah ibn ʿAqīl (§§50.1–3), Muḥammad ibn al-Ḥāzim al-Bāhilī (§35), the court poets of ʿAbd Allāh ibn Ṭāhir (§64.3), ʿAlī ibn al-Jahm (§31, §179), Ibn al-Rūmī, and al-Buḥturī (§39), were admirers. Those most vocal in the poet's defense were government scribes, such as al-Ḥasan ibn Wahb, who combined material support for the poet with vociferous defense of his odes.

The short texts that make up the collection depict real-life situations. They contain fascinating information about the professional life of poets, how they supported or competed with each other, and the etiquette of literary gatherings. They even include circumstantial details, such as how a poet composed (with ink on papyrus, or by heart), what sort of tools he had at his disposal, or which hurdles he had to brave to find a sponsor or get a promised reward disbursed. Most importantly, they touch on many more aspects than are reflected in the chapter headings. Notable are the recurrent topics of poetry and poetics, such as imitation and innovation, briefly characterized in what follows.

Criticism

In this evolving phase of poetics as a discipline, criticism often took the practical form of abridging odes to include only the best verses, as al-Ṣūlī tells us was done by the poets ʿUmārah ibn ʿAqīl (§30, §§50.1–3) and Ibn al-Muʿtazz (§§52.1–3), the secretary al-Ḥasan ibn Wahb (§§61.1–4),[19] and a Nuʿmānī scribe (§95.2). In his commentaries, al-Ṣūlī argues against criticism of specific metaphors, such as fever for generosity (§§21.1–6) and water for blame (§§22.1–10), and against criticism of motifs, such as the figs and grapes mentioned in the Amorium ode (§§20.1–6), a sword falling from the sky on one's head as an image of bravery (§§71.1–9), or the fallen moon as an image of the irreplaceable loss of General Muḥammad ibn Ḥumayd al-Ṭūsī (§69.5 and §§69.10–28). This last verse, part of Abū Tammām's lament for the general, is elsewhere condemned as a plagiarism (§§94.1–2). Thus al-Ṣūlī argues that criticism of the same verse as both a bad motif and a good theft shows that the criticism is gratuitous.

Meaning

The principal concepts that were to dominate the discipline of poetics were not yet defined. A good example is *maʿnā*: this term carries many meanings and nuances that are at times hard to distinguish.

In *The Life and Times of Abū Tammām*, *maʿnā* stands, first, for the general meaning of a passage; second, for a smaller theme within a poem, such as exile from home; and third, for the particular way in which a poet formulated this. Al-Ṣūlī notes how, for example, Abū Tammām transformed a familiar theme of exile as a painful experience into an individual's decision to enhance his appreciation through absence (§30).

Novelty

The most salient features of Abū Tammām's skill as a poet, those that were emphasized time and again, were his novelty, inventiveness, and self-reliance (§11.2, §23.2, §26.1, §52.8, §103); his development of motifs (§51.1);[20] and his skill at improvisation (§§110.1–2).

Imitation

Poetic experimentation and toying with older, existing motifs led to a debate about originality versus imitation and about authorship. Different terms, to wit, "taking," "stealing," "reliance" (§44.1), "emulating" (§69.13), "copying, transposing," "imitating," and "being inspired" (§55.1, §72.1)[21] reveal as much about attitudes to the influence of one poet on another as they do about specific opinions on individual cases of borrowing. It had already been established that it was not the act of poetic theft itself that mattered for the evaluation, since such a thing was literally unavoidable in a continuous poetic tradition, but rather the manner in which it was carried out, considered in terms of eloquence and invention. Al-Ṣūlī refers in this context to a "rule" (§26.1, §52.8) or "condition" (§81.5) posited by experts,[22] namely precedence in the authorship of a motif in terms of chronology, and among contemporaries, precedence in terms of quality (e.g., §13.4). A poet could thus "earn" the ownership of an existing motif if he outdid its creator. In this way the poet became "more worthy of it" (§34.1, §81.5). In other words, poetic excellence creates entitlement (§26.1, §34.2).[23]

The Presence of al-Buḥturī

A long section deals in particular with al-Buḥturī's borrowings from Abū Tammām (§44 and §§46–48).[24] Al-Buḥturī was a younger poet whom Abū Tammām took under his wing, but al-Buḥturī's fame among contemporaries would soon match Abū Tammām's. Al-Buḥturī poured the ideas that he borrowed from Abū Tammām, as al-Ṣūlī shows, into a more natural language than that of his mentor. Audiences and critics would compare the two, and each poet had his particular supporters, but al-Ṣūlī makes the point that in terms of creativity, al-Buḥturī was clearly second to Abū Tammām.

Poetic Themes

Most classical Arabic poems belong to a fixed set of larger genres, such as panegyric or lament, each of which included a catalog of common themes. Al-Ṣūlī also lists some themes that the Moderns rendered more successfully than the Ancients did (§§11.2–18). He assembles several series of motifs that show the versatility of poets when they return to the same themes over time, such as metaphors involving water (§§22.1–10), sounds that, though inarticulate, move their listeners (§§100.1–6), responsibility for endeavor but not success (§§25.1–6), and people who do not even merit a lampoon (§§24.1–30). One series lists poems describing robes (§§92.1–5).

Abridgments

Finally, the work features selections and abridgments of Abū Tammām's most famous poems in all genres (panegyric, apology, lament, boast, satire, love lyric), placed in the context of their first recitation and subsequent discussion in literary circles. It presents a lively picture of how hotly these were debated and how highly remunerated.

Factions

Al-Ṣūlī throws light on the two factions that attacked Abū Tammām. Language-centered philologists and transmitters made up one faction (§§9.1–2, §§69.6–9, §87.1), as confirmed by Ibn Abī Ṭāhir (§53). Self-promoting amateurs made up the other (§§19.1–4). Al-Ṣūlī dismisses their arguments as gibberish (§§70.1–3).

Conclusion

The Life and Times of Abū Tammām also affords a window on the academic world of Baghdad in the first half of the fourth/tenth century. In the course of his argument, al-Ṣūlī pronounces on professional ethics and his own scholarly etiquette. He lauds al-Mubarrad and Thaʿlab for not overstepping the limit of their competence by remaining faithful to their discipline (§§4.1–8, esp. §4.6), and he condemns religious and other biases against, or slander of, poets (§§86.1–7). He boasts of his own scholarly propriety, making a show of not criticizing colleagues openly (he toys with not naming them), but then does so, claiming a sense of scholarly duty. For example, after declaring that God would not ask him to explain scholars' and poets' unwarranted criticism of Abū Tammām (§69.9), he proceeds to do so a paragraph later, with "I will mention this" (see §9.1, §23.3, §24.1, and §28).

Al-Ṣūlī demonstrates great respect for the intellectual property of others (§46.1). Inversely, he complains that scholars like Abū Mūsā l-Ḥāmiḍ[25] did not treat him with the same respect, and used his works without giving him credit (§§6.1–2). But he misses no opportunity to promote his own expertise as a commentator of poetry (§2.4, §78.5, §101.2), mentioning the popularity of his edition of Abū Nuwās's *Collected Poems* (§27) and the failure of competitors to match his collection *The Life and Times of al-Farazdaq* with a similar work on Jarīr (§7.3).

Impressionistic and discursive, *The Life and Times of Abū Tammām* inaugurates a long line of poetic treatises that react to innovations in poetry. Along with Arabic grammar, premodern Arabic poetics never lost its dynamic character—ever unfolding in the wake of the seemingly inexhaustible creativity of its poets.

Note on the Text

The English translation is fairly free and idiomatic, supplemented by explanatory insertions implicit in the Arabic text but not obvious to the English reader. When the text uses a less recognizable form of an individual's name, the more common name is also supplied for clarity. The phrase "Al-Ṣūlī:" introduces explanatory comments inserted by al-Ṣūlī. Citations of Abū Tammām's poetry are identified in terms of their occurrence in the *Diwān* edited by ʿAzzām (4 vols., Cairo, 1951–65), and abbreviated as D in the endnotes to the translation. When poems are cited in abridged form this is indicated by an ellipsis at the end of the verse preceding an omission. Occasional (usually minor) variations in verses between *The Life and Times of Abū Tammām* and the *Collected Poems* are given in the endnotes, too, but are left unaltered in the accounts, as they were transmitted independently from the *Collected Poems*, and their differences attest to a different textual history.

Notes to the Introduction

1 Hermione Lee, *Virginia Woolf* (New York: Vintage Books, 1999), 386. The orthography follows Woolf's diary, whence the quote is taken.

2 The unpublished doctoral thesis by Naẓīr al-Islam [Naẓīrul-Islam] al-Hindī, "Die *Akhbār* von Abū Tammām von aṣ-Ṣūlī" (Breslau, 1940), includes a German translation of the prefatory epistle.

3 On his biography, see Meisami, "Abū Tammām," in *EAL*, 1:47–49; Ritter, "Abū Tammām" in *EI2*, 1: 153–55; Gruendler, "Abū Tammām," in *EI3*, s.v.; Larkin, "Abu Tammam"; and Sezgin, *GAS*, 2: 551–58; and on his works, see Stetkevych, *Abū Tammām and the Poetics of the ʿAbbāsid Age*.

4 Al-Marzubānī, *Muwashshaḥ*, 343–69.

5 Al-Āmidī, *Muwāzanah*, 1:6–56, and al-Ḥuṣrī, *Zahr*, 2:601–9.

6 On his biography, see Seidensticker, "al-Ṣūlī," in *EAL*, 2:744–45; Leder, "Al-Ṣūlī," in *EI2*, 9:846–48; Sezgin, *GAS*, 1:330–31; Osti, "Tailors of Stories" and "The Remuneration of a Court Companion." See also the further articles by Osti on al-Ṣūlī as historian, "The Wisdom of Youth" and "In Defense of the Caliph"; on his interactions at the court, "Al-Ṣūlī and the Caliph"; on his famous library, "Notes on a Private Library"; and on his literary reception, "Authors, Subjects, and Fame."

7 He is not otherwise attested (see al-Ṣūlī, *Akhbār*, preface, xviii) but must be identical with the military man to whom al-Ṣūlī's enemy al-Ḥāmiḍ bequeathed his books in 305/917 to prevent other scholars' access to them. Al-Ṣūlī mentions this bequest in §6.2. The dedicatee's name appears variously as Abū Fātik al-Muqtadirī (Ibn Khallikān, *Wafayāt*, 2:406) and Ibn Fātik al-Muʿtaḍidī (al-Qifṭī, *Inbāh*, 3:141).

8 See introd., n. 6.

9 Four are lost; others survive partially in citations in the *adab* literature.

10 Of Abū Nuwās, Muslim ibn al-Walīd, al-ʿAbbās ibn al-Aḥnaf, Ibn al-Muʿtazz, Ibn al-Rūmī, al-Ṣanawbarī, and others.

11 His collected *akhbār* of Sudayf ibn Maymūn, al-Sayyid al-Ḥimyarī, al-ʿAbbās ibn al-Aḥnaf, and the poets of Egypt have not survived; see Ritter, "al-Ṣūlī."

12 For more detail, see Gruendler, "Verse and Taxes" and "*Qaṣīda*," n. 20.

13 On practical criticism by literati contemporary with Abū Tammām, see Gruendler, "Abstract Aesthetics and Practical Criticism" and "*Qaṣīda*," 350–51.

14 On this debate, see Gruendler, "Arabic Philology through the Ages."

15 See introd., n. 7.

16 On the tension between philology and the emerging poetics, see Gruendler, "Meeting the Patron," 75–80, and "Arabic Philology through the Ages."

17 For a discussion of al-Ṣūlī's reaction to this criticism, see Gruendler, "Meeting the Patron," 75–80.

18 This has been published separately as *Sharḥ al-Ṣūlī li-Dīwān Abī Tammām*, edited by Khalaf Rashīd Nuʿmān, 3 vols., preceded by a study of Abū Tammām and al-Ṣūlī as his critic and commentator (ibid., 1:17–137). The edition by Muḥammad ʿAbduh ʿAzzām includes the commentary by al-Tibrīzī (see introd., n. 27).

19 See Gruendler, "Abstract Aesthetics and Practical Criticism."

20 The first three qualities are variously referred to as *ibdāʿ*, *badīʿ*, *ikhtirāʿ*, *iktifāʾ*, *ittikāʾ ʿalā nafsihī*, *yaʿmalu l-maʿānī wa-yakhtariʿuhā wa-yattakī ʿalā nafsihi*, and his development of motifs as *istikhrājāt laṭīfah wa-maʿānī ṭarīfah*.

21 "Taking" is referred to in Arabic as *akhdh*, "stealing" as *sariqah*, "reliance" as *lāʾidh bi-*, "emulating" as *muʿāraḍah*, "copying, transposing" as *naql*, "imitating" as *iḥtidhāʾ*, and "inspiration" as *ilmām*.

22 Referred to as *al-ʿulamāʾ bi-l-shiʿr, al-nuqqād li-l-shiʿr wa-l-ʿulamāʾ bihi* or elsewhere as *al-ḥudhdhāq bi-ʿilm al-shiʿr wa-alfāẓihī* (§18).

23 The concept of "entitlement" within the theory of poetic borrowing (*sariqah*), whose first development was prompted by Abū Tammām, came into full bloom with al-Mutanabbī; see Heinrichs, "An Evaluation of *Sariqa*" and "*Sariqa*"; Ouyang, *Literary Criticism*, 146–54; ʿAbbās, *Taʾrīkh*, 252–336.

24 One list collected by al-Ṣūlī is labeled *lawdh* and *naskh* (§§44.1–10). A following selection quotes an unnamed author of a book on thefts (§§46.1–6), probably identical with the one by Abū l-Ḍiyāʾ Bishr ibn Yaḥyā the Scribe, quoted and critiqued in al-Āmidī's *Muwāzanah*, 1:324–70; see n. 100 to the translation. A third section assembles the taking over (*naql*) of wording and meaning (or motif) (§§47.1–11). A fourth section displays stylistic matching or imitation (*iḥtidhāʾ*, *taqdīr al-kalām*, *ʿamila maʿnāhu ʿalayhi*) (§§48.1–4). Note that the terms *iḥtidhāʾ* and *ʿamila kamā ʿamila min al-maʿna* are elsewhere used more precisely for an item-by-item matching (§40.3). Another term for borrowing, *naql*, has many further applications, such as a reusing of wording and meaning in a different genre (§69.16), a reusing of a motif without wording (§25.5, §64.5), and a transposition of prose into poetry (§134.2). The inverse transfer of verse into prose is called *ilmām* (§§55.1–2).

25 A lexicographer of the Kufan school and assistant and successor to Thaʿlab, he authored several thematic dictionaries and was a book copyist known for his precision. However at his death he bequeathed his books not to a student or colleague but to a military man, Ibn Fātik al-Muʿtaḍidī (or Abū Fātik al-Muqtadirī; see introd., n. 7 above). He earned the nickname "Sourpuss" because of his unpleasant character. Al-Qiftī, who devotes two biographies to him, gives his name variously as Sulaymān ibn Muḥammad ibn Aḥmad and Muḥammad ibn Sulaymān (*Inbāh*, 2:21–22, no. 263, and 3:141–42, no. 649); the former name is used by Ibn al-Nadīm (*Fihrist*, 1:240) and Ibn Khallikān (*Wafayāt*, 2:406, no. 273).

Al-Ṣūlī's Epistle to Abū l-Layth Muzāḥim ibn Fātik

In the name of God, full of compassion,
ever compassionate

Praise be to God! He is due our praise in return for His grace. He grants favor to all His creation, and begins . . . .[1] He has made the way to the truth of His message clear and made it easy to obey Him. He created all that we behold, all that our hearts are drawn to, all that we ponder as evidence of His divinity and witness to His oneness. God bless and keep Muḥammad, seal of His prophets and best of His emissaries, and his blessed kin. 1

May God give you honor, prosperity, perfect happiness, and long life. May your deeds be pleasing to Him. May He preserve and keep you to adorn an age in which men such as you are rare. May He make your well-being a gift to men of culture. The last time we met, we talked at length about various areas of expertise, and argued about Abū Tammām Ḥabīb ibn Aws al-Ṭāʾī. You marveled at how people's views of him diverge so starkly. Most people, the leading scholars in the field of poetry and the evaluation of speech and experts in prose and verse, too, give Abū Tammām the praise he deserves and accord him his rightful status. They hold him in the highest regard and are struck by his poetic originality.[2] Some even place him on a par with his predecessors, while others go so far as to say he is unique, without precedent or equal. 2.1

Yet there are others who fault him and attack much of his poetry, citing some scholar or other in order to have an authority for what 2.2

are mere allegations since they are unverified and unsubstantiated. For my part, I considered both categories to be the same, given that neither group of scholars can understand Abū Tammām's poetry or clarify his intent, let alone dare to recite a single poem of his, which of course would put them at risk, for they have not studied and learned its references nor heard its pithy speech, nor are they familiar with its motifs.

2.3 Still, I conceded your point, and undertook to provide you with a full exposition to avoid any possible doubt on your part. When I saw how happy and pleased you were with this proposal, I was spurred to do it well and quickly, and to offer it to you as a gift in the form of an epistle followed by a report of everything ever said about every aspect of Abū Tammām: what makes him so good; a list of those who understood him, and adored and praised him; arguments against those who did not understand him, found him sorely wanting, and faulted him; and a list of the people he praised, corresponded with, and visited for favors. It would include everything said about him, my goal being to clarify his preeminence and to refute those who fail to appreciate him properly. This made you even happier and more enthusiastic.

2.4 Then I realized[3] that there was something else you were hoping for, which you had not told me. Maybe you were reluctant to burden me or did not wish to increase my labors, for I am sore pressed and tormented by an unjust fate, ruthless authorities, and friends who turned against me. I asked you to make your wishes plain and to charge me fully with what you wanted. You told me that what would satisfy you completely and fulfill all your desires would be, once I had finished *The Life and Times of Abū Tammām*, to edit his poetry, vocalizing it and glossing it so that it no longer contained any difficult vocabulary or obscure passages that blunt comprehension's blade or make one spit and cover one's ears.[4] I was quick to agree, my mind was made up, and after *The Life and Times of Abū Tammām* I appended an edition of his poetry, poems of praise and satire, boasting and love, description and lamentation. I began each of these genres with the rhyme letter *alif* and then *bā'* and continued in alphabetical order to make it easier for you to look things up should you so wish. I found no reason to disagree with you or depart from your will. I agreed to do this for you, no one else—I would not have done it for any other. It is not that I wish to withhold knowledge from scholars or that I am unwilling to disseminate it among those who deserve it. I am revealing what was hidden and removing its cover. It is something in which I am a reliable and trustworthy expert.[5]

I have found (God support you) that in our time most of those who wear culture as an ornament differ from what I was used to from the masters and learned scholars of the past. Nowadays someone studies one area of culture, receives his share of it and reaches a certain level. Then he thinks he will not be called a proper scholar or be thought of as a leader in his field without attacking other scholars, belittling the dead, and denigrating the living. He becomes so accustomed to voicing these attacks that they become the most important task he can perform, and they dominate his gatherings. He is not satisfied with the little bits of knowledge he has acquired but lays claim to it in its entirety. He keeps at bay anyone who would engage him in debate and expose his limited knowledge by besting him in an argument. He achieves this with the aid of people whom he has trained to pounce on those who ask a question or demand an answer. In this way he claims expertise in areas he has never thought of or put his mind to, or whose experts he has never met or was even known to have studied with. He thinks that if he does not know everything, he will not be considered a leading and preeminent scholar. 3

Abū l-ʿAbbās Muḥammad ibn Yazīd ibn ʿAbd al-Akbar al-Azdī l-Mubarrad and Abū l-ʿAbbās Aḥmad ibn Yaḥyā l-Shaybānī Thaʿlab (God show them mercy) were two of the greats—men we knew, frequented, and gained much knowledge from. They were of high 4.1

renown, recognized as scholars, and universally acclaimed. We never knew them to claim to be the most knowledgeable about ancient sagas, the rise and fall of dynasties, the study of who was first to do or say a thing, the stories of kings, or the history of Quraysh and the life of the Emissary (God bless him and keep him), his mission and campaigns, and knowledge of his kin and Companions (God show them mercy). Yet these are the most eminent subjects to study.

4.2 They did not claim to be the most knowledgeable about the history and genealogies of the Arabs, the battles of the pre-Islamic era, the history of Islam, the lives of the caliphs (God's blessings upon them) and their viziers, their governors and supporters, the Dissidents, and movements which had sprung up in their own lifetime.

4.3 Nor did they claim preeminence in jurisprudence, upon which people depend, or in Hadith, on which the religion of Islam hinges, and the knowledge of its scholars, methods, transmitters, and their chronology and lifespans, such that they would know if a transmitter were placed in the wrong order in a sequence or were put in contact with someone he never met. Nor preeminence in the science of transmitters' names and teknonyms, and knowing who among them is sound and reliable, and who weak and dubious.

4.4 They did not claim preeminence in the sort of knowledge that would seem to be the preserve of kings, to wit, which poems were intoned, which poets they are attributed to, the reasons they were composed, and who put which ones to song, as well as the explanation of the songs' modes, genres, and fingering on the lute strings. The people of Medina were conspicuous for their virtue, preeminence, and asceticism, and none of their legal experts ignored the fact that they deemed singing licit.

4.5 Nor did they claim preeminence in memorizing the things kings need and inquire about when something catches their eye and they expect to be instantly obliged. I mean, for example, questions about various kinds of drinks and their description, and about the best verses composed on the subject; or on the subject of fruits, fragrant herbs, and the seasons; descriptions of palaces and gardens, artificial lakes and literary gatherings, wine-drinking at morning and evening, clear skies and rain clouds, the sun and the moon, the constellations and rain-bringing stars; descriptions of horses and weaponry; and all the other topics of love poetry and so forth in the manner I have outlined. And they did not claim preeminence in the lore of amusing stories collected for kings or extemporized on the basis of recent events.[6]

They did not claim preeminence in the study of the modern poets and the pioneers from the beginning of the Abbasid dynasty (God prolong and safeguard it). And when they turned to this poetry, they did not claim that they had the ability to compose poetry like it. Nor did they claim that they had mastery of its entire lexicon and were able to distinguish between the rare, the mediocre, and the inferior, beyond rejecting a linguistic error or a lexical slip. 4.6

They did not claim that they had a better command than anyone else of the science of prosody and rhyme, genealogy, official and private correspondence, and rhetoric, and of how to spot when poets plagiarize and borrow from one another, and how to recognize which poets did it properly and which badly. Nor did anyone else make this claim on their behalf. What they were preeminent in was knowledge of syntax and lexicography, but they each knew something about these other fields. Neither of them declared, "I do not make mistakes," or felt embarrassed to say, "I do not know" when he did not know something. 4.7

Think then (God support you) about these two great, preeminent men. Think of how much they did not know of all these subjects I have listed for you. And then think of how highly they are revered among people, since they did not pretend expertise in anything they did not master, nor give answers about anything they did not know. 4.8

None of the contemporary scholars I alluded to is worth a tenth of either al-Mubarrad or Thaʿlab—they do not come close, not even 5.1

in the eyes of their most ardent and partisan supporters. And yet they claim to know everything and never admit, "We simply do not know." They are as the poet says:

He dabbles in everything yet masters nothing.
It's not his insight but his delusion that increases.

5.2 We might turn a blind eye to this as long as the scholarship is good and it is commonly acknowledged that they have studied properly and diligently with experts and scholars and have attended the right gatherings. But if they acquire learning by deceit, or by attacking and pillaging it, then God help us for having to depend on those who are unacceptable and unreliable!

6.1 Some things I dictated long ago about the motifs that poets contend with one another over had not been given a proper and systematic arrangement before I made them available. People had adopted such motifs without understanding them. Now I see that some individuals have broken them up and have made them available in a piecemeal fashion, strewn throughout their dictated lectures with no organization at all. The work that emanates from me is all too obvious when compared with the fruits of their own learning and stands out as distinct in their compilations—the setting speaks volumes that it does not belong.[7]

6.2 You (God support you) are my witness that Abū Mūsā l-Ḥāmiḍ insulted me in your presence, and you forbade it. He heaped blame and injury upon the other books I dictated, finding no good in any of them. When he passed away, and his books were brought to you, you discovered that he had written out in his own hand most of my *Compendium on the Knowledge of the Qur'an* and my *Book of Youths and Choice Anecdotes,* which I dictated, and the poetry of Abū Nuwās I had gone through. He had used my works as primary sources and would dispense smatterings of them to all who came to study with him and to benefit from his learning. You were astonished and found this offensive.

I consider next a class of people whose sole intention is to read poems, memorize some strange vocabulary, learn some problems of grammar, dip into a book of lexicography, and then attend literary gatherings, though not one of them has advanced in knowledge or derived any benefit from his reading. If the convener of the gathering has an idea or forgets something, the ignoramus jumps on him and takes him by surprise. He thinks that he is superior and more learned than the convener, because he has memorized a line of poetry or a motif that the convener has not. It may be that the convener knows over a thousand verses by heart. If this ignoramus were made convener and asked a thousand questions (all of which the convener could answer), he would not be able to get a single one right. 7.1

It seems to be the case (God support you) that the one person who knows least about my preeminent and unprecedented compositions is the one most in need of them. He claims my work as his own after I dictated it and makes formal pronouncements about it, after I explained its ideas. He does not make any reference to me or credit me. I do not care one jot about this. I enjoy your favor and have satisfied your request. You know only too well that these pretentious individuals are incapable of accomplishing the charge you gave me, and that none of them is bold enough to recite a single poem of Abū Tammām's and be sure to get its content right, let alone give an account of the poet's life and times, rebut his critics, comprehend and defend his entire corpus, preserve it intact, and highlight its merits, such that Abū Tammām's eminence in poetry and his peerless understanding become known. 7.2

I compiled *The Life and Times of al-Farazdaq*, a work of three hundred folios in length. I set myself the condition that I would not use a single word from the *Flytings* except what was absolutely necessary: his genealogy, wives, and so forth. This came to less than thirty folios *in toto*. I started with al-Farazdaq, and intended to move on to the *Life and Times* of Jarīr and al-Akhṭal, compiled in exactly the same format. I began with al-Farazdaq because of 7.3

his noble bearing, powerful and pithy language, rich motifs, and elegant style, and because during the Umayyad dynasty he was a supporter of the opposing Banū Hāshim, openly declaring their excellence and precedence, something I include in the book. I also consider his poetry to be superior to both Jarīr's and al-Akhṭal's. Yet I do not criticize anyone who places him second, for we do find that leading scholars hold divergent opinions on these three and prefer one over the other two. I for my part belong to the camp of those who prefer al-Farazdaq. I began to compile the *Life and Times of Jarīr*, then I learned that others had resolved to compile this according to the condition I had set for myself. They did this to oppose and outmaneuver me. So I held off completing the work, so that I could test their veracity. Some are dead, others still alive, but the work has yet to be compiled.

8 Your request is light indeed, though it would have been heavy if made by anyone else. You and your brothers Abū l-Fatḥ and Abū l-Qāsim (God support you all) are preeminent in knowledge, insight, faith, and truthfulness. I also acknowledge your favor, and am thankful for your kindness. You are as I described you all in a poem I once composed in your praise:

> Do not forget how God has favored you
> with noble, splendid brothers.
> Men shield their eyes from you—
> you are like fixed stars around a full moon.
> Three solid hearthstones, the epitome of majesty,
> fixed stars of Aquila.[8]
> Lions defending their lair,
> arrows of fate fired by an expert archer.
> Death is blind to you,
> Its sharp claws clipped.
> May your enemy ever be your servant,
> yoked, ignominious, the ally of defeat.

I will now begin to explain why some people disagree about Abū Tammām and the reasons for this, God willing. Some scholars are said to have avoided his poetry and found fault with it. I name no one. I mean to look out for, protect, and preserve scholars as a community. Do not be shocked that this actually happened. They mastered an extensive corpus of the poems of the Ancients in many recensions and identified authorities who had gone through the ancient poems and harnessed their motifs. Thus when they recite and explain them, specifying what is good and criticizing what is bad, they are simply following in the footsteps of others. The words of the Ancients resemble each other and are closely interconnected, even if they vary in excellence. Scholars therefore infer what they do not understand from what they do understand and conquer what is difficult by means of what is accessible. 9.1

They did not identify authorities or transmitters for the poetry of the Moderns from the age of Bashshār as well qualified as those they identified for the poetry of the Ancients. So they did not realize what Abū Tammām was capable of and could accomplish. They did not give him his due, but ignored him and opposed him, as God (Mighty and Glorious) says, «No; but they have cried lies to that whereof they comprehend not the knowledge»[9] and as the saying goes, "Man is the enemy of that which he does not understand, for he who does not understand a thing opposes it." When asked to teach the poetry of Bashshār, Abū Nuwās, Muslim, Abū Tammām, and others, these scholars demurred, saying "I do not not know this well" and reverted to abuse of Abū Tammām in particular, because he was their closest contemporary, and his poetry was the most difficult. What else could we expect of someone who says, "Study the poems of the Ancients with me," but then, when asked about any aspect of the poems of the Moderns, is unfamiliar with it? What else could he resort to but insulting what he does not understand? If he were fair-minded, he would have studied it with the experts, as he had other poets, and he would then have been preeminent in his knowledge of it. Learning is not confined to one individual: no one has a special right to it. 9.2

10.1 Thaʿlab was venerated by everyone, but I think by the Banū Nawbakht above all. Each of them acknowledged Thaʿlab as their principal authority. The Banū Nawbakht told me that Thaʿlab said to them, "I spend much time with scribes, in particular Abū l-ʿAbbās ibn Thawābah. Most of their gatherings are devoted to discussions of the poetry of Abū Tammām, which I do not know. Make me an anthology!" So we made a selection and gave it to him. He took it to Ibn Thawābah, who approved it. "It is not something I selected," Thaʿlab said to him, "the Banū Nawbakht selected it for me."

10.2 The Banū Nawbakht said: Thaʿlab used to recite to us a verse by Abū Tammām and then ask, "What did he mean by this?" and we would explain it to him. "By God," Thaʿlab would say, "he has done well and excelled!" This is a story they would tell of one of Abū Tammām's leading critics.

11.1 I will discuss the other sort of critic after the following section about the Moderns, God willing. You should know (God support you) that from Bashshār's era right up to today the lexicon of the Moderns seems to be moving toward more novel motifs, with a more accessible vocabulary, and more delicate speech, even if priority is given to the Ancients for their invention, innovation, natural talent, and self-sufficiency, as is right and proper. You should further know that they did not witness what the Moderns have witnessed, upon the observation of which they devised their images. So too the Moderns have not witnessed what the Ancients saw in their epoch and upon which they based their descriptions, as for example the evocation of deserts and open spaces, wildlife, camels, and tents. In these things the Moderns are forever second to the Ancients, just as the Ancients are forever second to the Moderns in what they have not seen. Abū Nuwās made this clear in his words:

> To describe an abandoned campsite is a dullard's eloquence.
> Devote your descriptions to the daughter of the vine!

He later says in this poem:

You describe the abandoned campsite by hearsay.
Does someone who sees it for himself understand it as you do?
If you describe a thing derivatively
you will slip up and resort to fantasies.[10]

Since poets who live later sail in the wake of their predecessors, cast with their molds, draw on their idioms, and are nourished by their speech, it is rare for them to take a motif from a predecessor and not do it well.

We have discovered in the poetry of the Moderns motifs the Ancients did not utter and others they hinted at, which the Moderns then used and excelled in. In addition, their poetry is more suited to its time, and people employ it more in their gatherings, writings, pithy sayings, and petitions. 11.2

People admire how (God support you) within one verse Imru' al-Qays makes comparisons between two things and two other things, and they say, "No one can match him in this." Here is how he describes a female eagle: 12.1

Bird hearts, moist and dry,
in her nest were like jujubes and withered dates.

He produced a most beautiful and excellent line.

Then Bashshār said: 12.2

The dust whirled up above our heads
and our swords were like a night whose stars had tumbled.

This from a blind man who did not have the power of sight and who did not actually see this. He composed his comparison by intuition and produced something excellent and beautiful, comparing within one verse two things with two other things.

Manṣūr al-Namarī followed suit, with the following: 12.3

A night of dust, with no stars or moon—
only your noble brow and the sharp spears, raised high, are visible.

12.4 And al-ʿAttābī said:

Their hoofs raised a canopy above their heads
where the stars are shattered swords.

13.1 People also admire the words of apology uttered by al-Nābighah to al-Nuʿmān in a classic ode:

You are like the night, engulfing me,
even though I imagined myself at a vast distance from you.
Iron hooks on twisted ropes are
pulled by hands that reach toward you.

13.2 Salm al-Khāsir composed several verses of apology to al-Mahdī, as follows:

I seek refuge among the best of all people:
you are that man by virtue of what you do and do not do.
You are like fate, whose nets are cast—
there is no escape or refuge from fate.
If I could control the wind I would turn its reins
in every direction, but still you would catch me.

13.3 This comes from the words of al-Farazdaq to al-Ḥajjāj:

If the wind were to carry me and you pursued me,
I would be like something trapped by its fate.

Salm thus successfully replaced "You are like the night" with "You are like fate" and replaced "iron hooks" with "If I could control the wind I would turn its reins" and produced excellent poetry.

13.4 ʿAlī ibn Jabalah, however, praised Ḥumayd with a motif similar to al-Nābighah's, as follows:

No one can escape you in pursuit,
even if ladders were to lift him to the sky,
Not even if he fled to a place where
neither darkness nor bright morning light could find their way.

In Ibn Jabalah's favor is the fact that he added to the motif and expanded it, but the fact that he turned it into two verses, whereas al-Nābighah had done so in one verse and had come first, counts against him.

The words of al-Buḥturī are similar to Ibn Jabalah's phrase, "If ladders were to lift him to the sky": 13.5

They were despoiled. Their blood shone red, like clothes—
it was as if they had not been despoiled.
Were they to ride the stars,
their fastest ones would not elude your intrepid grasp.[11]

Salm's words "You are like fate" are taken from al-Akhṭal: 13.6

The deeds of the Commander of the Faithful are like fate—
there is no shame in acts of fate.

The finest thing the Ancients said about homesickness and longing is a verse Abū Aḥmad Yaḥyā ibn ʿAlī l-Munajjim recited to me: 14.1

A land where the amulets of childhood were undone in youth,
the place where dust first touched my skin.[12]

Ibn Mayyādah later said: 14.2

If I only knew whether I would ever spend a night
in Layla's stony flatlands, where my people reared me.[13]
A land where amulets were hung from my neck
and then cut off, when maturity came.
If you are detaining me from my home,
give me ample sustenance and then reunite us!

and there are more lines like these.

14.3 Ibn al-Rūmī evoked his home, explained why it is beloved, and within the verses of a single poem brought together all this disparate material:

I have a house I swore I would never sell,
Nor live to see anyone own but me.
It was there I knew the carefree bliss of youth,
the blissful slumber of those who wake in your shadow.
My soul grew so used to it, it seemed like its body:
If I lost it, I would be left for dead.
What makes people love their homes
is what they accomplished there in their youth.
As they recall their homes, they bring to mind
their youthful lives—oh, how they miss them now![14]

15.1 People admire al-Nābighah's description of a topic rarely broached:[15]

When you thrust your spear, you thrust it into a high target,
rising to the touch and perfume-daubed.
And when you pull out, you pull out from a tight spot,
like a grown boy pulling on a twisted rope.[16]

15.2 Other poets used this motif and made it longer or shorter, then Ibn al-Rūmī brought together this disparate material in three verses:

She has a pussy that borrows its fire
from a lover's passionate heart and a chest full of hatred.
When you feel its heat
it's as if your own innards were on fire.
It gets tighter in the grip of love
like the noose of a rope.[17]

16 This poem contains a description of a black woman, to whom Ibn al-Rūmī refers in the preceding passage. He was the first to describe this in verse:

She wins love because she is dyed black,
the color of the pupil and the inner heart.[18]
She captivates minds and eyes,
oh, how they gallop after her!

I cite Ibn al-Rūmī because he is someone I myself encountered. Among the good poets, he is our closest contemporary, having died the most recently. If I went as far back as Abū Tammām, Muslim, Abū l-ʿAtāhiyah, Abū Nuwās, and Bashshār, I would discover many verses like this, but I would be digressing.

We cite Muḥammad ibn Saʿīd, who cites ʿUmar ibn Shabbah, who cites al-Aṣmaʿī as authority for the following: 17.1

People considered these words of Abū l-Najm outstanding:

Beneath her torn shift,
When she shows what she hides,
There's what looks like half a camel's hump with the other half
thrown on top.[19]
It bulges like the back of a head, has a fine straight line,
Like a nib cut on a penboard,[20]
Like a goatee on the face of a Yemeni shaykh,
Right where her belly is.

Then Bashshār said: 17.2

A heavy-bottomed woman, best of the clan of Mālik,
her pussy protrudes in front of her belly.
Its apex is graced by its elevation,
its watering hole tight and thin at the bottom.

Thus he consigned Abū l-Najm's poem to oblivion, as people preferred his and memorized it.

In the days before Islam and in its early period, the Ancients often evoked old age.[21] Those knowledgeable about poetry, experts of its 18 lexicon, are in complete agreement that the best verses on the subject are by Manṣūr al-Namarī. This is their consensus. The fact that he lived recently did not prevent his rendition from being deemed the best. Here they are:

Pain and regret are endless,
when I recall a youth I will never regain.
Youth departed. Time's evil treachery
stole its spark from me.
I had not lived my youth to its innocent full,
then it passed, and suddenly the world followed suit.
If you have not tasted the loss of youth
nor choked on its pain, you have no excuse.[22]
I weep, for I have been robbed of youth:
the world makes no restitution for its worth.
The sight of grey hair even on a loved one
is disgusting and repulsive.

19.1 It is a low and base person who uses a second type of critique of Abū Tammām to achieve prominence and attract notice by composing books defaming Abū Tammām and misleading others in order to gain notoriety through disagreement. He looks to earn a name through denigration, because he has nothing himself to contribute, and to profit from error because he has been barred from truth. It is said, "Disagree and you will become famous." Perhaps he thought that this behavior resembled the verse of ʿAbd al-Aʿlā ibn ʿAbd Allāh ibn ʿĀmir, namely:

If you can do no good, do harm,
for man is expected to do both harm and good.

19.2 Someone said, "If good is beyond you, fly the flag of evil." Another defended his bad poetry on the grounds that his only goal was fame. His are the lines:

I will satirize you for as long as I live, in poetry
    not worth a penny when assessed.
Let them say, "This is bad!"
    I am happy they call it bad, and yet it is transmitted.

'Abd al-Wahhāb al-Madā'inī said: 19.3

Wrongs are not all satisfied.
    Oh no, only nobles receive satisfaction.
To mention the sins of a scoundrel boosts his rank,
    even if he is guilty of wrong.

We cite al-Ḥusayn ibn al-Ḥasan al-Azdī, who cites Abū Ḥātim al-Sijistānī, who in turn cites al-Aṣmaʿī as his authority: 19.4

A Bedouin woman said to her son, "If in the company of others you can do well by going along with what they say, go ahead; if not, disagree and you will become famous, even if you have to hang a donkey's cock around your neck."

I will now discuss some unfounded criticism of Abū Tammām and explain it to you (God support you) before other instances that will follow in the relevant context of Abū Tammām's *Collected Poems*, God willing. 20.1

They found fault (God support you) with the following motif in a poem that is absolutely superb, a eulogy of al-Muʿtaṣim on the conquest of Amorium that begins: 20.2

The sword is more truthful than books,
    its edge marks the divide between earnestness and jest.

They faulted the following words in the poem:

Ninety thousand men like the lions of Mount Sharā
    ripe for victory, before the figs and grapes ripened.[23]

If the fault is that figs and grapes are not serious enough for poetry, we can cite the verse of Ibn Qays al-Ruqayyāt: 20.3

May rain fall upon the vines of Ḥulwān
and the rows of fig trees and vines that grow there!

20.4 And al-Farrāʾ recited a verse on the subject of a variant word form of "grapes" (*ʿinab*) that ends in long *ā*ʾ (*ʿinabāʾ*):

It resembled orchard fruits:
Choice grapes and figs.

So if the fault was that these objects were distinct from the subject matter of poetry, then these critics should have done their homework before voicing their criticism.

20.5 I never met anyone more knowledgeable about Abū Tammām's poetry than Abū Mālik ʿAwn ibn Muḥammad al-Kindī, the scribe of Ḥujr ibn Aḥmad. He had studied twenty of his poems with Abū Tammām himself, and I myself studied them with Abū Mālik in the year 285 [898]. I studied the Amorium poem with him and when I reached this verse, I asked him what it meant and why people found fault with it. He said that his father related to him the following:

I took part in the campaign at Amorium with al-Muʿtaṣim. He learned that the Byzantines who were under siege were saying, "By God, we have been told that our fortress will only fall to bastards! If this lot stay here until the figs and grapes are in season, none will escape." When al-Muʿtaṣim heard this he said, "I hope Almighty God will aid us to victory before the figs and grapes are in season! Let them say, 'Our fortress will only fall to bastards!'—I do not need more men than I have with me."

Abū Mālik then said: I think that Abū Tammām was referring to this idea in this verse.

20.6 Al-Ṣūlī: In view of the soundness of this account, it occurs to me that Abū Tammām took it as an opening for the poem. His phrase "The sword is more truthful than books" seems to allude to it.[24]

Abū Tammām's excellence should not be discounted as too fanciful or on account of some substandard verses. Scholars have found fault with Imruʾ al-Qays and inferior poets, ancient and modern, for numerous erroneous descriptions and other things that would take too long to explain, but they did not thereby forfeit their status. Would Abū Tammām be singled out like this if it weren't for zealous partisanship and prevailing ignorance?

The critics have found fault with the following verse and have consequently lowered him in their estimation: 21.1

His habit was to lavish gifts so nonsensically,
that we thought he was feverish.

Why then do they not lower their estimation of Abū Nuwās for his words about al-ʿAbbās ibn ʿUbayd Allāh ibn Jaʿfar: 21.2

You lavished riches until people said,
"He is insane."[25]

Fever is a better state than insanity. The feverish man gets better and regains his state of health, whereas the madman rarely recovers. Abū Tammām's comparison of excessive and lavish liberality with febrile ranting and raving is more excusable than Abū Nuwās's comparison of it with the behavior of a madman.

And why do they not fault these words by another poet? 21.3

Infantry men warn each other about a hero,
who rushes against the cavalry like a fool.

He compared his excessive display of courage with the behavior of a stupid and undiscerning man.

ʿUbayd al-Liṣṣ al-ʿAnbarī had previously used this motif but split it up: 21.4

None but a man of noble nature or a madman
gives someone like him gifts like these.[26]

So how can they approve these words by al-Buḥturī? 21.5

When other men are cautious with their liberality,
a mad zeal for giving leads him astray.

21.6 And these by Abū Nuwās:

You lavished so many riches,
people thought it stupidity.

22.1 They found fault with Abū Tammām's line:

Do not make me drink blame's bitter water!
I am an ardent lover who enjoys the sweet taste of his tears.

"What does 'blame's bitter water' mean?" they asked.

According to Yūnus ibn Ḥabīb people say, "words full of water"[27] and "How full of water the poetry of al-Akhṭal is!" The phrases "passion's water" and "desire's water" mean tears.

22.2 Dhū l-Rummah said:

Is it because you looked so long at a dwelling of al-Kharqā'
that your eyes shed passion's water?

He also said:

O abode in Ḥuzwā, you brought a tear to the eye—
desire's water drops in streams or floods.

22.3 'Abd al-Ṣamad ibn al-Mu'adhdhal, an excellent poet according to those who attack Abū Tammām and others, said:

Has your face not run out of water
after the humiliation of desire and beggary?[28]

He thus treated the water of the face as real water.[29]

22.4 People say, "the water of youth." Abū l-'Atāhiyah said:

A gazelle dressed in a beautiful dress,
cheeks flush with the water of youth . . .

22.5 This derives from the words of 'Umar ibn Abī Rabī'ah:

Hidden away, the water of youth pours down
the skin of her cheeks.

And Aḥmad ibn Ibrāhīm ibn Ismāʿīl said: 22.6

Slender, his cheeks stormy with the water of youth
but for his skin, he would turn to rain and fall in drops.

Muḥammad ibn ʿAbd Allāh al-Tamīmī on the authority of Ibn al-Sikkīt recited the following verse to me: 22.7

When the water of your love starts to shake,
and a drizzle falls from the low-lying clouds of youth, I said . . .

What is the harm then, if Abū Tammām adopts one of these phrases and uses it in the first half of his verse? Because the second half-verse is "I am an ardent lover who enjoys the sweet taste of his tears," he opened the first half-verse with "Do not make me drink blame's bitter water!"[30]

Sometimes, the Bedouins carry one word over and apply it to another whose meaning is not the same. God (Mighty and Glorious) says, «The recompense of evil is evil the like of it.»[31] But the second evil is not evil, because it is retribution. However, since He first said, «the recompense of evil,» He repeated «evil,» carrying over the meaning of one word and applying it to another. Likewise, «And they devised, and God devised»[32] and «Do thou give them the good tidings of a painful chastisement.»[33] Since He first said, "Give those the good tidings of paradise," He then said, "Give those the good tidings of a chastisement." "Tidings" is used only of good, not bad things, so He carried one word over and applied it to another. It is said, "They are called tidings, because they relax the face,[34] while bad and unpleasant things make it contract." Al-Aʿshā said: 22.8

Yazīd screws up his eyes in front of me
like a grimace caused by the cupping vessels.
May your knitted brows never relax,
and may your face be rubbed in dirt whenever you meet me.

God (Mighty and Glorious) said, «And lower to them the wing of humbleness out of mercy.»[35] This is the most magnificent and beautiful metaphor. The speech of the Bedouins works in the same way. What is the harm, then, if Abū Tammām said, "Do not make me drink blame's bitter water!"?

22.9 Al-ʿAttābī said:

> I suppress the pangs of love, but they are revealed
> by yearning's water as it seeps through my eyelids.

22.10 And Abū Nuwās said:

> When I invited you to generosity, you responded,
> "Here I am," and you found the water of my speech sweet.

This will contribute (God support you) to my defense of Abū Tammām and will give you an indication of my argument on his behalf, until you hear the whole argument in my edition of his poetry, God willing.

23.1 If these critics only knew the plethora of things people have objected to in poems by skilled poets, ancient and modern, they would deem the faults they find with Abū Tammām negligible—provided they believe in judging with an equitable eye. The position of someone who faults Abū Tammām is so contemptible that it is not worth blaming. It is beyond the pale.[36] Abū Tammām is a leading poet, the pioneer of a style subsequently followed by every excellent poet, even though they could not match it, to the point that it was labeled "the style of the Ṭayyite." Every skilled poet traces his ancestry back to him and follows in his footsteps.

23.2 Before Abū Tammām poets used to be innovative in one or two verses of a poem, and were held in the highest regard for doing so. Abū Tammām, however, pushed his talent to the limits and forced himself to be innovative in most of his poetry. I swear, he did so and did so well! And if he fell short in a few verses—which he did not!—then this piffle would drown in the oceans of his excellence. Is anyone so perfect as not to be allowed a mistake, except in the fancy of the unreasonable?

Some disciplines are restricted and some unrestricted, some are closely guarded and some are widely available. The scholar who studies the unrestricted must not ignore the restricted. The one who begins with the widely available must not be unaware of the closely guarded. I say this so no one should have the audacity to sit in judgment on poets, evaluating their words and passing verdict on what is good or bad in their verse, unless he, more than anyone else, is a consummate expert in poetry and prose, and completely qualified in every aspect he turns to; and unless he has committed to memory more varieties of poetic indebtedness and influence than anyone else, and is an unrivaled expert in their topics and their intent. 23.3

How can someone who cannot even put together a single good verse or write an eloquent missive, someone who cannot remember ten motifs out of the ten thousand which have been composed, have the audacity to make such a claim? How does he get his listener to accept it? If only Abū Tammām had been put to the test by the criticism of a high-ranking expert in the discipline of poetry or at least someone who properly understood it. But he was put to the test by those who cannot tell good from bad, but can only pretend to do so. 23.4

Ziyād ibn ʿUbayd Allāh al-Ḥārithī composed a few verses on a similar subject: 23.5

If only I had been put to the test by a Hashimite,
  whose maternal kin are the Banū ʿAbd al-Madān,
I would have put up with what he said.
  But come, look who tested me!

Al-ʿUtbī recited: 23.6

If only noble lions, hyenas, and jackals
  had toyed with my weak flesh,
This would have lessened my pain and soothed my affliction.
  But it is dogs that have finished off my flesh.

23.7 The ignorance of this generation of critics, and the silliness of those who believe their unfounded claims to understanding, bring to mind this line of verse:

How can he who does not know what he wants
know what we want?

The verse is preceded by the following:

Why do I see you free?
Where are your manacles and chains?
Is iron too expensive in your land,
or can no one clap you in chains?

23.8 I cite Abū Sulaymān al-Nābulusī:

A man appeared before Ayyūb ibn Aḥmad in Barqaʿīd and recited poetry to him, but Ayyūb had begun to reprimand his female slave and was not listening. So the man went away and said:

I swear, Barqaʿīd, what a bad education
you provide!
How can he who does not know what he wants
know what we want?
How can poetry pin down
someone no one can clap in irons?[37]
Reason wears itself out there,
foolishness is ever fresh and new.

23.9 Yaḥyā ibn ʿAlī recited the following verses to me about al-Zajjāj:

Good God in heaven! How dull this dimwit is—
unable to string two words together when asked to open his mouth!
His repeated claims of knowledge
are all the evidence we have.

24.1 Were I not under an obligation to provide the proofs you charged me with, people like this would not even cross my mind. I would not consider them worth a mention, let alone worth attacking. Muslim ibn al-Walīd composed some excellent verses on such a motif:

Tell me, little Mayyās, what kind of person are you?
You are neither known nor unknown.
Your honor is too small to be lampooned
while praise, as you know, is much beyond you.
Go then! You have been set free by your honor—
an honor with which you made yourself great, humble as you are.[38]

ʿAlī ibn Yaḥyā said: 24.2

Go! You have been set free by an honor
so vile it protected you.
He who lampoons you
wastes his poetry completely.
I will turn my lampoon to others
and keep it safe from you,
Asking Him who created mankind
to see you as I do.

These verses seem to be taken from the words of Abū Hishām to Bashshār: 24.3

You became great through the humbleness of your parents,
and because you are so vile you dare to talk back.

Muslim lampooned al-ʿAbbās ibn Aḥnaf: 24.4

Pretenders get no satisfaction through the Banū Ḥanīfah,
leave the Ḥanīfah alone and find yourself another ancestry.
Go to Bedouins—claiming them gives satisfaction,
I think you look like a Bedouin.
We ran a fierce race, I put you to the test,
by setting a goal you could neither pursue nor surpass.
Go then! You have been set free by my forbearance,
but I pledge a violent assault when I cannot control my anger.

24.5 Ibrāhīm ibn al-ʿAbbās al-Ṣūlī composed the following verses about Muḥammad ibn ʿAbd al-Malik al-Zayyāt:

Be what you like, say what you want,
explode on the right, thunder on the left!
You were saved by your vileness, like a fly
protected by shit from being caught.

24.6 These critics of Abū Tammām are as Abū Nuwās describes:

I am at a loss as to how to lampoon you;
my tongue just will not work.
When I think about your honor
I take pity on my poetry.

24.7 And also as ʿAlī ibn Yaḥyā describes:

When we put you down, we elevate you.
If we lampoon you, we praise you.
How does one lampoon a man of his standing?
God help us! God help you!

24.8 Also in this vein:

I did not think ugliness could be beautiful,
or that beauty could be ugly,
Until I lampooned Yaḥyā in verses full of filthy words,
and my lampoon turned to praise.

24.9 Al-Ḥuṭayʾah said:

Who are you? We have forgotten who you are.
What kind of wind are you?
Are you the kind of wind that comes with plants and locusts—
they fly away, but you do not appear to be flying away?
Give the land a rest and take your leave
after a scandalous act, just as fornicating slave-girls do.[39]

Another poet said: 24.10

A slave of the Banū Misma' insulted me,
but I held back and protected my honor.
I did not deign an answer.
Who bites a dog when it bites?

Yazīd al-Muhallabī said: 24.11

I am told that a dog who fears my aim
barks at me from a safe distance.
If you had any worth, or if you could even be seen or heard,
we would lampoon you.
So stop insulting me, for my equanimity comes
because I lack an equal.

Another poet said: 24.12

I will not lampoon you, you are no match for me.
Lampoon me however you can![40]
How can I lampoon you if Satire cries in fear
of smelling the stench of your provenance?

Muḥammad ibn ʿAbbād the Scribe composed the following verses about Abū Saʿd al-Makhzūmī: 24.13

You were certain that no matter how long you vilified others,
you would be protected from vilification by your vileness.
The only answer to a dog bark
is a simple, "Away with you, dog!"
Relax, stay where you are,
do not wander east and west!
Reveal the secret of your father!
You don't get a father on a raid.

The words of people like this do not harm Abū Tammām. Stones thrown into the sea do not harm it. The full moon does not wane because a dog barks at it. A poet said: 24.14

Stones thrown by a child
do not harm the raging sea.

24.15 Abū Dhakwān recited to me these verses from al-Mukhabbal on the authority of al-Tawwajī:

When they mention al-Ḥuṭay'ah, they count him
neither a modern nor an ancient poet.
Al-Ḥuṭay'ah is but a cur
whom God struck down for barking at the stars.

24.16 The following verses come from a poem of my own:

When a blow of fate strikes a people,
and a distinguished nobleman makes up for it,
his heart brimful of gifts and courage,
what can the envier say,
but spread sorrow from afar
like a dog barking at the stars?

24.17 And the same poet said:

I lampooned you to death, but you would not die—
dogs do have long lives.

24.18 Ibn al-Rūmī composed these verses lampooning Ibn Abī Ṭāhir:

I saw you barking at me pointlessly,
as you bark at the shining moon.
My bow is ready with sharp arrows
of tried and tested force.
But what protects you from their bite
is your paltry rank in my mind.
So do not fear the sure flight of my arrows,
but don't feel safe from a stray one.

Another poet said: 24.19

When I lampooned you, Satire said to me,
"Are you lampooning him with me or me with him?"
Insult too asked me in amazement, "Do you insult me
with one who is beneath me?"

Another poet said: 24.20

Those I love are gone
and I am left behind among those I do not love.
For a nobleman is never without
a dog that reviles him.

And Bashshār lampooned Abū Hishām al-Bāhilī as follows: 24.21

Does al-Bāhilī insult my honor with his?
I swear, I am the one insulted by that!
Is it not a harbinger of Judgment Day
to see a vile wretch jeer at a nobleman?

Manṣūr ibn Bādhān[41] al-Iṣbahānī said: 24.22

I wanted to lampoon you but
when I learned who you were, I was disgusted.
How can I lampoon you?
I spit every time I hear your name.
That's what saved you. If I wanted to lampoon you,
I would produce a wondrous lampoon.
I have scorched with my brand the hide
of many a man better than you.

Another poet said: 24.23

A dog would indeed be important,
if I shut him up,[42] whenever he howled and barked.

24.24 Al-Farazdaq said to al-Jarīr:

> It makes no difference to the Taghlib Wā'il whether you lampoon them
> or piss where the two seas clash.

24.25 Ḥassān ibn Thābit said:

> Do not insult me, you are not my equal—
> that would take a nobleman.
> I do not care whether a goat rattles in the highlands
> or a wretch jeers at me from a hidden spot.

24.26 Another poet said:

> I swear, you insulted me and won!
> Enjoy! You are cleverer at insults.

24.27 Mukhallad said:

> So much fault was found with you,
> that fault saved you from satire.
> Do not thank me—
> thank the abundance of your afflictions.

24.28 Khiyār the Scribe said:

> I am not chased away by every dog that barks,
> nor am I scared by every fly that buzzes.
> The lions of the thicket know
> that, alone, I pounce on them, when they are a pride.
> How did lowly hyenas show up,
> when hyenas only hunt with lionesses?

And he said:

> If I swatted a fly every time it passed,
> flies would indeed be important to me!

A Bedouin composed these verses on the former motif: 24.29

Slaves evade being lampooned by chiefs:
if you were to be lampooned, lampoon would be an ornament.
No matter what mankind can be accused of
worse could be said about you.

Diʿbil said: 24.30

I forced Satire upon a wretch,
and when it tasted how vile he was it spat him out.

Al-Buḥturī said: 25.1

My task is to carve rhymes from where they belong,
not that cattle understand me.
If the virtues in which I trust
are to be my sins, tell me, how then shall I apologize?[43]

He took the first verse from Abū Tammām:

No crowd, whatever their number, shall grieve you,
for most of them, nay, all of them are cattle.[44]

Al-Buḥturī also took his second verse from Abū Tammām:

If it be my sin that my best pursuit is bad
then bad judgment is my excuse.[45]

And Abū Tammām, or both Abū Tammām and al-Buḥturī, bor- 25.2
rowed this motif from the words of Abū Ḥanash al-Fazārī when he deserted Ḥudhayfah ibn Badr at the Battle of Habāʾah:

How often have the virtues of a good stance
been altered and counted as sins?

This poem contains a beautiful passage:

My stance reminded the women of Ḥamal ibn Badr
and his staunch companion buffeted by the shifts of fortune.

So I said to them, "In our opinion
a lover may not give a beloved an excuse."
If my love were true or I were free,
I would have died alongside Generosity in the Battle of the Well.
My fault is evident, nothing can hide it from anyone who looks for it;
my excuse has gone into hiding.
I tried as hard as I could,
but man's cunning ploy died.
There is no excuse that could be counted in my favor:
repeated excuses are the actions of a dubious man.
How often have the virtues of a good stance
been altered and counted as sins?

25.3 Abū Muḥallim recited this verse:

The hungry and thirsty man must ask for hospitality;
he does not need to make the clouds thunder with rain.

25.4 Abū Tammām alluded to this motif:

A troop like speartips, who took their rest on speartips,[46]
when the night turned pitch black,
For a matter which they must begin,
though they need not bring it to a close.

25.5 This couplet seems to be copied[47] from Ibn Abī . . . .[48] Aḥmad ibn Yaḥyā Thaʿlab recited it to us:

A man of war: he rushed in and put himself to the test.
But treacherous fate betrayed his attempt.
A brave man's task is courage in war;
he cannot control what fate wreaks.[49]

25.6 I composed some verses about consultation:

I consulted those I love about my affair—
he who does not ask for counsel meets with no success—

To find an excuse for what I did.
The actions of destiny are not my fault.

More than any other poet Abū Tammām (God support you) produced inventive motifs with no authority to rely upon but himself. And when he did borrow a motif, he enriched it, embellished it with his novelty, and perfected its meaning, so as to become fully entitled to it.[50] 26.1

According to the scholars of poetry this is the rule for how to borrow motifs. It applies to the words of Aws ibn Ḥajar:[51]

I compose poetry from what my clouds pour down on me.
I work hard to gather firewood in the clan's sandy track.

Abū Tammām then said:

If poetry could run dry, then the abundance collected in your pools
over the passing of the ages would have made it run dry.
But poetry pours from men's minds
when one group of clouds departs, another follows.[52]

Abū Tammām's style of borrowing is like the words of al-Nābighah 26.2
al-Jaʿdī in a poem describing war:

Do you not know what war robs its people of?
Men of forbearance have experience of this.
It overcomes and kills its noble leaders
and its galloping thoroughbreds.
It takes as plunder the black steeds prized so highly by their owner—
in war there are spoils.[53]

Abū Tammām then said: 26.3

The etymology of "war" is "spoils."[54]

Ibrāhīm ibn al-Mahdī said:

They stirred up war, and war gets its name, as they know,
from spoils—if knowledge were of any use.

Abū Tammām rarely borrows like this except from Muslim ibn al-Walīd.[55]

27 You do not need to bother (God support you) with the variety of opinions about Abū Tammām and how people have corrupted his poetry in handing it down. Once this recension is completed,[56] they will all agree on it and abandon all others. People used to disagree about the poetry and *Life and Times of Abū Nuwās,* but then they all reached agreement when I had finished them. A copy of Abū Nuwās's poetry, though not in the recension I produced, was sold for a couple of dirhams, whereas previously it had sold for the same number of dinars.[57] It may soon disappear from sight, discarded and unwanted.

28 I had even seen (God support you) some of these dimwits miscopy Abū Tammām's poetry and then fault him for things he did not say. I will mention this in the relevant context of his poetry, for I am afraid that I will alienate you and do not want to bore you. Still, I have prolonged this epistle (God support you) because I enjoy speaking to you, am keen to do your bidding, and want to let you know that I have fulfilled your desire and given you your due. I will append to this epistle the *Life and Times of Abū Tammām,* because its materials are precious and have virtually never been compiled for anyone else. These will be dealt with quickly, and then I will continue with my edition of his poetry, God willing.

The Life and Times of Abū Tammām

In the name of God, full of compassion, ever compassionate

The Superiority of Abū Tammām

His name was Ḥabīb ibn Aws of Ṭayy and he was of pure Arabian descent. He was born in a village called Jāsim, which will be mentioned in the accounts below,[58] God willing. 29

I cite Muḥammad ibn Yazīd ibn ʿAbd al-Akbar al-Mubarrad the Grammarian as follows: 30

The poet ʿUmārah ibn ʿAqīl came to Baghdad, and people flocked to him. They recorded his poetry, studied it with him, and showed him their own poetry for comment. One day, someone said, "There is a poet who some claim is the very best, while others claim the opposite." ʿUmārah said, "Recite some of his verse to me." So they recited the following:

> She took protection in tears from her anguish at tomorrow's separation.
> Every bed turned into thorns for her.
> What saved her from the throes of death
> was that my turning away was reluctant, and not by choice.
> Compassion made tears of blood
> run down rosy cheeks.
> She is a full moon, her dear face is enough for everyone she meets,
> so she need not endear herself . . .

Then the reciter stopped, and ʿUmārah said, "Let's have more!" So he continued:

But I possess no amassed wealth
to call my own, just a few scattered things
Nor did the days grant me restful slumber
to enjoy, only slumber chased . . .

"Excellent!" said ʿUmārah, "Your poet has outdone all previous poets who used this motif, though much has been composed with it, to the point of making exile appealing. Go on!" The reciter continued:

If a man lingers too long at home, it shows
on his face—so travel and refresh it!
People like the sun more, I know,
for not shining upon them perpetually.[59]

ʿUmārah said, "By God, he's perfect! If good wording, beautiful motifs, sustained intent, and balanced speech constitute true poetry, then this poet of yours is the very best. And if poetry is something else, well then I just don't know!"

31 I cite Muḥammad ibn Mūsā l-Barbarī, who said:

I heard ʿAlī ibn al-Jahm talk about Diʿbil and call him ungrateful, curse him, and malign features of his poetry. Muḥammad added: ʿAlī used to lie about Abū Tammām and invent stories about him, even though, by God, he meant nothing to Abū Tammām and did not have any ties to him. ʿAlī began to describe Abū Tammām, and someone said, "By God, if Abū Tammām were your brother you could not praise him better." "Even though he is not my real brother," ʿAlī said, "he is my brother in refinement, faith, and affection. Didn't you hear him address me as follows:

If a brother, recently met, skimps on affection,
ours is an ancient brotherhood we share, night and day

Or if the water of companionship alters,
ours, sweet, drips from a single cloud[60]
Or if a family bond is broken,
refinement is like a father to us."[61]

I once heard Abū Isḥāq al-Ḥarrī (God show him mercy) talk about 'Alī and relate an account about him and Abū Tammām—which I believe to be this one, or another along the same lines, though I do not remember it very well, nor can I find it; I think I wrote it down in one of my hadith books. I heard Abū Isḥāq say, "'Alī ibn al-Jahm is one of the most accomplished men. It is said, 'His knowledge of poetry is even superior to his poetry.'" 32

Consider then his high regard for Abū Tammām, given 'Alī's preeminence in poetry and knowledge of it; and consider 'Umārah ibn 'Aqīl's high regard for Abū Tammām, when scholars say, "'Umārah formed the last of the rearguard of poets."

'Alī's knowledge of poetry is further confirmed by what 'Abd Allāh ibn al-Ḥusayn ibn Sa'd said. 'Abd Allāh said that al-Buḥturī told him: 33

'Alī ibn al-Jahm sent me an invitation to his home, which I accepted. We talked at length about the poetry of the Moderns. When Ashja' al-Sulamī came up, 'Alī said, "He misses." He repeated this several times. I didn't understand the phrase, but I shied from asking what he meant. When I left, I thought about the phrase. I looked into the poetry of Ashja' al-Sulamī, and saw that his verse was largely bland and devoid of even one outstanding verse. This is exactly what 'Alī meant, that Ashja' came up with verses without hitting a superb one, the same way one says "He misses" about an archer who shoots without hitting anything. Al-Buhturī added: 'Alī ibn al-Jahm was a connoisseur of poetry.

I cite Abū Bakr Hārūn ibn 'Abd Allāh al-Muhallabī, who said: 34.1

We were at one of Diʿbil's gatherings when the subject of Abū Tammām came up. Diʿbil said, "He used to seek out my motifs and lift them." Someone at the gathering asked, "Which one, for example—God support you?" Diʿbil replied, "Mine is

> A man who grants me a favor through an intermediary
> and hopes for gratitude from me is foolish.
> Give thanks to one who intercedes for you in time of need!
> He shields you from adversity by giving of himself."[62]

The man then asked him, "And what did Abū Tammām compose?" Diʿbil replied, "He said:

> I found sweet gifts in your presence,
> while in my presence you found a bitter request.
> When a man makes me a gift of his dignity
> it is as if he is giving me all his wealth."[63]

The man said, "Abū Tammām excelled."

"You lie—God disfigure you!" replied Diʿbil.

And the man said, "By God, had Abū Tammām used this motif first and you followed him, you would not have excelled. If he has borrowed it from you he has done well and deserves it more than you."

Diʿbil got angry and upped and left.

34.2 Al-Ṣūlī: The verses of Abū Tammām are better, so he is more entitled to the motif, whether he was the first to devise it or copied it. There is a famous account about Diʿbil and these very verses, which I will mention because of the preceding account. I cite Muḥammad ibn Dāwūd ibn al-Jarrāḥ, who cites Yaʿqūb ibn Isḥāq al-Kindī, who said:

Al-Qāsim ibn Muḥammad al-Kindī used to pay Diʿbil a yearly stipend, but was late with it one time, so Diʿbil spoke to me about it. I reminded al-Qāsim. Diʿbil received it soon thereafter and said,

"When a man gives me his dignity as a gift." Muḥammad then quoted the couplet.

Al-Buḥturī followed Abū Tammām, and used the same motif:

> The gifts from another are gifts from you,
> if you make an effort for them.[64]

I cite Abū Jaʿfar al-Muhallabī, who cites Ibn Mihrawayh, who cites ʿAbd Allāh ibn Muḥammad ibn Jarīr al-Ṭabarī as follows: 35

I heard the poet Muḥammad ibn al-Ḥāzim al-Bāhilī describe Abū Tammām as first in poetry, knowledge, and eloquence, and say, "I have heard no opening to a lament by either an ancient or a modern poet like this one by him:

> The herald of death deafens you as he forces you to hear.[65]

"or any love poetry[66] like these lines:

> Before her, people had never seen a sun set
> that did not leave them in darkness . . .
> If they could, they would crawl to her, face to the ground,
> rather than walk on their feet."[67]

I cite Sawwār ibn Abī Shurāʿah, who cites al-Buḥturī as follows: 36.1

My career and my fame as a poet started when I sought out Abū Tammām in Homs and I showed him my verse. He held regular gatherings, and every poet sought him out and showed him his poetry for comment. When he heard my poetry, he left the others and approached me. When everyone dispersed, he said, "Out of all those who have recited to me, you are the best. How are you faring?" I complained of my penury. So he wrote a letter on my behalf to the people of Maʿarrat al-Nuʿmān, attesting to my skill and said, "Go eulogize them." When I got there, they treated me with respect because of his letter and allotted me a stipend of four thousand dirhams. This was the first money I ever earned.

36.2 I cite Abū ʿAbd Allāh al-ʿAbbās ibn ʿAbd al-Raḥīm al-Alūsī, who cites a group of people from Maʿarrat al-Nuʿmān as follows:

We received Abū Tammām's letter regarding al-Buḥturī. It went, "My letter reaches you through al-Walīd ibn ʿUbādah.[68] Despite his threadbare clothes, he is a true poet. Treat him with respect."

37 I heard Abū Muḥammad ʿAbd Allāh ibn al-Ḥusayn ibn Saʿd speak to al-Buḥturī when they met in his mansion in the Khuld quarter, with al-Mubarrad the Grammarian in attendance. They mentioned a motif both al-Buḥturī and Abū Tammām had used in their poetry, and Abū Muḥammad said, "Your version is better than Abū Tammām's."

"Absolutely not, by God!" al-Buḥturī protested, "He is the leader and master. He is the sole reason I can earn my daily bread."

"Abū l-Ḥasan," al-Mubarrad chimed in, "you show everyone respect."

38 I cite Abū ʿAbd Allāh al-Ḥusayn ibn ʿAlī, who said:

I asked al-Buḥturī, "Who is the better poet, you or Abū Tammām?"

"His good poetry is better than my good poetry," al-Buḥturī answered, "but my bad poetry is better than his bad poetry."

Al-Ṣūlī: In this al-Buḥturī is absolutely correct, nobody came close to the poetry of Abū Tammām in his time, but here and there his formulation—though not his content—was less than perfect. With al-Buḥturī, however, this never occurred.

39 I cite Abū l-Ḥasan al-Kātib as follows:

The poet Ibrāhīm ibn al-Faraj al-Bandanījī was a great expert in poetry and used to visit us often, as did al-Buḥturī and ʿAlī ibn al-ʿAbbās al-Rūmī. At the mention of Abū Tammām, they would extol him and rate him highly as a poet, placing him ahead of most other poets. Everyone acknowledged Abū Tammām's leadership and agreed that they had all learned from him.

Abū l-Ḥasan commented: These were the greatest poetry experts of their day and the best poets.

I cite Abū l-Ḥasan ʿAlī ibn Muḥammad al-Anbārī, who heard al-Buḥturī say: 40.1

Abū Tammām recited to me his verses:

> A galloping horse, smooth and flowing in his run,
> trusted, not letting you down in the race,
> His joints throbbing, his legs unweary;[69]
> let your eyes roam over one both thirsty *and* saturated.[70]
> If you were to see him advance and
> place his hoofs carefully between heaps of stones, one by one, or in pairs,
> You would be sure—if you didn't look too close—
> that his hoof was made of Palmyra rock or ʿUthmān's face.[71]

Then he asked me, "Do you know what sort of poetry this is?"

"I don't," I replied.

"This is digressing" (or he said, "digression").

"What does that mean?"

"On the face of it the poet is describing a horse, but what he really intends is to lampoon ʿUthmān."

Al-Buḥturī imitated this in his description of a horse in his praise poem for Muḥammad ibn ʿAlī l-Qummī. It begins: 40.2

> Welcome, approaching apparition,
> whether you do our bidding or not.

Then he describes the horse:

Because of a noble, splendid man
I was mounted upon a horse with noble blaze and bright white legs[72]
A temple well built, though in beauty
like an effigy within the temple . . .
He hurls himself forward, like an eagle when it spots its prey,
holds his head high like a falcon on the fist
Listening for a faint sound with fine ears
like paper-thin sheets attached to him . . .
As if the red wine of Baradān or Quṭrabull[73]
has spread its color over him . . .
He commands all eyes; when he appears they look at him
like a lover at an approaching sweetheart . . .
With eyes untroubled by dust motes,
even if one day you gave him the squinty eyes of Ḥamdawayh.[74]

40.3 This Ḥamdawayh was an enemy of the person al-Buḥturī was praising. ʿAbd Allāh ibn al-Ḥusayn related the following to me when we met in Qirqīsiyāʾ:

I said to al-Buḥturī, "In your poem (the one from which we just cited) you imitated Abū Tammām and produced a motif like his. Some people have faulted you for this."

"Am I to be faulted for following Abū Tammām?" al-Buḥturī asked me. "I have not uttered a single verse without having his poetry in mind. But I will go ahead and drop the lampoon from my poem."

He did not recite it thereafter, though it remains in most copies of his poetry.

41.1 I cite Muḥammad ibn Saʿīd Abū Bakr al-Aṣamm, who cites Aḥmad ibn Abī Fanan, who said:

I visited Abū Tammām, who had just received two hundred dinars and given one hundred away to a man who was with him, saying,

"Take it." Later I was told that he was a friend of his, but I knew Abū Tammām was hard up and reprimanded him for giving away what he had been given: "Even if he had been your brother, I would not excuse you, in view of how dire your circumstances are." Abū Tammām responded in verse:

Friend and relative are equally dear to me;
brothers and brethren are one ideal to me.
A group whose refinement is a close neighbor of mine,
though they be spread out across the earth, they remain my neighbors.
Our spirits inhabit one place,
though our bodies may travel to Syria or Khurasan.[75]

Aḥmad ibn Abī Fanan commented: Abū Tammām had the quickest wit of all.

Ibrāhīm ibn al-ʿAbbās al-Ṣūlī excelled with this motif when he said the following: 41.2

I side with friendship's ties against my cousin
and judge in favor of my friend against my brother.
I make a distinction between giving and mentioning my gifts
and use my wealth to meet my obligations.
If you don't find me a free man to be obeyed,
you find me the servant of a friend.

I cite Abū l-Ḥasan al-Anṣārī, who cites Ibn al-Aʿrābī the Astrologer as follows: 42.1

When spoken to, Abū Tammām used to reply before the speaker had finished his words, as if he knew what the other person was going to say and had readied his response. Someone said to him once, "Abū Tammām, why don't you compose poetry that can be understood?"

"And you," Abū Tammām retorted, "why can't you understand the poetry that is composed?" reducing him to silence.

42.2 I cite Abū l-Ḥusayn al-Jurjānī as follows:

It was Abū Saʿīd the Blind who made this comment, in Khurasan. He was a scholar and connected to the Ṭāhirids.

43.1 After Abū Tammām I know of no poet whose expression was more vigorous, whose embellishment more beautiful, whose talent more innate, or who was more gifted as a poet than al-Buḥturī. His verse is balanced, his wording sweet, his expression apposite. By consensus he is first. Nonetheless he does lean on Abū Tammām for his motifs. What stronger proof can there be for the preeminence and superiority of Abū Tammām?

For instance, Abū Tammām said:

He calls down far-flung hope with his shining face;
the good tidings of a cloud, promising copious spring rains.
Such are clouds. Rarely do they call scouts to their gifts of rain
without flashing lightning.[76]

Abū Tammām embellished and perfected this motif.[77]

43.2 Then he rendered it plainer and pithier on another occasion, when he said:

A smiling face is but a garden:
if gifts follow, it becomes a garden with a lake.[78]

43.3 Al-Buḥturī often repeated this motif in his poetry, following Abū Tammām, but still coming in second in most cases. In a poem praising Rāfiʿ he said:

Your smiling face announced the good news first,
then we received gifts,
Like a cloud that holds back its water at the first promise
but then, after steady rain, pours down in streams.[79]

He thus followed Abū Tammām's motifs closely. They attracted him and compelled him to imitate Abū Tammām's phrasing, and so al-Buḥturī's formulation ended up being quite similar, though as a rule it is easier.

Al-Buḥturī then repeated this motif, but borrowed it to describe a sword: 43.4

A bright signal of generosity,
for the sword's iron must shine for him who draws it;
Laughter with gifts in its wake,
for the lightning of clouds comes before the thunder.[80]

Then al-Buḥturī repeated the motif. He dropped the smiling face and replaced it with thunder in a poem composed for Abū l-Ṣaqr Ismāʿīl ibn Bulbul: 43.5

At the start of day he gives you the limit of wealth
with favors that yesterday were but promises,
As morning clouds cross your path, and the thunder
booms as the lightning flashes.[81]

He then repeated the former motif as it was and composed a brilliant verse about al-Muʿtazz: 43.6

Joyous and laughing, when he promises wealth with a
smiling face
his gifts follow,
Like a cloud, when its bolts of lightning flash
they give us a steady rain or a downpour.[82]

It was Abū Nuwās who first devised this motif. He composed a *rajaz* poem in praise of members of the Quraysh, in which he described carrier pigeons as follows: 43.7

Their joyfulness precedes the arrival of gifts
Like the appearance of lightning before rain.
Rainfall is hidden to the observer
Without lightning to guide you to it.[83]

44.1 Anyone who immerses himself in Abū Tammām's poetry will find that the poets who excelled after him relied on him, in the same way that every poet who excelled after Bashshār relied on him and traced his achievement back largely to him. Abū Tammām said:

My answer to one who did not call
and my call from the depths to one who does not answer
are the same.[84]

Al-Buḥturī copied him:

You asked one who does not answer, so your asking was
like giving an answer to one who did not ask.[85]

44.2 Abū Tammām said:

Odes may, one day, become the praise of people
but you, by my life, are the praise of odes.[86]

Then al-Buḥturī said:

Let others boast about all the kinds of poetry they are mentioned in—
it is you poems boast about.[87]

44.3 Abū Tammām said:

When God wants to spread a hidden virtue
he predestines it for the tongue of an envious man.[88]

Then al-Buḥturī said:

You will see where a favor was placed only
when guided to it by an envious man.[89]

44.4 Abū Tammām said:

You worship miserliness, bitter or sweet,
as if it were part of God's oneness.[90]

Then al-Buḥturī said:

Miserliness is worshipped so much that I imagine it
a duty by which God is worshipped and adored.[91]

Abū Tammām said: 44.5

Or, if the water of companionship changes,
ours drips sweetly from a single cloud.[92]

However, he took this from the words of al-Farazdaq: 44.6

Bishr,[93] you are the hero of all Quraysh;
we are both feathers on the same wing.

Al-Buḥturī then said: 44.7

The very least that unites both you and me
is that we attack the tribes from the same side.[94]

Abū Tammām said: 44.8

They produced a noise that boomed in the east
and frightened the hearts of those in the west.[95]

He took this, however, from the words of Muslim: 44.9

When you settle in the nearest border of their land,
the furthest borders open up to you.

Then al-Buḥturī said: 44.10

When he rose at forenoon in the lands of the east
he caused a conflagration in the farthest west.[96]

One day I engaged in a debate with a person who preferred other poets to Abū Tammām without understanding anything, and was prejudiced against him, as a result not of his own comprehension but of accepting someone else's opinion. "Can Abū Tammām," he asked, "compose like al-Buḥturī, who said: 45

He rushed forward so hastily that a witness to the mêlée wondered,
'Is it a meeting of foes or of lovers?'"[97]

I retorted, "Did anyone possess[98] this motif before Abū Tammām said:

He longed for death so much that anyone who did not know him
thought he was yearning passionately for home."[99]

46.1 If a book about al-Buḥturī's borrowings from Abū Tammām had not already been composed by a man of letters, I would have adduced a lot more of this sort of material. But I hate to repeat what has been written and abstain from appropriating[100] literary knowledge that has been laid claim to before me. But, God willing, I will cite some verses from this collection that give an impression of the whole work.

Abū Tammām said:

Despite his absence, I witnessed mighty deeds;
had he been present, he could have been absent.[101]

Then al-Buḥturī said:

I would advise you, but does anyone listen to advice
in the presence of someone whose understanding is absent.[102]

46.2 Although Muḥammad ibn 'Ubayd Allāh al-'Utbī had earlier said:

A people who are present but absent in their minds
for which there are no padlocks.

46.3 Abū Tammām said:

If your foe does not praise you humbly on my behalf,
then know that I am not truly praising you.[103]

Then al-Buḥturī said:

May you always be celebrated in famous poetry,
of such beauty your foes transmit it about you.[104]

This motif seems to derive from the saying, "A man's excellence consists in the fact that his enemies agree upon it," and the saying, "The best praise is that transmitted by friend and foe alike."

Abū Tammām said: 46.4

The sound of someone asking his favor
is sweeter to his ears than sung melodies.[105]

Then al-Buḥturī said:

He is intoxicated by requests,
as if they were songs by Mālik of Ṭayy or Maʿbad.[106]

Zuhayr was the first to portray the joy and laughter of someone receiving a petition. Then others borrowed and developed the motif and said, "The request of a favor is sweeter to him than song, and the petitioner dearer to him than the benefactor." Zuhayr said: 46.5

You find him joyous when you come to him,
as if you are giving him what you are requesting.

Abū Tammām said: 46.6

He served up his boldness to seasoned men—
but when they met in battle, they were like novices.[107]

Then al-Buḥturī borrowed it and composed the following verse:

A king who, in every adversity, possesses
the novice's impetuousity and the seasoned man's resolve.[108]

Al-Buḥturī copied verses of Abū Tammām wholesale, that is, taking both the wording and the meaning, such as Abū Tammām's following line describing his poetry:[109] 47.1

Free from hidden theft,
too noble to be derivative.[110]

Then al-Buḥturī described eloquence as follows:

He does not employ repeated meaning in it
or reuse words.[111]

47.2 Abū Tammām said:

Deserts, camels, and the long night,
three things forever yoked together.[112]

Then al-Buḥturī said:

Search for a third besides me:
after camels, darkness, and desert, I am the fourth.[113]

47.3 Abū Tammām had borrowed this motif from the words of Dhū l-Rummah:

I dressed in robes of night like a bride's gown
with four things that are one to the eye:
A black ʿIlafian saddle, a sharp blade,
a Mahrian mount, and an awe-inspiring hero.

47.4 Abū Tammām said:

His generosity overflows when the cloud skimps,
and he cuts when the sharp saber rebounds.[114]

Then al-Buḥturī said:

They burn when stars have faded
and cut when swords rebound.[115]

47.5 Abū Tammām said:

They only call out to Nūḥ ibn ʿAmr for assistance
when fate deals a mighty blow.[116]

Then al-Buḥturī said:

Abū Jaʿfar, you are only called on
for a momentous affair.[117]

Abū Tammām said: 47.6

You sought his glory and strove;
but it was as lofty as Mount Abān and Mount Yalamlam.[118]

Then al-Buḥturī copied both wording and meaning:

Enviers will not take your glory away
after Mount Raḍwā stands firm, Mount Mutāliʿ immutable.[119]

Abū Tammām said: 47.7

You bring honor to great deeds. Can it be any other way
when you are their guardian?[120]

Then al-Buḥturī said:

His body is restless in quest of great deeds,
so that he becomes their guardian.[121]

Abū Tammām said: 47.8

He dons noble traits so virtuous
they protect his honor like armor.[122]

Then al-Buḥturī composed this verse without fully capturing the motif—just as he falls short in most of the cases that I have cited:

When they don armor for battle,
they are armor for noble traits.[123]

Abū Tammām said: 47.9

To escape death had been simple—
but grim resolve and rugged character brought him back to
face death.[124]

Then al-Buḥturī said:

Had he intended life for himself
he would have found it cheap.[125]

47.10 This also goes back to another poet's words:

Had they fled, they would have remained powerful
but they thought it more noble to face death.

47.11 Abū Tammām said:

Kindness delayed is like a sweetheart you get over
when she is too far to visit.[126]

Then al-Buḥturī said:

I hoped for a gift from Murr,
like one asking for generosity from a sweetheart who refuses to meet.[127]

48.1 The following borrowings of Abū Tammām's words are compositions by al-Buḥturī in the style of Abū Tammām, matching his speech and modeling his content, such as Abū Tammām's line:

An ambition that touches the stars
and luck habitually low to the ground.[128]

Then al-Buḥturī said:

Disoriented, he has a resolve that stands up to every blow of fate
and luck that sits down.[129]

48.2 Abū Tammām said:

You are followed on your heels in pursuit of great deeds and glory
while the feet of other men fall in step.[130]

Then al-Buḥturī said:

You won the race for great deeds, others came second;
after him the feet of other men fall in step.[131]

Abū Tammām said: 48.3

Your petitioners give to petitioners,
and every morning your visitors befriend visitors.[132]

Then al-Buḥturī matched him:

Their guest entertains guests,
and their visitor shows kindness to visitors.[133]

Abū Tammām said: 48.4

They lowered tents over full moons
and confined behind dark curtains the light of shapely houris.[134]

Then al-Buḥturī said:

Bright women lit up the tents
like full moons at night chasing away black darkness.[135]

I cite Ibn al-Muʿtazz, who cites Abū Saʿīd the Grammarian, known as Ṣaʿūdāʾ, who cites Abū Tammām of Ṭayy as his authority for the following: 49.1

Once I was traveling to Samarra during the reign of al-Wāthiq. As I drew near I met a Bedouin. I was curious to ask him about the people of Samarra. He turned out to be extremely astute and articulate. "Which tribe are you from?" I asked.

"The tribe of ʿĀmir," he replied.

"How come you know so much about the Commander of the Faithful?"[136]

"To know is to control."[137]

"What say you about him?"

"He trusted God, who sufficed him: he caused rebels misery, crushed his every enemy, treated his subjects justly, and made pen-wielding officials fear death for their treachery."[138]

"What about Aḥmad ibn Abī Duʾād?"

"A high plain one dare not tread, a hard wood that cannot be harmed. Knives are whetted for him, nets are laid for him, calamities are wished on him, but when one says 'Done deal!' he lunges like a jackal and pounces like a lizard."

"What about Muḥammad ibn ʿAbd al-Malik?"

"His evil engulfs the near, and his harm kills the distant. Every day he strikes men down with no sign of bite or claw marks."

"What about ʿUmar[139] ibn Faraj?"

"Big in giving, all-devouring, one who relishes reprimand."[140]

"What about al-Faḍl ibn Marwān?" I continued, since I found his language pleasing.

"A man resurrected after burial; life and violent death are both against him."[141]

"What about Abū l-Wazīr?"

"The ram in the herd of heretics, as you know. Whenever the caliph paid him no heed, he paraded and caroused. Whenever the caliph roused him, he produced rain and herbage."

"And Ibn al-Khaṣīb?"

"He ate like a glutton and shat in revulsion."

"What about his brother Ibrāhīm?"

"«Dead, not alive, and they are not aware when they shall be raised.»"[142]

"What about Aḥmad ibn Isrāʾīl?"[143]

"How excellent he is! What a prompt helper! He was nurtured in the nurseries of nobility, and when he grew to youthful vigor, they cut him down."

"What about Ibrāhīm ibn Rabāḥ?"

"His nobility ruined him and his glorious deeds ruled him, but he does not give up his kindness.[144] His Lord does not forsake him; his caliph does not mistreat him."

"What about Najāḥ ibn Salamah?"

"What an excellent man! What a mighty avenger! He burns like a firebrand. He holds a seat near the caliph from which he cancels grace and inflicts retribution."

"Bedouin, where is your home?"

"Heavens above, what a question!—when darkness spreads, I sleep wherever sleep overcomes me."

"How satisfied are you with the army?"

"I do not humble my face by asking them for aid.[145] Haven't you heard the words of the Ṭayyite whose poetry fills the world:

> The best speech is the truest. I do not care
> whether you spare my lustrous face or spare my blood."[146]

"I am the Ṭayyite who composed this poetry," I said, and he rushed to embrace me. "God reward the father who made you!"[147] he exclaimed, "Are you not the one who said:

> The generosity of your palm, whether it gives or withholds,
> is no substitute for my lustrous face when I humble myself."[148]

"I am," I replied,

"By God, you are the best poet alive," he exclaimed.[149]

I took the Bedouin back with me to Ibn Abī Du'ād the Judge and 49.2
told him his story. He introduced him to al-Wāthiq, who asked him about his encounter with me. The Bedouin narrated it to him. The caliph ordered that he be given money[150] and showed him generosity. Ibn Abī Du'ād gave him a gift too.

"God has made you a great blessing to me," the Bedouin acknowledged.

I cite Muḥammad ibn al-Qāsim ibn Khallād Abū l-ʿAynā', who said: 50.1

One day I left the home of Ibn Abī Du'ād and went to see Muḥammad ibn Manṣūr, finding his close friend ʿUmārah ibn ʿAqīl there. He was reciting to Muḥammad one of his poems about al-Wāthiq, which begins:

> He recognized their habitations, their traces decayed,
> winds and raindrops at play there.

When he had finished we told him, “We never heard a poem better than this one rhyming in *R*. God favor you, ‘Umārah!”

“By God,” he said, “the *R* poem by this Ṭayyite of yours has blown away any poem in its style.”

“Which one?” we asked.

“His classic lampoon of al-Afshīn,” ‘Umārah replied.

“I know it by heart,” Muḥammad ibn Yaḥyā ibn al-Jahm interjected.

“Let’s hear it!” ‘Umārah exclaimed, and Muḥammad recited:

> Truth shines bright and swords are bared,
> beware the lion of the thicket, beware!

‘Umārah interrupted, “Recite his description of fire,” so Muḥammad recited:

> Unbelief remained a secret within his ribs
> until it ignited the hidden fire-stick:
> A fire, whose hot flames like one half of a coat dyed red
> devoured his body.
> Sparks flew and consumed his being in a blaze,
> that left no ashes behind . . .
> They disjointed him, bit by bit,
> and wreaked calamity upon each vertebra.

50.2 Al-Ṣūlī: Abū Tammām used “wreaked,” specifically choosing this word, because God (Mighty and Glorious) said, «Thou mightest think the calamity has been wreaked on them,»[151] and people say, “Calamities have been wreaked on him,” that is, time’s vicissitudes.

> They stared at the top of his gibbet, as if they were looking for
> the crescent moon on the eve of breaking the fast.

50.3 Then Abū Tammām referred to those who were gibbeted:

> With black garments, as if the sun
> had woven shirts of tar with its own hands,

Mounted day and night on spindly steeds
with halters tied by the carpenter.
They do not stop, and he who sees them
imagines them forever on a journey . . .
They did not realize, no, they didn't bother
to build long lives through proper obedience.[152]

"How brilliant, by God," said ʿUmārah, "he found what had been lost to other poets, as if it had been set aside for him."

Muḥammad ibn al-Qāsim said: From that day on I was convinced that Abū Tammām was the best poet. I had not thought so before.

I cite Abū l-ʿAbbās ʿAbd Allāh ibn al-Muʿtazz as follows: 51.1

Muḥammad ibn Yazīd al-Mubarrad visited me one day. We discussed Abū Tammām, and I asked al-Mubarrad about Abū Tammām and al-Buḥturī. "Abū Tammām," he responded, "has developed with great subtlety novel motifs the likes of which al-Buḥturī does not compose, though al-Buḥturī has sound ideas and a good intuition. Al-Buḥturī's poetry is more balanced, while Abū Tammām composes unusual and refreshing material. This is the style that impressed al-Aṣmaʿī. I would compare Abū Tammām with a diver who dives for pearls and nacre. Abū Tammām and al-Buḥturī have so many beautiful verses that if they were to be measured against most of the poetry of the Ancients, there would be no match."

Al-Ṣūlī: Abū l-ʿAbbās al-Mubarrad took his words "I would compare him with a diver" from those of al-Aṣmaʿī about al-Nābighah al-Jaʿdī, "You will find in his poetry both robes worth thousands and cloaks worth a dime."[153] 51.2

I cite ʿAbd Allāh ibn al-Muʿtazz for the following: 52.1

Ibrāhīm ibn al-Mudabbir was prejudiced against Abū Tammām and used to put him down. One day he had an argument with me about him. "Are you saying this," I asked, "about the person who said:

White hair drew a line on my temples:
the path of mortality, the road to death.
It is an apparition[154] one drives away, a companion one dislikes,
an acquaintance one hates, a new gown that's already been patched.
Radiant white to the eye
but black and stained in the heart.[155]

52.2 "And who said:

If a life, whose span draws to a close, betrays you,
wants you no more, and dispatches you,[156]
You are a sword that strikes a victim and cuts him to pieces,
then bends and falls to pieces.[157]

52.3 "And about him who said:

They submit to your power, which to them resembles
approaching death; there is no shame in this.
People tread softly, call out with silent gestures,
and talk in hushed tones for fear of your reprisal.
Our days, from dawn to dusk, are illuminated by you,
and our nights are daybreak.
Your petitioners give to petitioners,
and every morning your visitors befriend visitors."[158]

I recited other things as well and, by God, I shut him up.[159]

52.4 Abū Bakr al-Ṣūlī commented: Abū Tammām's words "and cuts him to pieces, then bends and goes to pieces" are borrowed from the words of al-Baʿīth:

We give the Mashrafī swords their due;
in our right hands they cut and are cut to pieces.

52.5 Al-Baʿīth also said:

Fate brought him honor through his feats:
But a sword strikes time and again, till finally it breaks.

His words "our nights are daybreak" derive from ʿAbd al-Malik ibn Ṣāliḥ. When al-Rashīd asked him, "What is night like in Manbij?" he responded, "Perpetual daybreak." 52.6

Ibn al-Muʿtazz had borrowed this and said: 52.7

Many a night was continuous daybreak
the full moon bright, the breeze lazy.

If it were permissible to forgive any one poet his plagiarism, then it would have to be Abū Tammām in view of his great novelty, inventiveness, and self-reliance. But the ruling of critics of poetry, the experts, dictate that when two poets exchange or share motif and wording, precedence is given to the older of the two, the one who died first, while the later poet is deemed to have borrowed, because this is the way it usually occurs. If they are contemporaries, then precedence is given to the one with the more appropriate wording, and if this proves difficult to decide, they concede authorship to both. 52.8

I cite ʿUbayd Allāh ibn ʿAbd Allāh ibn Ṭāhir as follows: 53

Faḍl al-Yazīdī brought me poems by Abū Tammām, read them to me, and made me wonder about those who do not understand his worth. "Those who do not understand this," I said to Faḍl, "are as Abū Tammām says himself:

No crowd of theirs, however great, shall grieve you,
for most of them, nay, all of them, are cattle."[160]

"Abū Tammām was criticized by a clique of poetry transmitters," he said to me.

"Transmitters know how to explain poetry," I concurred, "but they do not know its formulations. Only a few of them possess this discernment."

"That explains their behavior," he said.

54 We were at the home of Abū ʿAlī l-Ḥusayn ibn Muḥammad ibn Fahm and the subject of Abū Tammām came up.

"Who is the better poet," one man asked, "al-Buḥturī or Abū Tammām?"

"I heard an expert of poetry being asked this same question," al-Ḥusayn responded, without giving the expert's name, "and he answered, 'How can al-Buḥturī be measured against Abū Tammām? He needs Abū Tammām to survive and his words belong to Abū Tammām, but Abū Tammām neither needs al-Buḥturī to survive nor pays any attention to his words.'"

55.1 I cite al-Qāsim ibn Ismāʿīl Abū Dhakwān as follows:

I heard your uncle Ibrāhīm ibn al-ʿAbbās al-Ṣūlī say, "In my letter writing I relied solely on my ideas and impulses, except when I said, 'What once shielded them exposed them, and their barricades turned into their prison bars,'[161] and when I said in another letter, 'They forced them in shackles from their stronghold and gave them death for hope.' I borrowed my words 'death for hope' from those of Muslim ibn al-Walīd:

> Descending on hearts' blood on a day of strife
> like death attacking hope.

"And with 'stronghold' and 'in shackles' I borrowed from the words of Abū Tammām."

55.2 Ibrāhīm then recited:

> If he heads for the desert, you welcome him
> with blades and spears, and his watering holes are pools of death.[162]
> If he builds walls around himself,
> he is not protected but confined by them.[163]
> Otherwise, tell him how angry you are,
> and abandon him, for, no doubt, fear will finish him off.

Guidance has a long reach in the hand of Abū Isḥāq,[164]
the backbone of religion is straight, its shoulder sturdy.
From whichever direction you approach him, he is the sea:
his depths are gifts, and his shores munificence.
So accustomed is he to opening his hands that if he tried
to close them, his fingertips would rebel.[165]

Then he asked, "Aren't you listening, Qāsim?"
"By God, I am my lord."
"Death cut him down before he had realized all his ideas. The wells of his thought had not run dry before his life's thread[166] was cut."

I cite Abū l-Ḥusayn ibn al-Sakhī, who cites al-Ḥasan ibn ʿAbd Allāh as follows: 56

After Abū Tammām had recited some of his poetry about al-Muʿtaṣim, I heard Ibrāhīm ibn al-ʿAbbās say to him, "Abū Tammām, the princes of speech are governed by your excellence."
"This is so," Abū Tammām returned, "because I take my light from your insight and draw water from your spring."

I cite Abū ʿAbd Allāh al-Huṣayn ibn ʿAlī, who cites Sulaymān ibn Wahb as follows: 57

Abū Tammām saw me write a letter. He studied it carefully and said, "Abū Ayyūb, your prose is my poetry in molten form."

I cite Aḥmad ibn Yazīd al-Muhallabī, who said: 58

I asked my father about Abū Tammām, or he said, My father heard me argue with someone about Abū Tammām, and he said to me, "No poet could earn a single dirham in the days of Abū Tammām. On his death, the poets each took a share of what he used to earn."

I cite Abū l-Ḥasan ʿAlī ibn Ismāʿīl, to whom al-Buḥturī told the following: 59

The first time I saw Abū Tammām—whom I did not know before—was when I appeared before Abū Saʿīd Muḥammad ibn Yūsuf to praise him with a poem, which begins:

> Does a man in love recover from passion? Perhaps I too can recover!
> Does he betray a bond or obey a brother?[167]

I recited it to him, and when I had finished, Abū Saʿīd exclaimed with delight, "God favor you, young man!" Then someone in the gathering said, "God support you, this is my poetry. This man memorized it and came to you first." Abū Saʿīd turned pale. "With your ancestry and family connections you don't need to try to get access to us like this," he said. "Don't do this to yourself!"

"God support you," I said, "this is my poetry."

"Glory be to God, don't say that," the man insisted and then began to recite verses from the poem.

"We will do whatever you want," Abū Saʿīd said to me, "just don't do this to yourself!"

I left speechless and confused and resolved to find out the man's identity. But I had not gone far before Abū Saʿīd called me back. "I have wronged you," he said. "Be brave, do you know who this is?"

"No."

"This is your cousin, Ḥabīb ibn Aws of Ṭayy. Stand up and greet him."

I rose and embraced him, upon which he started to commend me and compliment my poetry. "I was only joking with you," he said. Thereafter I remained close to him. I was regularly amazed by how quickly he could commit things to memory.

60 I cite Aḥmad ibn Ismāʿīl as follows:

I was at al-Buḥturī's home, reciting poetry, but he seemed pensive:

> Women like best
> men whose cheeks most resemble theirs.

Find calmness in motion,
and sleep awake on reddish she-camels
That give you night after night
a pace[168] that banishes all sleep . . .
They were headed for the lush spring camp of Rabīʿah
and arrived at Rabīʿah's lengthening shade . . .
Rabīʿah of Dhuhl,[169] of Murrah, of Maṭar,[170]
their right hand—Khālid ibn Yazīd.
His ancestry is bright as the light of the morning sun
and the beam[171] of breaking dawn
Clear as a bare tract where no guide stumbles out of blindness
or needs pathfinders.
An honor as old as time
(it is shabby for one's ancestry to be recent) . . .
Your forefather Maṭar is father to the crescent moons of Wāʾil;[172]
he fills the flat earth with weaponry and numbers . . .
They inherited pedigree and good fortune,
thus their glory combined forebears and fortune . . .
Rhymes and great deeds last forever
like a string when fitted with a center pearl.
They are scattered jewels; when strung into verse
they become necklaces and ornate chokers.[173]

"What is this?" al-Buḥturī asked anxiously.

"Don't you know it?" I replied, "It's by Abū Tammām."

"You've made me happy by reminding me of it. Only he can achieve such excellence."

I cite Muḥammad ibn Mūsā ibn Ḥammād al-Barbarī as follows: 61.1

I was in the company of al-Ḥasan ibn Wahb when Abū Sulaymān Dāwūd ibn al-Jarrāḥ, the scribe of Abū Isḥāq Ibrāhīm ibn al-ʿAbbās, came to see him. Al-Ḥasan inquired about Abū Isḥāq. Dāwūd answered his queries and then said, "Abū Isḥāq had a debate with a man about the relative merits of Umayyads and Abbasids (God prolong their rule) today.

"'Who nowadays can match the poets the Umayyads had in their time?' the man had said.

"'If the Umayyad dynasty was the time of poets,' Abū Isḥāq retorted, 'the dynasty of the Banū Hāshim is the time of scribes.'"

"Abū Isḥāq will never give up his partiality for the early poets," al-Ḥasan said, "even though, by God, the Umayyad dynasty had no one like him. Isn't he the one who said, 'I can enumerate the poets of the Abbasid dynasty, but you try and count the scribes of the previous dynasty!'" Al-Ḥasan turned toward us, "The people of this dynasty are unrivaled for eloquence in prose writing. For all the love and praise I have for the ancient over the modern poet, I know of no verses more beautiful than Abū Tammām's words on al-Muʿtaṣim, with their novel motifs, perfect praise, and fluid wording." Then he recited the following verses:

> Conquest of conquests: beyond the grasp
> of compositions in poetry or sermons in prose

(Abū Bakr al-Ṣūlī commented: The only version of this account I know uses the word "beyond," though normally people transmit it as "elevated above.")[174]

61.2 A conquest for which the gates of heaven open wide
and the earth comes out in new attire
O Battle of Amorium,
hope leaves you replete with honeyed milk.
You have raised high the fortune of the children of Islam
and lowered the polytheists' fortune and their territory.
She was their mother: if they ever expected to redeem her,
they would do so with their own mothers and fathers.
Cheekily she shows her face;[175] the quest to tame her has baffled Chosroes;
from Abū Karib[176] she turned away in scorn.

From the age of Alexander or even before,
the forelocks of time had turned white but hers had not.[177]
A virgin, not deflowered by misfortune's hand,
nor were the calamities ambitious enough to attain her . . .
At the battle of Ankara the auguries were ominous:
Ankara's courtyards and open spaces were left devastated.
She saw her sister destroyed yesterday:
destruction passed on to her faster than mange . . .[178]
You gave her over to fire, Commander of the Faithful,
a battlefield of burst rock and wood.
You left dark night behind as forenoon—
driven away by a dawn of flames in its midst,
The robes of darkness seemed to crave
a different color; the sun seemed not to have set.
Fire shone bright as darkness hovered bewildered,
dark smoke in a pallid forenoon.

(Abū Bakr al-Ṣūlī commented: Abū Mālik has "shone bright" here but the correct reading is "made morning.")

On one side, the sun rises when it has set, 61.3
on the other, the sun sets, though it has not set . . .
The ruined site of Amorium is more splendid than the hills of
Mayyah's campsite
when they were inhabited and Ghaylān[179] roamed there.
The dust-smeared cheek of Amorium is more delightful to
the eye
than any cheeks, burning with shame,
An ugliness that makes the eye have no need for
outward beauty or pleasing sight.
The beauty of a reversal of fate, whose repercussions will last,
derives its splendor from the reversal's very wickedness . . .
The doing of "Protected-by-God,"[180] avenging God,
fearing Him, and humble before Him . . .

When he attacks a people or rises against a land
he is preceded by an army of fear:
If he did not lead an army into battle,
he would be a one-man army . . .
When Theophilos saw war for himself—
the etymology of "war" is "spoils"[181]
He wheeled around speechless; the Khattian spears had silenced him,
and his bowels churned in turmoil . . .
You saw the great place of rest, and you saw
it could only be reached by a bridge of toil.
If the acts of fate are connected through blood,
or bound through protection unsevered,
Then there is close kinship between your victory days
and the days of Badr.[182]

"Is a single word of this poem flawed?" al-Ḥasan asked. "The Ancients became famous when two verses from a poem happened to be admired, whereas this entire poem is innovative and excellent."

61.4 Abū Aḥmad al-Barbarī said: I never saw anyone have greater affection for another than did al-Ḥasan ibn Wahb for Abū Tammām. Al-Ḥasan committed most of Abū Tammām's poetry to memory, apparently selecting from each poem portions to memorize.

62 Abū Tammām was asked, "Did you really praise Dīnār ibn Yazīd?"[183]

"I only praised him," Abū Tammām retorted, "in order to expose ʿAlī ibn Jabalah's poetry about him. So I said:

Oryxes of al-Naqā—were it not for their legs and the backs of their knees."[184]

Abū Tammām praised him with no other verses.

63 I cite ʿAḥmad ibn Ismāʿīl, who cites ʿAlī ibn al-ʿAbbās al-Rūmī, who cites Mithqāl as follows:

I visited Abū Tammām at home, when he had just composed a poem that was the most beautiful thing I ever heard. But one of the verses was not like the others, and he knew that I had noticed this.

"Why don't you drop that verse," I said.

"Do you think you know more about this than I do?" he retorted with a laugh. "This is like a father who has several sons, each accomplished, handsome, and brilliant. But one of them is ugly and mediocre. The father is conscious of this and well aware, but still he does not wish him to die. A similar thing happens with poems, for the same reason."

I cite Abū Aḥmad ʿUbayd Allāh ibn ʿAbd Allāh ibn Ṭāhir for the following: 64.1

When Abū Tammām arrived in Khurasan, the poets flocked to him. "Let us hear the poetry of this Iraqi," they said and asked him for a recital.

"The governor promised that I can recite for him tomorrow," he responded, "so you will hear it then." When he appeared before ʿAbd Allāh ibn Ṭāhir he recited to him the following verses:

> They are the temptresses and companions of Joseph.
> Determination! Someone who pursues a quest always achieves it.

And then he reached the words:

> The long way to Khurasan shook her composure.
> So I said, "Be calm, the lushest meadow is the farthest one."
> A troop like speartips, who took their rest on speartips
> when the night turned pitch-black,[185]
> For a matter which they must begin,
> though they need not bring it to a close.
> Riding every camel mare whose shoulders move as they amble,
> towering humps travel-worn, udders shriveled.

The wastelands now feed on her. For a year she had fed on them,
as heavy rain beat down on the meadows.[186]

64.2 Al-Ṣūlī: Both versions are transmitted "the deserts feed on her" and "the wastelands feed on her."[187]

64.3 The poets shouted to the governor Abū l-ʿAbbās, "The governor, God support him, merits such poetry, no else does." One of the poets, known as al-Riyāḥī, said, "The governor, God support him, promised me a reward which is still outstanding: it should go to Abū Tammām in return for his composition." "We will double it for you," the governor said, "and do right by Abū Tammām." When he had finished the poem, a thousand dinars were scattered over Abū Tammām, but he touched none of them and the servants picked them up. The governor resented this, "He scorned my kindness and belittled the riches I gave him."[188] After this, Abū Tammām did not get what he wanted from the governor.

64.4 His words "a troop like speartips" are taken from al-Baʿīth:

Unkempt, thin as speartips, they roamed through
the dusty wastes of a desert strewn with mounds of stone.

64.5 And these two verses:

A troop like speartips, who took their rest on speartips
when the night turned pitch-black,
For a matter which they must begin,
though they need not bring it to a close

are copied from the words of a poet:

A man of war: he rushed in and put himself to the test.
But treacherous fate betrayed his attempt.[189]
A brave man's task is courage in war;
he cannot control what fate wreaks.

65.1 I cite al-Mubarrad, who heard al-Ḥasan ibn Rajāʾ say:

I never saw anyone more knowledgeable about fine poetry, both ancient and modern, than Abū Tammām.

I cite al-Ḥusayn ibn Isḥāq, who heard Ibn al-Daqqāq say: 65.2

I was visiting Abū Tammām, while he was compiling a selection of modern poetry. When he came across an effortless poem by Ibn Abī ʿUyaynah in which he lampooned Khālid, Abū Tammām looked at it and put it to one side. "The whole poem is a keeper," he said.

This is the best proof of Abū Tammām's knowledge of poetry, for Ibn Abī ʿUyaynah could not have been more unlike him. He composed with natural talent, without too much thought; he literally breathed poetry. Abū Tammām on the other hand exhausted himself, strained his talent, and thought long and hard, crafting and developing motifs. But he made this comment about Ibn Abī ʿUyaynah because he knew good poetry, whatever its type.

I cite Muḥammad ibn Mūsā, who heard al-Ḥasan ibn Wahb say: 66.1

Abū Tammām appeared before Muḥammad ibn ʿAbd al-Malik and recited to him his poem which begins:

Easy it is for us to speak and for you to act . . .

and then he reached the words:

We find your hands to be more generous than those of other men
and your face more handsome and appealing when we make requests.
You shine when times are black,
while some men think it death to give generously or smile.
By God, what I offer you is a religious duty,
while I offer other people only voluntary works.
No man who carries you as his weapon
faces life's uncertainties unarmed.[190]

"By God," Muḥammad said, "now that I am familiar with your praise, I no longer like anyone else's, because of your quality and novelty. But you spoil your praise by bestowing it on those who are unworthy." "I won't make excuses, though I could do so eloquently,"[191] Abū Tammām replied and continued with the poem, and Muḥammad ordered that he be given five thousand dirhams.

66.2 Afterward Muḥammad wrote to the poet:

> I see you are a generous and easy-going vendor,
> but a high price is only achieved when a merchant hangs on to his goods.
> If he gives his merchandise little value
> he runs the risk that his merchandise will stay with him.
> Such is water: sweet when you let it collect in a pool
> but free access pollutes it.

67 I cite Abū Bakr Aḥmad ibn Saʿīd al-Ṭāʾī, who said:

Ibn ʿAbd Kān and Ismāʿīl ibn al-Qāsim—two paragons of secretaryship and literature—used to say, "Al-Buḥturī is a better poet than Abū Tammām."

When I mentioned this to al-Buḥturī he said to me, "Don't say this, cousin, by God, he is the sole reason I can earn my daily bread."

68 I cite ʿAbd Allāh ibn al-Ḥusayn, who cites al-Buḥturī:

I heard Abū Tammām say, "The first poetry I ever said was:

> Beware of my willfulness! I do not obey him who rebukes me . . .[192]

"I praised ʿAyyāsh ibn Lahīʿah with it, and he paid me five thousand dirhams."

69.1 I cite Muḥammad ibn ʿAbd Allāh al-Tamīmī, Abū ʿAbd Allāh al-Ḥazanbal, who cites Saʿīd ibn Jābir al-Karkhī, who cites his father as follows:

I was with Abū Tammām when he recited his praise poem rhyming in *B* to Abū Dulaf, in front of a group of Arab and Persian nobles. It begins:

Over encampments and places of play such as this
tears long suppressed are poured forth.
Place of my pleasure, who let you decay
and become a place for the south and east winds?

And then he reached the words—

When red camels bring me face to face with Abū Dulaf
I am safe from all vicissitudes . . .
At forenoon he makes his cherished wealth a bride
though she be led to the lowest suitor . . .
His bright gifts in response to dark requests are more beautiful
than white blossoms opened by the dew.[193]
When the Lujaym[194] one day harness their steeds,
surrounded by the children of the fortress, offspring of chaste noblewomen,
Death, sharp swords, and spears
are their true relatives in fear . . .
When the Tamīm, one day, boast with their bow[195]
and embellish the virtues they firmly secured,
Your swords in the Battle of Dhū Qār
toppled the throne of him who took Ḥājib's bow in pledge.[196]
When the achievements of others are held
next to their glorious achievements, they look like defects.
Noble deeds soaring ever higher as if they were
trying to exact revenge from a star.

Al-Ṣūlī: ʿAlī ibn al-Jahm borrowed this to describe a fountain: 69.2

A fountain which shoots high and seeks revenge in the skies
and never fails.[197]

69.3 "Clan of Rabīʿah," Abū Dulaf cried, "never have you been praised with such poetry! What will you give the one who said this?" They grabbed their shawls and turbans and threw them toward Abū Tammām.

"He has accepted these," Abū Dulaf said, "and lends them to you for you to wear. I will give him a good reward on your behalf. Finish, Abū Tammām!" And when Abū Tammām reached the words:

If poetry could run dry, then the abundance collected in your pools
over the passing of the ages would have made it run dry.
But poetry pours from men's minds:
when one group of clouds departs, another follows.[198]

Abū Dulaf said, "Pay Abū Tammām fifty thousand dirhams, though, by God, this is not enough for his poetry."[199]

69.4 He turned to Abū Tammām, "Nothing compares to this composition except your lament of Muḥammad ibn Ḥumayd."

"Which passage does the commander mean?" Abū Tammām asked.

"Your words:

He did not die before his sword edge broke[200] from striking,
and he twice served drink to tawny spears.
To escape death would have been simple—
but grim resolve and rugged character brought him back to face death . . .[201]
He placed his foot in the swamp of death
and said to it, 'Beneath you lies the resurrection.'
In the early morning he clothed himself in praise,
and did not leave before the shrouds were his reward . . .
On the day he died, the Banū Nabhān[202] were like the stars
from whose midst the full moon had fallen
Consoled for a man dwelling in a tomb for whose loss Greatness too must be comforted,
and over whom Magnanimity, Bravery, and Poetry weep.[203]

"By God, I wish that you had said this about me!"

"I and my kin will give our lives for the commander, may death take me before him!"

"A man lamented with such poetry is not dead."[204]

Al-Ṣūlī: The most astonishing thing, the most offensive outrage, is that some people found fault with his words: 69.5

> On the day he died, the Banū Nabhān were like the stars
> from whose midst the full moon had fallen.[205]

"He meant to praise him but lampooned him instead," they said. "It is as if his kin were obscure during his lifetime, and when he died they shone by virtue of his death. He should instead have said something like al-Khuraymī's verse:

> When one of their moons fades or is eclipsed
> another moon appears on the horizon, shining."

I cannot excuse a person in his right mind and master of a scholarly discipline for saying such things. Nor do I excuse anyone who listens and does not protest—unless, by God, he wanted to blame and insult Abū Tammām. In the first place, why does the person guilty of such misjudgment devote himself at all to the subject of poetry, debating its motifs, and evaluating its formulations? Perhaps he imagines that this knowledge comes to the brightest and cleverest people without any need of instruction, serious effort, and long study with its experts. But what then about a dull and slow student? Anyway, someone who is by nature suited for one or two kinds of knowledge is not necessarily suited for others. 69.6

Most agree that among Arabs and foreigners, al-Khalīl ibn Aḥmad was the wisest scholar of his time. He was so talented that he mastered everything he took up. Then he started to write about theology, and his natural aptitude failed him. He went off track, and even now his disciples are busy defending some of his utterances. 69.7

69.8 If only I knew when these people had sat with an expert in the discipline of poetry or studied with him and listened to what he had to say. Imagine: They think that anyone who explains the rare vocabulary of a poem or supplies its case endings can pick out what is good in it, recognize the mediocre and the inferior and evaluate its formulations! Who among their authorities was an expert in this art? Was it the one who lampooned al-Aṣmaʿī and claimed:

I raise myself today above a man
who is not my match—no, he misses.
Of vices he has no lack and it serves him right,
because he is a liar whom only liars wish well.
When we meet for a fiercely contested race,
the noble steed comes in first, before the stumbling nag.

Or was it the one who attended the gathering of an illustrious scribe and was asked by the host if he composed poetry and beseeched to recite some of it? The guest asked to be excused, but the host insisted, and the guest recited his ditty:

Who will buy an old goat of a scholar[206] for two dirhams,
Advanced in years, with only two milkings left in him,
And just two teeth?

69.9 Such are the poems of their authorities. I do not think that anyone with a smattering of learning is in the dark about why they blame Abū Tammām. Nor had I thought that God (Mighty and Glorious) would ever put me in the position of having to explain such a thing.[207] The philosophers said, "If the ignoramus kept quiet, people would be left in peace," and "To keep saying 'I do not know' produces fewer mistakes." One of the Ancients said: "I liked saying 'I do not know' so much that I even wanted to apply it to the things I do know." A poet said:

I will convey a truth whose path people will follow:
the ignorant benefit from the informed.

If you do not know and do not ask him
who appears to know, how will you ever know?

I will explain this, God willing.[208]

It is related that a person of distinction was mentioned to Caliph ʿAlī ibn Abī Ṭālib (God's blessings upon him). ʿAlī commented, "You are right, but a lamp does not shine by day." He (God be pleased with him) did not mean that there was no light in the lamp or that it had ceased to be what it was. The lamp is dim in comparison with the light of day.[209] He was not attacking daylight or lamps, but he meant someone of modest distinction as opposed to someone who is more distinguished. A poet excellently said: 69.10

Ṣafrāʾ, your love was freely given
in nights when your departure was still a jest.
While you were among them, the maidens of the quarter were ugly,
but became beautiful when you were gone.[210]

He wanted merely to set her above them without insulting anyone, for ugly people do not become beautiful in an instant. Rather, he meant that they *were* beautiful, but she was more so, and when they were all together, they were inferior to her.

Ibrāhīm ibn al-ʿAbbās al-Ṣūlī said: 69.11

Among them you were a center pearl,
and they, left and right, were below you.

Abū l-ʿAbbās Aḥmad ibn Yaḥyā Thaʿlab recited these lines from Ibrāhīm ibn al-ʿAbbās—Abū l-ʿAbbās used to dictate Ibrāhīm's verses to his students, and he always praised this verse. Ibrāhīm did not want to blame the other women—they were after all strung on the string beside her—but to elevate her. Thus Abū Tammām wanted to place Muḥammad ibn Ḥumayd above his clan, even if they were all excellent. The light of the full moon does not make the stars vanish altogether nor change their nature. But one sees better with moonlight than with starlight, and when there is no full moon, one uses the light of the stars, though it is not as strong. Abū Tammām appears to have meant: "Though the full moon has left them, they still have stars."

69.12 A poet composed some excellent verses:

I do not chide the Banū Kaʿb.
  Peace be with the Kaʿb and their poet!
God placed us higher than the house of our fathers,
  just as the camel's hump is raised upon its back.
So it is with people who have a brother
  but only they are noble.

This is the motif Abū Tammām was aiming for.

69.13 Al-Nābighah had also expressed the very same thing, and if Abū Tammām is guilty of error, so is al-Nābighah, for he apologized to al-Nuʿmān for going to the Ghassanids and managed to avoid belittling them. He elevated al-Nuʿmān above them and said:

But I was a man who roamed
  through the land, following his quest.
When I visit brethren and kings, I am honored
  and put in charge of their riches.

Don't you see how he praised them all? He then said:

As you do with people to whom I see you grant favors,
  and do not consider their gratitude a sin.

This is the most beautiful emulation[211] and clearest argument by al-Nābighah. It means, "Do not blame me for expressing gratitude to them in your presence, in the same way as it is not a sin when you grant people favors and they show you gratitude in the presence of your enemies." Then al-Nābighah elevated al-Nuʿmān above the other kings.

Don't you see that God gave you a station
  below which you see every monarch tremble?

You are a sun, other kings stars:
When the sun rises, the stars cannot be seen.

All the things al-Nābighah explained hinge on a single motif: your superiority over the kings is like the superiority of the sun over the stars. It was said, "He meant, 'As long as you are good to me, I don't need these kings, even if they have a degree of excellence, as someone on whom the sun shines does not need to wait for the light of stars.'" 69.14

I cite al-Qāsim ibn Ismāʿīl, who heard Ibrāhīm ibn al-ʿAbbās say: 69.15

If an eloquent scribe wanted to rephrase in prose the motifs which al-Nābighah composed, he would need many more words to do so.

Al-Ṣūlī: Ibrāhīm used to prefer this poem to any other. Al-Nābighah was preceded in this motif by the poets of Kindah. One of them praised ʿAmr ibn Hind in a classic poem:

The earth underneath the people almost shakes
when they see ʿAmr ibn Hind's troops and he is in a rage.
He is the sun that rises on an auspicious day,
and blinds the light: other kings are dim stars.

Abū Muḥallim recited these verses.

Abū Tammām copied[212] the motif expressed in al-Nābighah's words, which Ibrāhīm had explained, except he applied it to the subject of love: 69.16

"Will you forget the full moon?" she asked.
"As long as the sun has not set," I bravely replied, "the moon has not yet risen."[213]

This is what Abū Tammām had in mind.[214]

Al-Najāshī said: 69.17

What a man you are! But the two of you
differ in excellence like sunlight and moonlight.

69.18 Abū Muḥallim recited the following verses of Ṣafiyyah al-Bāhiliyyah, and al-Gharīḍ, I believe, put them into song:

The uncertainties of time betrayed Mālik;
time lets nothing remain as it is.
We were like the stars of the night with a moon in our midst[215]
that dispelled the darkness, but the moon fell from
our midst.[216]

This is the very wording and meaning of Abū Tammām.[217]

69.19 Jarīr lamented al-Walīd ibn ʿAbd al-Malik as follows:

A dusty vault with sloping walls
conceals the virtues of a caliph.
So immense was their loss that his sons became
like stars from whose midst the moon had fallen.

Do you think al-Jarīr meant to lampoon al-Walīd, or say that his sons benefited from his death?

69.20 Nuṣayb said, taking the very motif expressed in al-Nābighah's words:

He is the full moon; the people around him are stars.
Do stars resemble the shining moon?

69.21 Next the critics said: "Why didn't he say something like al-Khuraymī's verse:[218]

When one of their moons fades or is eclipsed
another moon appears on the horizon, shining."

69.22 To this statement one must respond, "Why didn't he who said:

The stopping places and dwellings of the encampments are
effaced . . .[219]

"instead say:

Bring the bowl and pour the morning draught . . .?[220]

"And why didn't Imru' al-Qays, instead of saying:

> Stop! Let us weep for the memory of a beloved and a dwelling . . .[221]

"instead say:

> Vestiges of Khawla's camp lie on the sandy hill of Thahmad . . .?"[222]

The point is that the motif Abū Tammām intended is not the motif al-Khuraymī intended. Abū Tammām wanted to express superiority in leadership, whereas al-Khuraymī had equality in mind. Abū Tammām said, "A leader died and a lesser leader ascended," whereas al-Khuraymī meant, "A leader died and his equal arose." How, once he has finally understood, can anyone who missed the point of this deign to utter a word about poetry? Still, I find this sort more excusable than those who listen to them and mouth their words. 69.23

Al-Khuraymī was imitating Aws ibn Ḥajar: 69.24

> When one of our noble stallions[223] loses his teeth,
> another noble stallion bares his teeth in a roar.[224]

This is like what Abū l-Ṭamaḥān Ḥanẓalah ibn al-Sharqī l-Qaynī said: 69.25

> I belong to a people who are what they are;
> when one of their chiefs dies, his equal arises.
> Stars in the darkness, when one star vanishes
> another appears and his fellow stars take refuge there.
> Their faces and their deeds brighten up the dark night,
> so that one can thread gems on a string by their light.[225]

Another poet said: 69.26

> The caliphate is passed down among the inhabitants of the earth;
> when one of our leaders dies another one rises.

Ṭufayl al-Ghanawī said: 69.27

Stars in the darkness: when one falls
another appears and drives the dark away.[226]

69.28 Another poet said:

When one of our leaders passes away,
another leader raises the pillar of glory.

This is what al-Khuraymī meant.

70.1 If it were not certain that such things[227] do happen to the critics without them noticing it, and that they speak gibberish if they overstretch themselves, it would be difficult for me to make those who are not experts and are not privy to it understand this. We have the books left by the members of the group who have passed away. Did they utter a single word of this criticism at all? Or did they claim it? Or did anyone else claim it on their behalf? Or did they practice it? Their silence is enough for anyone who has renounced[228] partisanship, found it within himself to be just, considers with the mind's eye, and ponders my words. For the memory and imagination of the heart see better than the eye, once it no longer has something in its sight.

70.2 Ibn Qanbar put this excellently in the following verses:

Even if you are not with me, my memory of you is.
My heart sees you, even though you are absent from my sight.
The eye sees, then no longer sees the one it loves,
but the heart's eye never fails to see.

70.3 This appears to derive from Bashshār's words:

They say, "You rave about Salmā, without having seen her—
how far your thoughts have run away with you!"
I said, "A few words can make me besotted,
because the heart sees what the eye does not."[229]

71.1 Equally detestable is when the critics blame Abū Tammām's words:

If a drawn sword fell from Capella[230]
it would land on their heads.

People have also transmitted, "it would land on their right hands," but I will clarify the verse's correctness and the error of its detractors according to the former version, which, to my mind, is what Abū Tammām had said.

Abū Tammām meant that every war is either fought alongside them or against them, and that every sword attempts to rob them of their power.

On such a theme, a man from the Banū Abī Bakr ibn Kilāb uttered the following verses, which al-Mubarrad the Grammarian recited to me: 71.2

Kings rejoice when they strike us dead,
and seize the pinnacle of merit.
Every clan is after us,
makes killing us its goal.
Violent is our death, endurance is our mark.
We are not frightened when warriors[231] are red with blood.

By this he meant that the Banū Abī Bakr will not die in their beds—the Arabs reviled this—and that swords strike their faces and hands as they advance, rather than their backs and the backs of their heads as they retreat.

This is why Kaʿb ibn Zuhayr said something similar in his poem in praise of the Emissary (God bless him and his kin), who then granted Kaʿb protection after he had pronounced a death sentence upon him. It begins: 71.3

Suʿād is gone and my heart today is distraught,
left enslaved by her, shackled beyond redemption.

In this poem he praises the Quraysh:

Spear thrusts to their chests not their backs;
they do not shun the pools of death.

Why do the critics of Abū Tammām not blame Kaʿb for his poetry, which the Emissary (eternal peace be his) listened to and rewarded?

71.4 I cite Muḥammad ibn al-ʿAbbās, who cites Abū Ḥātim, who cites as his authority Abū ʿUbaydah as follows:

One of the descendants of Ḥabīb ibn ʿAbd Allāh ibn al-Zubayr[232] boasted: I have the longest history of violent death;[233] five of my forefathers in a row have been killed.

71.5 Another poet said:

People who, when spears fly,
bare their hearts to receive them:
They wear their hearts
over their armor to shield it.

71.6 I cite Abū ʿUmar ibn al-Riyāshī, who cites his father, who cites al-Aṣmaʿī as his authority, who in turn cites Abū ʿAmr ibn al-ʿAlāʾ as his authority for the following:

When ʿAbd Allāh ibn al-Zubayr learned of the killing of his brother Muṣʿab and of his steadfastness in battle, he said, "By God, we do not die from gluttony like the Umayyads,[234] but we die a quick death among spears in the shadow of swords." ʿAbd Allāh would not have boasted about it if it were something to be ashamed of.

71.7 Among those who reviled dying in bed was Sahm ibn Ḥanẓalah, who said, chastising Ṭufayl ibn ʿAwf:

Praising, not blaming, the point of your spear,
Abū Qurrān, you died in bed all the same.[235]

71.8 The following verses are attributed to al-Samawʾal, but belong to al-Ḥārithī:

Our souls flow forth on the blades of swords.
Only iron can make them do this.

Love of death brings us close to our allotted spans
but the allotted spans of others loathe death and remain at bay.
None of our chiefs has died in his bed,
nor did his death, wherever it occurred, go unavenged.[236]

Another poet made the souls of his tribe the food of death. He said: 71.9

Death finds our souls sweet
but finds others bitter, and will not taste them.
We are made of a hard wood[237] death loves to chew on:
All but a few of its roots have vanished.

Abū Tammām and Aḥmad ibn Abī Du'ād

72.1 I cite Abū Bakr ibn al-Khurāsānī, who cites 'Alī al-Rāzī as follows:

I was present when Abū Tammām's assistant recited the following verses to Ibn Abī Du'ād:

The virtues of Aḥmad ibn Abī Du'ād have consigned
the vices of all ages to oblivion . . .
I travel the horizons
with your generosity for my camel and my provisions.
Thoughts and desires remain at home with you,
even if my mount moves restless through the lands.[238]

"Abū Tammām, did you invent or borrow this last motif?" asked Ibn Abī Du'ād.

"It is mine," Abū Tammām replied, "though I drew inspiration from the words of Abū Nuwās:

If our words praise anyone
other than you, it is *you* we mean."[239]

72.2 Al-Ṣūlī: One day I attended a gathering with a group of literati who fervently championed Abū Nuwās.

"Abū Nuwās is a better poet than Bashshār," one of them declared. I objected and apprised him of Bashshār's excellence and superiority, noting that all Moderns borrowed from him and followed in his footsteps. He had been unaware of this.

"Abū Nuwās was the first and only one to use certain motifs," he retorted.

"Which ones?" I asked and proceeded to give the origin of everything he recited, including Abū Nuwās's verses:

> When we praise you for a good deed
> you are as we praise you—but better.
> If our words praise anyone
> other than you, it is *you* we mean.[240]

"The first verse," I stated, "derives from the words of al-Khansā':

> When praise is dedicated to people, even if it is exaggerated,
> something nobler can always be said about you.

"and from the words of ʿAdī ibn al-Riqāʿ:

> I praise him but I know—the fact does not escape me—
> that he is superior to what I say and praise him for.

"The second verse is from the words of al-Farazdaq addressed to 72.3
Ayyūb ibn Sulaymān ibn ʿAbd al-Malik:[241]

> My soul does not bid me travel
> to anyone without having you in mind."

I cite Aḥmad ibn Ibrāhīm, who cites Muḥammad ibn Rawḥ al-Kilābī, 73
who said:

Abū Tammām came to stay with me and told me that after the conquest of Amorium he had praised al-Muʿtaṣim in Samarra. Ibn Abī Du'ād had mentioned him to al-Muʿtaṣim.

"Isn't this the man with the rough voice who recited to us in al-Maṣṣīṣah?" the caliph asked.

"Commander of the Faithful, he is accompanied by a transmitter who recites beautifully."

The caliph granted Abū Tammām an audience and his transmitter recited his praise of the caliph. (Muḥammad did not mention the exact poem.) The caliph ordered that he be given many dirhams in the form of a check payable by Isḥāq ibn Ibrāhīm al-Muṣʿabī.

"I took the check to him," Abū Tammām narrated, "and recited to him a poem in his praise, which Isḥāq appreciated and ordered that I be given a sum that was a little less than what al-Muʿtaṣim had ordered.

"'By God,' Isḥāq exclaimed, 'if the Commander of the Faithful had ordered that you be given the same sum in dinars instead of dirhams I would have done the same.'"[242]

74 I cite ʿAlī ibn al-Ḥusayn ibn Yaḥyā the Scribe, who cites Muḥammad ibn ʿAmr al-Rūmī, who said:

I have seen no one quicker to gain consensus or win an argument than Ibn Abī Duʾād.

"Abū ʿAbd Allāh," al-Wāthiq said to him, "I have received a note containing lots of lies."

"It is no wonder," the judge replied, "that I am envied for my standing with the Commander of the Faithful and that people lie about me."

"They claim that you appointed a blind man to a judgeship."

"Indeed. I had decided to dismiss him when he lost his sight; then I heard that he had gone blind from weeping so much for Commander of the Faithful al-Muʿtaṣim and kept him in his position."

"Further, according to the note, you gave a poet a thousand dinars."

"Indeed not! I gave him less. The Emissary (God bless him and keep him) gave a reward to the poet Kaʿb ibn Zuhayr and said about another poet, 'I will silence his tongue with money.'[243] The recipient is an effective and superb panegyrist of the Commander of the

Faithful, even if I were to base my judgment solely on his composition for al-Muʿtaṣim (God's blessing upon him) about you, Commander of the Faithful[244] (God support him):

> Secure the caliphate for Hārūn!
> He gives its unruliness calm and stability.
> I knew this son was a wrist
> that you would not leave unadorned by bracelets.[245]

"I gave him five hundred dinars."

Al-Rūmī continued: Abū Tammām appeared before Aḥmad ibn Abī Du'ād when he had just been administered medicine and recited to him the following verses: 75

> God provide you with bodily health
> for as long as doves coo in the branches.
> How was the medicine?
> May God cure you with it until the end of time!
> May God not prevent you from
> any good deed which you may confer[246]
> May you always glow with good health,
> which shields you from unforeseen trials.
> The long life of Aḥmad the Generous
> is a gift we are indebted for.
> If our lifespans were to do our bidding,
> the lords of Yemen would give him a share of their lifespans.[247]

I cite Abū ʿAbd Allāh Muḥammad ibn ʿAbd Allāh, known as "the Visitor," who cites his father: 76

Abū Tammām appeared before Aḥmad ibn Abī Du'ād, who had reprimanded him for something. The poet apologized to him. "You are all humankind," he said, "and I could not bear the anger of all humankind."

"Excellent! Where did you borrow this from?"

"From the words of Abū Nuwās:

By God, it cannot be denied
that He gathered the whole world in one man."[248]

77 I heard Muḥammad ibn al-Qāsim say:

Ibn Abī Du'ād said to Abū Tammām, "Some of your verses were recited to me. If you had uttered them in a moment of worldly renunciation or in contemplation or as a call to obey God (Mighty and Glorious) pure and simple, you would have outdone yourself. Recite them for me!"

"Which verses?"

"Those rhyming with *fa-adkhulahā* (allow me to enter)." Abū Tammām recited to him as follows:

Say to Ibn Ṭawq, the pivot of auspicious fortune,
when the vicissitudes of time trample high and low,
You have become Ḥātim in generosity, Aḥnaf in sagacity,
and Kayyis and Daghfal in knowledge.[249]
Why is it that I see the spacious chamber locked to me,
when I have long asked for it to be opened?
It is like the garden of paradise opened wide,
but I have done no pure deed which will allow me to enter.[250]

78.1 I cite ʿAwn ibn Muḥammad al-Kindī, who cites Maḥmūd al-Warrāq, who said:

I was sitting outside Ḥayr castle in Samarra with a group of people to watch the cavalry. Abū Tammām passed by and sat with us.

"Abū Tammām," one of us asked him, "what sort of man would you be if you weren't from Yemen?"

"I want only the place God chose for me," Abū Tammām replied, "Who would you like me to be descended from?"

"From Muḍar."

"Muḍar is noble because of the Emissary (God bless him and keep him). Were it not for him, they could not measure up to our kings: we have So-and-so and So-and-so." Abū Tammām went on to boast of his own tribe and mention the faults of several individuals from Muḍar.

Maḥmūd continued: The incident was reported to Ibn Abī Du'ād in an embellished form.[251] 78.2

"I don't want Abū Tammām to appear before me," the judge said. "He shall be denied entry."

Abū Tammām then apologized to him and praised him with the following verses:

Distant exile is fortunate with Su'ād
as she heeds the call of Tihāmah and Najd . . .
My hair turned white; I think the whiteness of the head
comes only from the intense whiteness of the heart.
The heart precedes the body
in every bit of comfort and ill luck.[252]
I was unfamiliar with white for so long. Now that I have lived a little,
I no longer recognize the color black . . .[253]
Abū 'Abd Allāh, you lit the fire stick in my hand,
which had never struck fire before.
You made darkness stray from the path of hope,
when guides and caravan-leaders go astray . . .
The light of hope shines farther for eye and heart
than the light in the sky.

Then Abū Tammām described members of Ibn Abī Du'ād's entourage and described himself as more in his favor.

They attended generosity's summit and core,
while time's hostile vicissitudes turned me away from it and its like.

Hills are closer to the first drop of rain;
my luck is that of the low ground
After the backbiters bared their swords
and, though blunt, cut me up.
There are certain hadiths which,
when probed judiciously, have a weak chain of transmission.[254]
May your ear, open only to truth,
banish fabricated speech from you.
Sagacity and dignity erect barriers around the ear
against ugly speech.
Greatness forbids that your person
be called a steed ridden by resentment.[255]

78.3 Composing what, to my mind, is the most beautiful apology, Abū Tammām spelled out the accusation and apologized for it to Ibn Abī Duʾād:

May rain after rain fall[256] where we knew shelter
and transform into gardens town and desert dwellings alike.

Then he said:

My wing may belong to the Banū Udad,
but it is tightly feathered by the Banū Iyād . . .[257]
When death roams among the spears,
the Iyād are as impetuous as lions and wise as ʿĀd.
Aḥmad ibn Abī Duʾād's virtues have consigned
the vices of all ages to oblivion.[258]
When you dwell with him you inhabit a region
nursed by morning and evening clouds . . .
I travel the horizons
with your generosity for my mount and my provisions.
Thoughts and desires remain at home with you,
even if my mount moves restless through the lands.

(Al-Ṣūlī: This is derived from the words of Abū Nuwās:

If our words praise anyone
other than you, it is *you* we mean.[259])

The paradise that follows resurrection is well known, 78.4
but your generosity is my paradise on earth.
I heard a stray piece of news, a blighting catastrophe
brought at night by scorpions . . .
That I had spoken ill of Muḍar,
and my complaint raced to you like a thoroughbred steed . . .
Apparently I requited good with bad
and blackened your kindness,[260]
Drove camels laden with ignominy,
made ingratitude settle in the abode of sacred effort . . .
My froth does not float on watered-down milk
nor is my live-coal smothered by ashes . . .
Look closely! Before your time
false accusations about Ziyād were made to Nuʿmān . . .[261]
I have sent you virgin motifs
followed by the swift guide and the caravan-leader . . .
Thought is yoked to them and when they refuse to move,
it tames them by mentioning you, and they become docile . . .
Free from hidden theft,
too noble to be derivative,[262]
Their lord supplicates you, guilty of no crime
other than good counsel and affection.
He who listens to backbiters
has his ear cut by sharp tongues.[263]

Ibn Abī Du'ād was angry with Abū Tammām for a long time and would not be reconciled, until Khālid ibn Yazīd al-Shaybānī interceded. Abū Tammām composed a poem in praise of Ibn Abī Du'ād, mentioning the intercession of Khālid ibn Yazīd, but inserted in his apology obscure passages that no one has yet been able to explain. I 78.5

thought I would provide them because I happen to know what they refer to, as I have memorized accounts of the events to which Abū Tammām alludes. Such knowledge is accessible only to those who memorize historical accounts. The poem begins:

Did you see which cheeks and necks
came our way in Liwā and Zarūd?

In this poem he said:

Listen to the words of a visitor
whose eyes are not deceived even in a confusing desert . . .
One who fled at night chased away by the shame of their claim,
not a fugitive in fear.
You were the spring rain before him,
and behind was Khālid ibn Yazīd, the full moon of the tribes.
Thus the rain was from Zuhr, the gentle cloud,
and the ground was of Shaybān, the iron mountain.

Zuhr and Ḥudhāq are two clans of Iyād, the people of Ibn Abī Du'ād.

Tomorrow the pristine nature of my courtyard would become clear,
if you were to check my tracks in Tihāmah and Najd.[264]
Al-Walīd thought carefully
when they said, "Yazīd ibn al-Muhallab must die."

Abū Tammām meant al-Walīd ibn ʿAbd al-Malik. When Yazīd ibn al-Muhallab fled from imprisonment by al-Ḥajjāj, he sought the protection of Sulaymān ibn ʿAbd al-Malik. Al-Ḥajjāj wrote to al-Walīd to have Yazīd executed, but Sulaymān ibn ʿAbd al-Malik and ʿAbd al-ʿAzīz ibn al-Walīd intervened with al-Walīd on Yazīd's behalf. "You must hand him over to me," the caliph demanded. Sulaymān complied but sent his son Ayyūb along with Yazīd. "Do not leave his side," he instructed his son, "and if anyone seeks to harm him, defend him with your life."

The lie put before him collapsed, 78.6
for the fabrication was not well built.
Ibn Abī Saʿīd was in a strong position, protected by a king,
indebted to the offspring of kings.

"Ibn Abī Saʿīd" means Yazīd ibn al-Muhallab, because the teknonym of his ancestor al-Muhallab is Abū Saʿīd. "Protected by a king" refers to Sulaymān ibn ʿAbd al-Malik,[265] and "grateful to the offspring of kings" means that Sulaymān would be fortunate to enjoy the gratitude of the House of Muhallab for all time.

To me Khālid is no less a man than Ayyūb or ʿAbd al-ʿAzīz, 78.7
nor are you second to al-Walīd.

Abū Tammām says, "My intercessor is Khālid ibn Yazīd, and he means as much to you as ʿAbd al-ʿAzīz ibn al-Walīd and Ayyūb ibn Sulaymān meant to al-Walīd. In fact he is even closer to you than they were to al-Walīd. And you are no less astute or forgiving than al-Walīd."

My life is yours—have you not been given the key 78.8
to unlock any catastrophe? . . .
When your cloud cast its shadow over me
the witnesses against me became witnesses for me
After they had thought
that I would suffer from their iniquity as ʿAbīd suffered.[266]

He means ʿAbīd ibn al-Abraṣ,[267] who met al-Nuʿmān on an ill-omened day. On that day the king would ride out and kill anyone he encountered, especially the first person he saw. He encountered ʿAbīd and killed him.

They took aim with an arrow fletched with disobedience: 78.9
the arrow did not fly true.
Whenever God wants to spread a hidden virtue
he predestines it for the tongue of an envious man.[268]

If fire did not burn its surroundings
    we would not know the sweet smell of incense-wood.
If we did not have to fear fate's outcomes,
    the envious, not the envied, would benefit.[269]

Praise be to God and God bless and keep
Muḥammad the Emissary and his progeny.

Abū Tammām and Khālid ibn Yazīd al-Shaybānī

In the name of God, full of compassion, ever compassionate

We cite al-Mubarrad the Grammarian for the following. He had written some entertaining books, from which I used to choose passages I would study with him.[270] They included the following passage from one such book, titled *Trials and Tribulations*. 79.1

Abū Tammām traveled to Khālid ibn Yazīd ibn Mazyad,[271] the governor of Armenia, and praised him. Khālid ordered that he be given ten thousand dirhams along with travel expenses. Khālid gave instructions that the poet need not stay if he did not want to, and bade him farewell. Some time later Khālid went out hunting and spotted Abū Tammām sitting under a tree drinking from a skin of date wine with a servant playing a tanbur in front of him.

"Ḥabīb?"

"Your servant and slave, my lord."

"Where did the money go?" Abū Tammām responded in verse:

Your generosity taught me munificence;
  I have nothing left of your gift.
Before a month had passed I gave it all away,
  as if I had power like yours.
In a day, in one hour you dispense
  gifts it takes you a year to acquire.

Were our Lord not to add to your gifts,
I do not know where you would get your gifts from.[272]

Khālid ordered Abū Tammām to be given another ten thousand dirhams, which the poet accepted.

79.2 Al-Ṣūlī: Abū Tammām's words "he taught me munificence" derive from those of Ibn al-Khayyāṭ al-Madīnī. He had praised al-Mahdī, who ordered that he be given a reward. The poet gave it away in the palace,[273] with the following verses:

I touched his hand with mine in a request for riches
not knowing that his generosity would be contagious.
He infected me and I scattered all I had:
I did not profit from him as the wealthy do.

News of this reached al-Mahdī, who doubled the poet's reward and had it delivered to his home.

80.1 I cite ʿAbd Allāh ibn Ibrāhīm al-Mismaʿī l-Qaysī, who cites his father, who cites Abū Tawbah al-Shaybānī—the most articulate man I have ever met—who said:

I visited our friend and commander Khālid ibn Yazīd, and he was in the company of a man full of jokes and pleasant conversation to whom I took an immediate liking. "Haven't you heard his poetry about us?" Commander Abū Yazīd inquired. "I haven't come across eloquence more brilliant or a tongue more articulate than his:

What happened to the dune of the precinct toward the sloping sands
and to the sandy track near the bare ground?"

He continued until he reached the passage where the poet says:

What a fine banner you came back with
on Thursday, as high noon approached.[274]

In my mind's eye I see it as a white eagle
flying from royal chambers and lofty porticos.
It beat the air, its home,
and battled the wind, its support.
Its forelocks swirl over its brown spine,
blood-stained in battle . . .
Its folds flutter above a king
who hunts heroes for sport . . .
Can any king match your mighty deeds
when your heart is greater than his domain?
Your noble traits alone without your kin are more plentiful
than those of any king, including his kin and troops.

I had never heard anything like this, and was beside myself with joy in the hope that the poet hailed from Rabīʿah. "Who, Sir, are you descended from?" I asked.

"From Ṭayy, but my allegiance is to this commander."

"What a pity! Why can't you be from Rabīʿah or Nizār?"

Then Commander Abū Yazīd ordered that Abū Tammām be given ten thousand dirhams in silver coin. By God, he deserved more.

Al-Ṣūlī: In this poem Abū Tammām recounted Khālid's intercession with Ibn Abī Du'ād, as we have already mentioned:[275] 80.2

By God I will never forget[276] how he rejected the lies,
ravings, and ugly words of hate.
The clans of Yemen will not forget
how he helped and rallied round them.
He showed me preference when I took refuge with him;
he is every man's support.[277]

I cite Abū Bakr al-Qanṭarī, who cites al-Mubarrad as follows: 81.1

Khālid ibn Yazīd al-Shaybānī's honor and generosity were legendary, and he rewarded poets most liberally. He gave ʿUmārah ibn ʿAqīl a thousand dinars for compositions in his praise:

Khālid's nature and his deeds
shun every unseemly affair.
Should we arrive at his gate during the midday meal,
we are admitted to the meal despite his chamberlain's protests.[278]

And Abū Tammām received a sum many times more than this for praising Khālid.

81.2 I came across the following in the handwriting of Ibn Abī Sa'd, who cites Ismā'īl ibn Muhājir, who cites an agent of al-Ḥasan ibn Sahl, known as al-Balkhī:

Khālid ibn Yazīd asked Abū Tammām to recite his poem about al-Afshīn in which he mentioned al-Mu'taṣim and which begins:

The houses and courtyards of the realm have come alive,
resplendent with lush gardens and sweet springs.

Abū Tammām reached the words:

He wears forbearance next to his skin
and in adversity fastens a sharp sword over it.
The eagle-standards are overshadowed
by eagles, quenching their thirst[279] for blood in the forenoon.
The birds camp beside the banners until they seem
to be part of the army—although they do not fight.[280]

Khālid asked, "How much did you receive for this ode?"

"Not enough to slake thirst or stave off poverty."

"I will reward you for it."

"Why? My hope has been fulfilled by praising you."

"Because I have sworn that, whenever I hear good poetry that a man was praised with but did not pay what it was worth, I will make up for it."

"And what if it's awful poetry?"

"I consider the case, and if the poet received anything for it, I ask for it back."

Al-Ṣūlī: Abū Tammām excelled in this motif and outdid previous poets by saying "although they do not fight." Muslim before him had said: 81.3

He trained the birds to habits they grew to trust
and they follow his each and every move.

Even better than this is the composition of Abū Nuwās about al-ʿAbbās ibn ʿUbayd Allāh: 81.4

When spears spit black blood
and death shows itself in its guises
His ample coat of mail is draped around
a lion whose claws drip with blood.
At forenoon the birds follow him as a sign,
confident they will be sated from his kill.[281]

However I do not know anyone who expressed this motif better than al-Nābighah. He deserves its authorship, even if he was not the first to use it, because he did it better (the conditions of borrowing have already been mentioned).[282] Al-Nābighah said: 81.5

When they march off with the host,
squadrons of birds circle above them, following the troops.[283]
The birds hover, confident that
when the hordes meet, his tribe will be first to win.

The motif derives from a poem by al-Afwah al-Awdī that begins: 81.6

Sons of Hagar, it is a bad plan
to demand justice and withdrawal from us.

In this poem he said:

You can see the birds following us,
assured that they will be fed.

Praise be to God, Lord of the worlds, and God bless and keep Muḥammad the Emissary and his progeny.

Abū Tammām and al-Ḥasan ibn Rajā'

In the name of God, full of compassion, ever compassionate

We cite 'Awn ibn Muḥammad al-Kindī, who cites Muḥammad ibn Sa'd Abū 'Abd Allāh al-Raqqī, a scribe of al-Ḥasan ibn Rajā', who said: 82

Abū Tammām presented a praise poem to al-Ḥasan ibn Rajā', and I saw he was a man whose knowledge and intellect were superior even to his poetry. It was at a drinking party, and al-Ḥasan ibn Rajā' asked Abū Tammām to recite, which he did as follows:

> Stop the clamor, woman. I dislike you.[284]
> My resolve is not now how it began.
> I am the one you know, and if you have been stricken with ignorance—
> I now take the place of the accusers.

When he said:

> His days turned so black
> that he thought they were nights.

Al-Ḥasan said, "By God, from this day forth they shall no longer be black for you." And when he recited:

> Do not be surprised at seeing the noble stripped of wealth,
> for torrents cannot flow uphill.

Look at how the camels trot: the reviver of poetry
drives them to the killer of wealth.

Al-Ḥasan stood up and exclaimed, "By God, you will have to finish the poem with me on my feet." Abū Tammām stood up too and continued:

When we reached the courtyard of al-Ḥasan
the kingdom of dearth lost its rule over us.
He gave us hope[285] despite the vicissitudes
that often strike it down.
He pays dearly for the virgins of poetry;
even when cheap, their dowries are expensive in the eyes of noble men.
With him expectations are confirmed,
and hope reigns over wealth.
Your father's name[286] has come true in you
through profit most splendid and fortune most auspicious.
You saw me and asked your soul to pour over me,
you gave me rich gifts, without waiting for me to ask.
Like the cloud that has no choice but to produce showers,
whether or not it is begged for rain.[287]

They embraced each other and sat down together. "By God how beautifully you have presented this bride!"

"By God," Abū Tammām replied, "had she been one of the dark-eyed beauties of paradise, the most perfect dowry she could have would have been when you stood up in her honor."

Muḥammad ibn Saʿd[288] concluded his account as follows:

Abū Tammām remained with him for two months and received ten thousand dirhams disbursed by me as well as many other gifts that I know nothing about—even though al-Ḥasan ibn Rajāʾ was a stingy man.

I cite Abū l-Ḥasan al-Anṣārī, who cites Nuṣayr al-Rūmī, the freed slave of Mabhūtah al-Hāshimī, who said: 83

I was with al-Ḥasan ibn Rajā' when Abū Tammām came to stay with him. Al-Ḥasan had instructed his chamberlain that no petitioner should stand at his gate without his being informed. One day the chamberlain came in laughing.

"What's the matter with you?" al-Ḥasan asked.

"There is a man at the gate, asking for admission. He claims he is Abū Tammām al-Ṭā'ī."

"Ask him what he wants."

"He says, 'I have composed a poem in praise of the commander (God support him) and have come to recite it to him.'"

"Send him in." The man entered, a meal was brought, and al-Ḥasan bade him eat with him.

"Who are you?" he inquired.

"Abū Tammām Ḥabīb ibn Aws al-Ṭā'ī. I have composed a poem in praise of the commander (God support him)."

"Let's have your praise poem." The man recited a beautiful ode. Al-Ḥasan approved, said, "You've done well," and ordered that he be given three thousand dirhams. The man thanked him and blessed him. Al-Ḥasan had earlier instructed all present to say nothing.

Abū Tammām then said to the man, "We want you to improvise a verse matching this one," and Abū Tammām extemporized a verse.[289] The man began to stutter.

"Shame on you! Are you not ashamed?" said Abū Tammām, "You have claimed my name, my father's name, my teknonym, and my ancestry? *I am Abū Tammām!*"

The old man laughed. "Don't be too hasty to judge me before I can tell the commander (God support him) my story. I had a comfortable life, but then my circumstances changed. A friend of mine, a man of letters, suggested that I come before the commander with a praise poem.

"'I do not know how to do this,' I objected.

"'I will compose a poem for you,' my friend offered, and he composed this poem and gave it to me, saying 'Perhaps you will get something from it.'"

"You have what you wanted," al-Ḥasan declared, "I have doubled your reward." Thereafter the man became his intimate companion, and people grew fond of him and called him "Abū Tammām."

84 I cite Abū Bakr al-Qantarī, who cites al-Mubarrad as follows:

Every time I heard al-Ḥasan ibn Rajā' mention Abū Tammām he would add, "He is the 'Father of Perfection.'[290] I have never met anyone who knew more about any subject."

85 I cite ʿAlī ibn Ismāʿīl al-Nawbakhtī, who said:

Al-Buḥturī said to me, "By God, ʿAlī, if you saw Abū Tammām, you would have seen a man of the most consummate intellect and culture, and you would know that poetry was the least of his accomplishments."

86.1 I heard al-Ḥasan ibn al-Ḥasan ibn Rajā' tell Abū Saʿīd al-Ḥasan ibn al-Ḥusayn al-Azdī that one day his father saw Abū Tammām abbreviate his prayer.

"Complete it, Abū Tammām!" al-Ḥasan ibn Rajā' said. Upon his return from prayer, the poet defended himself, saying, "Fleeting wealth, lengthy hope, declining youth, and increasing sorrow all forbid the completion of prayer, especially when we are traveling."

"I wish he cared about his religious duties as much as he does about his poetry!" my father deplored, "How can a creditor not be burdened by his debt?"[291]

86.2 Al-Ṣūlī: Some people accused Abū Tammām of unbelief and even claimed to have proof. They made it a pretext for attacking his poetry and for calling its beauty ugliness. I do not think unbelief detracts from poetry, or that faith adds to it. We hear Abū Tammām cursed for unbelief by those who never saw or heard him, or even studied him with any reliable person, so how can Abū Tammām's unbelief be proved? This is the opposite of what God (Mighty and Glorious) and his Emissary (eternal peace be his) commanded, and what all Muslims practice. People are to be judged at face value until their unbelief is established by something they say or do, something one sees or hears, or something for which there is unequivocal proof.

They based their argument on the authority of Aḥmad ibn Abī Ṭāhir. A number of people told me that he said: 86.3

I visited Abū Tammām while he was composing, the poetry of Muslim and Abū Nuwās laid out in front of him. "What is this?" I asked.

"Al-Lāt and al-ʿUzzā whom I have venerated for thirty years instead of God."[292]

If this statement is true, its form is ugly and its content and expression wicked, because these are the words of a libertine besotted with poetry. It means, "These two goddesses have distracted me from venerating God (Mighty and Glorious)." But it is absurd to think that Abū Tammām would venerate two poets to whom he might have considered himself superior, equal to, or nearly so. Nonetheless, one must not utter with one's tongue in earnest or in jest or believe in one's heart something that will incur the wrath of God (Mighty and Glorious), and for which one must atone. 86.4

How can the critics give credence to someone's unbelief so as to curse him in their gatherings, a man whose entire corpus of poetry attests to the opposite of what they allege? If it is a matter of religion, they should busy themselves cursing poets whose unbelief is a plain and true fact—poets the caliphs (God's blessing be upon them) executed after receiving confessions and unequivocal proof. But even then, the status of their poetry did not suffer as a consequence, nor did its excellence vanish. Rather it was the poets themselves who were at fault and doomed in their unbelief.

86.5 Unbelief does not detract from the poetry of the four poets whom scholars agree are the best of all time: Imru' al-Qays, al-Nābighah al-Dhubyānī, Zuhayr, and al-Aʿshā. They are harmed by their unbelief, not by their poetry. I don't think Jarīr and al-Farazdaq are put before al-Akhṭal because they were believers and al-Akhṭal was not. Their precedence derives from their poetry. Some scholars have placed al-Akhṭal ahead of them. Indeed all three are peers on one level, and people have different opinions about whom to rank first.

86.6 I cite al-Qāsim ibn Ismāʿīl, who cites Abū Muḥammad al-Tawwajī, who cites as his authority Khalaf al-Aḥmar, who said:

Ḥammād al-Rāwiyah was asked which of the three, Jarīr, al-Farazdaq, or al-Akhṭal, was the best poet. "Al-Akhṭal," he answered, "what can you say about a man whose poetry endeared Christianity to me?"

86.7 This too is a joke by Ḥammād and shows his extreme partiality for the poetry of al-Akhṭal. If people scrutinized his conduct as intently as they do Abū Tammām's, then his words would appear ugly indeed.

87.1 Abū Tammām's poetry is excellent. People are unanimous about it. I do not think that his poetry suffers at all from attacks on it in this day and age. I have seen many well-known scholars attack and belittle Abū Tammām throughout his life and theirs, but people did not take them seriously. I presented their justification for their lack of knowledge[293] about poetry and its criticism and evaluation earlier, when I showed that this was not part of their vocation. Meanwhile in return for the poetry for which they attacked him Abū Tammām received highly coveted gifts from learned kings and leading officials, who know prose and poetry best. In fact it was Abū Tammām himself who gave gifts to contemporary poets and interceded for them—every excellent poet was his apprentice and followed in his footsteps.

87.2 People's extreme bias against him appears in the following incident that Ibn al-Muʿtazz recounted to me:

When I saw Ibrāhīm ibn al-Mudabbir appreciate Abū Tammām's poetry without giving him full credit for it, I related an account related to me by Abū ʿAmr ibn Abī l-Ḥasan al-Ṭūsī. I did this as a way to hold up a mirror to him. Al-Ṭūsī said:

"My father sent me to Ibn al-Aʿrābī to study poetry with him. I admired the poems of Abū Tammām, so I recited to Ibn al-Aʿrābī poems of the Hudhayl tribe and then the following *rajaz* poem by Abū Tammām, which I pretended was by a Hudhaylite poet:

> I admonished an admonisher for admonishing me,
> He thought me ignorant of his ignorance.[294]

"I recited the whole poem. 'Write it down for me,' he demanded, and I did.

"'Isn't it beautiful?' I asked.

"'The most beautiful thing I ever heard.'

"'It is by Abū Tammām.'

"'Tear it up! Tear it up!' he cried."

ʿAbd Allāh ibn al-Muʿtazz wrote an appendix to this account, which 87.3
I copied from him. He wrote:

Such behavior by scholars is utterly disgusting. One must not deny anyone's excellence, friend or foe. Rather, one must draw benefit from those placed both high and low.

The Commander of the Faithful, ʿAlī ibn Abī Ṭālib (God's blessings 87.4
upon him), is reported to have said:

Wisdom is the believer's lost camel. Retrieve your lost camel, even from the polytheists![295]

Buzurgmihr is reported to have said:[296] 87.5

"I took the best anything had to offer—even a dog, cat, pig, or raven."

"What did you take from the dog?"

"His closeness to his family and his defense of what he protects."

"What did you take from the raven?"
"His extreme watchfulness."
"What did you take from the pig?"
"That he gets up early to attend to his needs."
"What did you take from the cat?"
"Her gentle way of asking and her soft purr."

87.6 Ibn al-Muʿtazz commented: Anyone who maligns poetry that cheers the heart, gladdens the soul, excites the ear, and focuses the mind, does himself a disservice and insults his own knowledge and taste.

87.7 ʿAbd Allāh ibn al-ʿAbbās (God have mercy upon him) is reported to have said, "Caprice is a deity adored," basing himself on the words of God (Mighty and Glorious) «Hast thou seen him who has taken his caprice to be his god?»[297]

88.1 I cite ʿAlī ibn Muḥammad al-Asadī, who cites Thaʿlab, who said:

Ibn al-Aʿrābī stopped as he passed by al-Madāʾinī. "Where are you headed, Abū ʿAbd Allāh?" al-Madāʾinī inquired.

"To one who is as the poet says:

Camels carry our bodies to a king
from whom we receive riches and learning."[298]

88.2 Al-Ṣūlī: Ibn al-Aʿrābī unwittingly quoted Abū Tammām's poetry. Had he known it was his, he might not have done so. Ibn al-Aʿrābī did the same thing in his miscellany on lexicography,[299] in which he cites many poems of the Moderns. Had he known he might not have cited them.

89.1 We have known people to tell the truth about their enemies' merits, not with the intention of placing them first, or out of a desire to elevate or praise them, or even out of respect for their faith. Rather, they did so out of self-respect and to call attention to their own excellence and knowledge.

One such case is what ʿUmārah ibn ʿAqīl said after listening to the recitation of a poem by al-Farazdaq in which he satirized Jarīr, "By God, he devoured my father! By God, he devoured my father!"[300] 89.2

Another such case is what al-Farazdaq said when he heard a composition by Jarīr—I cite al-Faḍl ibn al-Ḥubāb, who cites Muḥammad ibn Sallām, who cites Maslamah ibn Muḥārib ibn Salm ibn Ziyād as follows:[301] 89.3

Al-Farazdaq was with my father in one of his upper chambers, when a man entered. "Today a poem by Jarīr circulated in the Mirbad market. People were reciting it to each other." Al-Farazdaq turned pale.[302]

"It is not about you, Abū Firās."

"About whom then?"

"About Ibn Laja' al-Taymī."

"Do you remember anything of it?"

"Yes, I memorized two verses."

"Which ones?"

The man recited:

> If for a while Taym enjoyed a carefree life,[303]
> Taym has now been pressed hard.
> Let not the lion attack the ʿUkl and bite them unawares,
> while the ʿUkl sniff the bite-marks of wounded prey.

Both Abū Khalīfah and Abū Dhakwān explained this motif to me, on the authority of Ibn Sallām as follows:[304] 89.4

When a lion bites an ewe and is chased away, the sheep gather to sniff at the bite-mark. Then the lion takes them by surprise and kills another sheep. ʿUkl is a sister tribe of Taym, ʿAdī, and Thawr, all descending from the Banū ʿAbd Manāt ibn Udd. Jarīr meant, "Do not help the Taym, because if you do, I will leave them alone and lampoon you instead."

Ibn Sallām commented: The line by Jarīr is similar to this:

I cautioned the Banū ʿAdī,
"Keep your clothes away from being splattered with the victim's blood."

89.5 "What a devil!"[305] al-Farazdaq cried, "He is unstoppable when he goes about it this way," meaning, this poem's *B* rhyme.[306]

89.6 Ibn Sallām added, citing someone from the Banū Ḥanīfah, who cites al-Farazdaq:

"I considered the *B*-rhyme to be Jarīr's father and mother." That is, he excelled when he adopted it.[307]

89.7 Another example[308] is what al-Rāʿī said about Jarīr after Jarīr had lampooned him. I cite Judge Abū Khalīfah al-Faḍl ibn al-Ḥubāb, who cites Muḥammad ibn Sallām, who cites Abū l-Baydāʾ al-Riyāḥī as follows:

A rider passed by, chanting the following couplet:

At a dog who howled for no reason
I shot a rhyme, inflicting a bloody wound,
A steed racing forth from the mouths of men,
like the feast thrown by an Indian blade: once brandished, it severs limbs.

"Whose couplet is this?" al-Rāʿī asked.
"Jarīr's."
"What a devil!"[309] al-Rāʿī replied, "Men and jinn combined could not best him!"

Ibn Sallām commented: Al-Rāʿī meant, "How can I be blamed if someone like him beats me?"

89.8 We cite Muḥammad ibn al-Faḍl, who cites ʿUmar ibn Shabbah, who cites Muḥammad ibn Bashshār as his authority as follows:

"Recite to me some verses by Ḥammād ʿAjrad," Bashshār bade his transmitter.

> You are traced to Burd, but this is not your ancestry.
> Let's assume you are from Burd—may I fuck your mother—
> who the hell is Burd anyway?[310]

"Can anyone hear me?" Bashshār asked.

"No."

"That whoreson did well."

This is very common, and I have provided a sample to give an idea of the rest. This sort of thing[311] detracts from excellent and outstanding practitioners of any profession. It is ugly if done by anyone, but more so by scholars. I seek God's protection from following caprice, furthering error, babbling about scholarship, and clinging to prejudice. 89.9

I cite ʿAwn ibn Muḥammad as follows: 90

I saw Diʿbil belittling Abū Tammām at al-Ḥasan ibn Rajāʾ's place. ʿIṣābah al-Jarjarāʾī confronted him. "Listen to how Abū Tammām praised Abū Saʿīd Muḥammad ibn Yūsuf, and if you like it, there you go! And God forbid you don't like it!" Then he recited to Diʿbil the poem that begins:

> If it were not for neighbors taking their leave . . .

When he reached Abū Tammām's words:

> The glory of Muḥammad ibn Yūsuf aggrieved his enemies;
> the deficient in this world begrudge the excellent.
> He is like the river; when you meet it head on, it carries you along.
> But if you redirect it from the banks, it follows you.[312]
> I see no benefit in him who cannot harm,
> nor do I see harm in him who grants no benefit . . .

Paradise follows after death.
But before death, his rain is our paradise.[313]

Diʿbil conceded, "We don't deny this man's excellence, but by placing him first, you elevate him above his rank and attribute to him things he stole."

"His peerless excellence has made you malign and vilify him."

Praise be to God and God bless and keep
Muḥammad the Emissary and his progeny.

Abū Tammām, al-Ḥasan ibn Wahb, and Muḥammad ibn ʿAbd al-Malik al-Zayyāt

I cite ʿAbd al-Raḥmān ibn Aḥmad as follows: 91.1

I came across a passage in al-Mubarrad's hand that Abū Tammām wrote the following verses to al-Ḥasan ibn Wahb asking for date wine:

My life is yours! ʿAbd Allāh[314] is with me again
after he had withdrawn and distanced himself.
He has splendid comrades among the scribes
who discharge the duties of visiting and friendship properly.
But, unless you are generous to them, I think
they will face a dry reception.
Many's the night star that brought wine from you
while other stars brought the rain of kindness in the morning!
One star slaked my thirst,
the other fed my wealth . . .
I invited the scribes at your expense,
since we have made you responsible for stored treasures.[315]

Ibn Wahb sent him a hundred amphoras and a hundred dinars. "One dinar for every amphora," he explained.

I cite Ibn al-Muʿtazz, who said: 91.2

Al-Mubarrad the Grammarian paid me a visit, as he often did, on his way home from the house of Judge Ismāʿīl. He informed me that al-Ḥārithī—the one about whom Ibn al-Jahm had said:

> Al-Ḥārithī and the Deneb star
> rise only for extraordinary events[316]—

had appeared before Judge Ismāʿīl and recited to him a poem by Abū Tammām addressed to Ibn Wahb with a request for date wine. The grammarian had never seen a better treatment of this motif, but he had been loath to ask al-Ḥārithī to repeat it or write it down in the judge's presence.

"Do you remember any of it?" I asked.

"Yes," al-Mubarrad replied, "it begins:

> My life is yours! ʿAbd Allāh is with me again . . ."

I recited the verses to him, as I had memorized them, and he wrote them down in his own hand.

Al-Ṣūlī: These are the verses quoted above.

91.3 We cite Aḥmad ibn Ismāʿīl, who cites ʿUbayd Allāh ibn ʿAbd Allāh, who said:

Abū l-ʿAynāʾ asked me for a gift of cooked food and I sent him some, but he did not think it was enough and wrote to me:

"I repeat to the commander the words of Abū Tammām to Muḥammad ibn ʿAlī ibn ʿĪsā l-Qummī when the poet had asked him for a gift of wine and the messenger took forever. Finally al-Qummī sent him a little blackish wine[317] and Abū Tammām wrote back in verse:

> We saw the evidence of denial,
> or what looks like denial, in delaying the messenger.
> We are disgraced by this plonk:
> a horrid sort of wine that he evidently enjoys.

A few miserable drops! Were they a lover's tears,
they wouldn't soothe his burning desire . . .
So we have written you this guarantee:
'You will never be asked for this wine again ever.'
We have enjoyed the hospitality of many an ignoble man,
and we know from the little he gives what he thinks is a lot."[318]

I made it up to Abū l-ʿAynāʾ afterward, ʿUbayd Allāh added.

An incident Aḥmad ibn Ibrāhīm al-Ghanawī related to us resembles the line, "A few miserable drops! Were they a lover's tears." 91.4

Abū Mālik al-Rasʿanī (his maternal uncle is the poet Dhū Nuwās al-Bajalī) asked one of his friends for date wine. He sent him a few pints, and Abū Malik wrote back in verse:

If you had given me antimony
it would just be enough for one eye.
By God, you gave small relief,
but then we asked for a small favor.

Al-Buḥturī composed something similar for Abū Ayyūb ibn Ukht Abī l-Wazīr: 91.5

Be well! What can I do, what will my excuse be,
when the House of Ḥumayd visits me, the least of people?[319]
One *Ṭ* after another *Ṭ*: Ṭūs and Ṭayy,
whether you say he hails from Khurasan or Najd.[320]
Friends visit me out of the blue,[321]
with no wine to drink, they will have to leave with just a promise.
I have never met a friend like wine;
if it deserts you, its friends and lovers desert you too.
Youths are delighted that the start of the rose season
is now at the end of Shaʿban.[322]
Tomorrow plain water will be banned,
but upon arrival faces will grow sad at the loss of pleasures.

Come to our aid against a day that lays our joys to rest
and leads to a night that holds their final moment.[323]

92.1 I cite Muḥammad ibn Mūsā ibn Ḥammād as follows:

When Abū Tammām was in Mosul, al-Ḥasan ibn Wahb sent him a robe of honor trimmed with silk and brocade, and the poet praised him with a poem in which he described the robe. It begins:

Abū ʿAlī, you are the spring rain for pasture-seekers.
They may dwell anywhere in your valley, it makes no difference!

Then he described the robe:

The messenger brought me the stately garb
for both winter[324] and summer . . .
Had it been bestowed on Uways[325]
his piety would have been overcome by pride . . .
Splendid, skillfully fashioned silk, its fabric ripples like water;
the east wind bows before its wearer.[326]
Choicest brocade; now and then it seems
as if my poetry were kin to its artful rosettes . . .[327]
Thanks to its beauty, you have allowed me to look down
on infinite time, ever ancient yet new.[328]

He means "on pre-eternal time." Time is called "infinite" because of its length, both ancient and new, for every day is new. Laqīṭ al-Iyādī said:

People, may your best leader not be taken from you!
I fear time ancient yet new.

92.2 Abū Tammām composed an even better description of another robe and excelled in it. I cite ʿAwn ibn Muḥammad, who cites al-Ḥusayn ibn Wadāʿ (al-Ḥasan ibn Rajāʾ's scribe):

I was with Muḥammad ibn al-Haytham in Jabal province when Abū Tammām recited the following to him:

May your meeting grounds be watered by the first spring rains
from a cloud
whose company is blameless among the dwellings.[329]

When Abū Tammām had finished reciting, Muḥammad ordered that he be given a thousand dinars and dressed in a handsome robe of honor. We passed the whole day with Muḥammad, as did Abū Tammām. He left and on the next day wrote the following verses to Muḥammad:

We were dressed in the garb of summer
by a generous man whose own garb is noble and heroic deeds.
A Sābirī gown and a tunic
like eggshell or snakeskin,
Like a shimmering mirage in its beauty
but unlike its false promise,
Finest linen, trembling in the wind
by unknown Fate's heeded command,
Fluttering, as if it were ever
the heart of a man in love or the innards of a man in fear.
Hugging the body,
it seems part of your ribs and elbows.
Protection against the burning midday heat,
though its heat burns like a day of parting.
A robe from an illustrious, awe-inspiring man,
a generous heart in a great chest, and a mighty arm.
I will dress you in a tailor-made mantle of praise,
so much finer than my tailor-made robe.
The beauty of one is for the eyes,
the beauty of the other for hearts and ears.[330]

"Who wouldn't give everything he owns for this?" Muḥammad ibn al-Haytham cried. "By God, I will give every piece of clothing in my house to Abū Tammām," and he ordered the poet to be given every single garment he owned at that time.

92.3 Abū Tammām's last verse is similar to the following verses of ʿAbd al-Ṣamad:

With the most auspicious augury and the happiest omen
in the loftiest station,
You drank sesame oil and then emerged
like a blade from the burnishing.[331]
He was revealed to you and you saw him,
as clouds part to reveal the crescent moon.
May you attain long nights
in long life and enduring well-being!
I dedicate to you the fresh and fragrant flowers
of my words which challenge my listener's wit:
It is nothing but an *Ḥ* after a *Y*,
after an *M* before a *D*,[332]
Fresh flowers live for a day:
the flowers of speech never die.
Do not prefer flowers fragrant to the nose
to flowers fragrant to men's ears.

92.4 I wrote some verses describing garments in a poem praising a friend of mine. I was not aware that anyone had described garments until I read Abū Tammām's poetry, in which he utterly excelled in this. I had said:

Where is the Dabīqī cloth, stretched by women's hands,
obediently rolling off the spindle?
Its thin weft makes its borders invisible
without any ribbing or fraying.
The dress's thin weft mimics
a spiderweb in an abandoned place.
Kings were obsessed with it,
artisans, unhurried, were allowed to take their time with it.
Lightly woven it comes to you,
kept hidden from a quick and easy purchase.

As light as air, when clear and calm,
made translucent by the weaving of the winds, autumn's approach.
Or like the weft of the sun's rays which exhaust
and weary the observer's eye.
Or like an accident[333] existing in-and-of itself
with no body to inhere in.

I know of no description of a garment or spun fabric any earlier than Abū Tammām's apart from the one al-Mubarrad the Grammarian told me about: 92.5

ʿAmr ibn Ḥafṣ al-Minqarī recited to me the following verses by Abū Ḥanash al-Numayrī about a weaver who became governor:

How excellent is your sword!
How blunt its stroke on battle-days when you could not use it to kill
Threads, twirled and braided by fingertips
into twisted loops.
White, like fine vellum delicately spun on a spindle;
its weft vies with the spider's web.
May you long strike spun fabric with its edge,
till your back bends and your wrist weakens,
While your pot cooks porridge, sweet, soft
without pepper's bite.

I cite Muḥammad ibn Mūsā l-Barbarī as follows: 93.1

Abū Tammām loved a Khazar page who belonged to al-Ḥasan ibn Wahb, whereas al-Ḥasan swooned over a Byzantine page belonging to Abū Tammām. One day Abū Tammām saw al-Ḥasan fool around with his page. "By God, if you rush to the Byzantines, we will hasten to the Khazars," he warned.

"Why don't you let me be the judge, and submit to my ruling?" al-Ḥasan replied.

"I think you are David and I his rival."[334]

"If you had said this in verse, we would be afraid," al-Hasan said. "But as it is prose, it is evanescent and without substance." Abū Tammām then said:

Abū ʿAlī, come to my aid against the twists and turns of fate,
its events, its days and warnings!
You reminded me of the affair of David,
when I was a man whose heart was devoted to love and remembrance.
Will you hold onto the sun which never sets,
yet be in turmoil over the moon?
If you do not stop your pressing journey to the oryxes of Byzantium
we will rush to the Khazars.
His frown is where my desire resides;
it takes the place of my hearing and my sight.
The pants of many better-protected companions
and sacred groves have been put in danger by me.
I showed them the armies of my bare resolve,
and their hidden battlefield yielded a trifling fuck.
By God whom all limbs glorify
how greedy your eye and cock are!
You stay at home, your camels do not travel,
but your cock never stops wandering.[335]

93.2 I cite Aḥmad ibn Ismāʿīl, who cites Muḥammad ibn Isḥāq as follows:

I said to Abū Tammām, "Your page obliges al-Ḥasan more than al-Hasan's page obliges you."

Abū Tammām replied, "Because my page gets from him what his page doesn't get from me. I give his page chitter-chatter, and al-Ḥasan gives mine money."[336]

93.3 This story is also told in a different version. I cite Abū Jaʿfar al-Muhallabī, who cites Aḥmad ibn Abī Fanan as follows:

Abū Tammām recited a praise poem to Muḥammad ibn al-Baʿīth, who had a Khazar page. Muḥammad started winking at Abū Tammām's page, and Abū Tammām delivered these verses rhyming in *R*.

Al-Ṣūlī: But the former version is the correct one.

I cite Abū l-Ḥasan al-Anṣārī, who cites his father and Abū l-Faḍl the Scribe, known as Fanjākh, for the following: 93.4

Al-Ḥasan ibn Wahb was secretary to ʿAbd al-Malik ibn al-Zayyāt when he served al-Wāthiq as vizier. Ibn al-Zayyāt had learned about what was going on between al-Ḥasan ibn Wahb and Abū Tammām and their pages. The vizier instructed two of his sons, who were companions of al-Ḥasan ibn Wahb, to inform him of what was going on between them. They reported that Abū Tammām's page had decided to be cupped.[337] The page wrote to al-Ḥasan about this, and asked him for some date wine. Al-Ḥasan sent him a hundred jars, a hundred dinars, a robe of honor, and incense, and wrote the following verses:

> I'd love to know, my most beautiful one,
>   did you go to the cupper to be cured from me?
> God avert all evil from you from dawn to dusk, for my sake,
>   even if you have betrayed my bond!
> I concealed my love as much as I could
>   but though I did not show it, it showed,
> I stopped trying
>   that all would know of my pure affection for you.
> Let them say what they please, as long as you are amenable
>   and don't scare me with rejection!
> Who will protect me from your black eyes
>   and your shining-white smile beneath a rosy cheek?

Al-Ḥasan hid the note under his prayer mat, but Muḥammad ibn ʿAbd al-Malik al-Zayyāt heard about the note and wrote to al-Ḥasan, busying him with some task. Then he ordered someone to bring him the note. When he had read it, he wrote on the note the following verses in the voice of Abū Tammām:

I'd love to know about this "I'd love to know" of yours:
  was it earnest or jest?
If your words were true, Ibn Wahb,
  you mounted a surprise attack in my absence:
You imitated me—I thought I was
  unique as passion's slave.
I gave up aiming at all goals, and but for the slips of passion
  I had been able to see my goal clearly.
I have no love for him who reprimands me,
  if he is only keen for me to struggle and succumb.
I love instead the brother who shares in my love,
  even if his passion is not like mine.
Like the two confidants of Abū ʿAlī[338]—
  I hope my confidant will not share in my misfortune:
My master is another man's slave.
  Were it not for my bad luck, my master would be *my* slave.
My lord and master is he
  who humbled and abased me!

"Put the note back where it was," the vizier ordered. When al-Ḥasan ibn Wahb read it, he exclaimed, "God help us! O God! I am disgraced before the vizier!" He let Abū Tammām know how things stood and passed the note onto him. Then they both met with Muḥammad ibn ʿAbd al-Malik. "We used these page-boys as a pretext to write poetry to each other," they pleaded.

"Who would have expected you to do anything else?" the vizier countered. His words really cut them to the quick.

94.1 I cite Muḥammad ibn Mūsā ibn Ḥammād, who said:

I was with al-ʿAmrawī[339] at Diʿbil ibn ʿAlī's place in the year 235 [850],[340] when he had returned from Syria. We were discussing Abū

Tammām, and Diʿbil began to insult him and accuse him of stealing poetry. "Hand me that sack," he said to his servant Nafnaf.[341] The servant brought him a sack full of notebooks. Diʿbil rummaged through them and pulled one out. "Read this!" he said. We looked at the notebook, and it read:

Muknif[342] Abū Sulmā, descendent of Zuhayr ibn Abī Sulmā, had lampooned Dhufāfah al-ʿAbsī in verses, including the following:

> Tribe of al-Qaʿqāʿ, your lucky star rose in al-Durāṭ,[343]
> pride yourself then on the fart!

Later Muknif mourned Dhufāfah:

> Can Fate taste sweet after Abū l-ʿAbbās?
> After him Fate is all bad and has no excuse.
> You who announce the death of Dhufāfah, the death of generosity,
> Perish! May all your ten fingers wither!
> Are you announcing the death of a rock of the Qays ʿAylān
> which pulverized the mountains of our enemies?
> When Abū l-ʿAbbās leaves his place,
> no female shall be fertile and conceive!
> Rain shall not water the earth, nor stars travel,
> nor wine delight the drinker!
> On the day he died, the Banū l-Qaʿqāʿ were like stars in a sky
> from which the full moon had fallen.[344]
> Hope died with him,
> now travelers have no reason to travel.[345]

"Abū Tammām stole most of this ode and incorporated it into his poetry," asserted Diʿbil.

Muḥammad ibn Mūsā told me this story another time and added: 94.2

I told al-Ḥasan ibn Wahb this. "I know this poem by Muknif," he responded, "and I own a copy of his poetry. Abū Tammām used to recite it to me. None of Muknif's poem appears in Abū Tammām's ode.[346] Rather, Diʿbil mixed up the odes, since they have the same meter and both are laments, in order to falsely accuse Abū Tammām."

95.1 I cite ʿAbd Allāh ibn al-Ḥusayn, who cites Wahb ibn Saʿīd as follows:

After Abū Tammām's death Diʿbil came to Abū ʿAlī l-Ḥasan ibn Wahb with a request. "Abū ʿAlī," a man interrupted, "you insulted the one who says:

> Your places, I swear, have decayed after my time with you,
> and have faded like the threads of a coat.
> You went to Najd after pitching camp in Tihāmah—
> Tears, help me deal with the inhabitants of Najd!"[347]

"He excelled, by God," Diʿbil cried and began to repeat, "'Tears, help me deal with the inhabitants of Najd!' God have mercy upon him." Then he added, "If he had left me any of his poetry, I would have called him the best poet ever."

95.2 There is a story about this poem. I cite ʿAbd Allāh ibn al-Muʿtazz, who said:

Al-Mubarrad the Grammarian visited me. I wouldn't let him leave, so he stayed. The subject of Abū Tammām came up in conversation. Muḥammad did not give him his due. A scribe from the Nuʿmān tribe was present at the gathering. I have never met anyone who knew more of Abū Tammām's poetry. He said to the grammarian, "Think of a poet, then ask yourself whether he could compose anything like the following apology which Abū Tammām addressed to Abū l-Mughīth Mūsā ibn Ibrāhīm al-Rāfiqī:

> Your places, I swear, have decayed after my time with you,
> and have faded like the threads of a coat.
> You went to Najd after pitching camp in Tihāmah—
> Tears, help me deal with the inhabitants of Najd!"

Then he continued till he reached Abū Tammām's apology:

Riders brought me something to think about—glory
before which I covered my head in shame and disgrace:
Betrayal is said to have destroyed Trust within my courtyard
and I let Blame roam loose in the plains of Praise . . .[348]
I am supposed to have denied many of your kindnesses,
like the kindnesses that bring the distant lover close,
To have denied that in which you dressed me—
looking back, it was a time of roses . . .
How on earth could I? My wits did not fail me after I had left,
and your favor did not fail.
Would I dress in foul speech someone
whose good deeds would lampoon me, were I to
lampoon him?
A noble man: when I praise him, the world joins me.
Were I to blame him, I would do so alone . . .
And if there was any mistake or unintended slip on my part,
I beg forgiveness.[349]

"I have never heard anything more beautiful," al-Mubarrad admitted. "Only two kinds of men would do Abū Tammām an injustice, either someone who knows nothing of the discipline of poetry and the science of proper speech or a scholar who has not studied or immersed himself in his poetry."

Ibn al-Muʿtazz commented: Before al-Mubarrad died he retracted everything he had said about Abū Tammām and attested to his excellence and skill.

Abū Tammam's words 95.3

Would I dress in foul speech someone,
whose good deeds would lampoon me, were I to lampoon
him?[350]

are taken[351] from a beautiful poem that is unsurpassed. I cite Muḥammad ibn Zakariyyā al-Ghalābī, who cites ʿUbayd Allāh ibn al-Ḍaḥḥāk, who cites al-Haytham ibn ʿAdī on the authority of ʿAwānah as follows:

A group of Dissidents, disciples of Qaṭarī, were brought to al-Ḥajjāj. One of them was al-Ḥajjāj's friend. Al-Ḥajjāj ordered that they be executed, but pardoned the man, gave him a gift, and let him go. The man returned to Qaṭarī. "Return to fighting God's enemy al-Ḥajjāj," he commanded. "Never," the man said, "someone who unties a hand shackles it, and someone who frees a slave enslaves him." Then he said:

Shall I fight the power of al-Ḥajjāj
 with a hand that affirms he has set it free?
I would then be a base man
 one whose foolishness ill rewards kindness received.
What shall I say when I stand facing him in the battle line
 and his deeds argue in his favor?
Shall I say, "He did me an injustice"? No!
 I would then truly deserve the injustice of rulers
And people would say that a good deed was planted in my soil
 but its palm tree turned into bitter colocynth.
Take that! Cowardice is not my way,
 I am battle's hammer and anvil.

96 I came across the following in the handwriting of Aḥmad ibn Ismāʿīl ibn al-Khaṣīb.

Muḥammad ibn ʿAbd al-Malik conveyed to al-Wāthiq a praise poem by Abū Tammām. It begins:

I swear by the encampments,[352] they spell sorrow,
 and speak clearly though dumb.

The ode was read to the caliph, including the verses:

She was offered you as a necklace, two strings of treasured pearls,
the tongue has strung together
Cut like pointed Ḥaḍramī slippers
with a narrow arch and tapered tip;
Tame and wild, the people of the earth take her everywhere,
while she stays still and serene.
When read out, her motifs are virgins
but her rhyme words matrons,
A gift to you from a mind that draws
from a brimming cistern when speech dries up.
Though this mind does not think highly of what it fashions,
unlike someone besotted with his children or his verse.
Its hope, ever intent on you,
directs its zeal and sorrow to you.
Perhaps what it hopes for, which does not yet exist,
will sooner or later exist through you.[353]

"Pay him two hundred dinars," the caliph said.

"He has high hopes and is very grateful," Muḥammad replied.

"Double it."

Another source tells us that the caliph ordered that he be given a hundred thousand dirhams.

Muḥammad ibn Dāwūd recited to me the following couplet by Abū Tammām about the House of Wahb, which he admired: 97

House of Wahb, every mountain pass you tread
belongs to me and every man of culture . . .
For you my heart thirsts like a lover's,
but for others it is like any other heart.[354]

If this second verse had been about the family of the Emissary (peace be upon them) and the grief they suffered in the Battle of Karbalāʾ and after, Abū Tammām would have been the best poet.

98 Masʿūd ibn ʿĪsā transmitted the following, citing Abū Tammām's page Ṣāliḥ (who was Abū Tammām's reciter and had a beautiful face):

I was with Abū Tammām when he appeared before al-Ḥasan ibn Wahb. An elegant slave stood behind al-Ḥasan, waiting on him. Al-Ḥasan gestured to her, egging her on against Abū Tammām, and she improvised the following line:

> Ibn Aws, you are as depraved as the Aws[355]
> because you have taken a page as confidant and bride.

Abū Tammām answered:

> Do you shine for me since I have no one to take a shining to[356]
> in order to rekindle our passion?
> I did not sin when I was young—
> could old age then give me license to sin?
> My ambition forbids it as does my pedigree
> whose origin does not disappoint it.[357]

Abū Tammām and the House of Ṭāhir ibn al-Ḥusayn[358]

We cite Muḥammad ibn Isḥāq the Grammarian, who cites Abū l-ʿAynāʾ, who cites ʿAlī ibn Muḥammad al-Jurjānī as follows: 99.1

We, poets and petitioners, were gathered at the gate of ʿAbd Allāh ibn Ṭāhir. Abū Tammām was present. The commander kept us waiting outside for days, then Abū Tammām wrote to him the following verses:

«O mighty prince, affliction has visited us»
  and our people are scattered.
In our saddle bags we bring «a father aged and great with years»
  and «merchandise of scant worth»
Its buyers are few, so it has turned to loss
  and our goods are now a mockery.
Calculate our fee, «fill up to us the measure
  and be charitable to us», for we are dying.[359]

ʿAbd Allāh laughed when he read the poem. "Tell Abū Tammām not to repeat this sort of poetry again," he said. "The words of the Qurʾan are too lofty to be used for poetry."

Abū Tammām resented him for this.

We cite Abū ʿAbd Allāh Muḥammad ibn Mūsā l-Rāzī, who cites Muḥammad ibn Isḥāq al-Khuttalī[360] (a tax agent of ʿAbd Allāh ibn Ṭāhir) as follows: 99.2

When Abū Tammām came to ʿAbd Allāh ibn Ṭāhir, the sum the commander ordered that he be given did not satisfy the poet, so he gave it away. ʿAbd Allāh was angry with Abū Tammām for treating his gift as an insult and giving it away.[361]

Abū Tammām complained about this to Abū l-ʿAmaythal,[362] the Ṭāhirids' poet laureate and favorite, who went to see ʿAbd Allāh ibn Ṭāhir. "Commander," he said, "are you angry with someone who came with hope all the way from Iraq, who exhausted his body and mind for your sake, and who said about you:

> In Qūmis my friends said to me,
> after the fatigue of the night journey on well-trained Mahrian camels,
> 'Are you taking us to where the sun rises?'
> 'No,' I replied, 'to the place where generosity rises.'"[363]

That very day ʿAbd Allāh summoned Abū Tammām to drink with him, gave him a robe of honor, and awarded him a thousand dinars and a precious ring that he wore.

100.1 I cite Abū ʿAbd Allāh Muḥammad ibn Ṭāhir, who said:

When Abū Tammām entered the city of Abrashahr he fell for a skillful singer with a beautiful voice who sang in Persian. Whenever ʿAbd Allāh inquired about Abū Tammām, he was told that the poet was with her, and Abū Tammām lost standing in the eyes of the commander. Abū Tammām composed the following lines about her:

> Sleepless night of Abrashahr,
> you put to shame a day spent anywhere else!
> I thank you for a night, beautiful and sweet,
> when joys lingered while sleep fled.
> If your happiness lies in the lowlands
> don't long for the hills!
> There I heard a song
> so powerful it stole my soul,

A singer who beauteously fed the ear.
    She did not fall on deaf ears—may her voice never be
        silenced!
She played her strings, sorrowful and yearning;
    had they been able, her listeners would have given their life
        for her.
I did not understand what she meant, but it set my heart[364] on fire,
    for I understood her sorrow.
All night long I was like a blind man, broken-hearted,
    in love with beauties he cannot see.[365]

Abū Tammām excelled in these verses—although after hearing a Persian singer al-Ḥusayn ibn al-Ḍaḥḥāk had said something similar (some people transmit the verses as belonging to Abū Nuwās, though I don't know them as his, and Abū Jaʿfar al-Muhallabī recited them to me as al-Ḥusayn's): 100.2

A song[366] for the freeborn,
    men of model lives,
Mournful, it devours the chords
    till each one dies.
I cannot tell:
    does his right or left hand make a sadder sound?
I do not understand
    what our singer means when he sings,
Only that my love for him
    makes me find beauty in his meaning.

"Only that my admiration for him . . ." is also transmitted.

Ḥumayd ibn Thawr was the first person to utter this motif and claim that he had been affected and saddened by something incomprehensible. The difference is that he was describing a dove: 100.3

I marveled at how her song could be so eloquent,
    when no speech left her mouth.

I have never known such a little thing with such a voice
to make a sad man feel so much yearning, pain, and agony.
I have never known something like her to stir up someone like me as she did,
nor any Arab moved by a foreign voice.[367]

100.4 Abū Tammām's words "a singer who beauteously fed the ear" derive from the saying "Song feeds the ears, just as food nourishes bodies."

100.5 I cite Muḥammad ibn Saʿīd and others, who cite Ḥammād ibn Isḥāq al-Mawṣilī as their authority for the following:

Marwān ibn Abī Ḥafṣah used to visit my grandfather Ibrāhīm, who when he ate his midday meal used to say, "You have given me a feast of tasty things, now give my ears a feast of beauty."

100.6 Ibn Abī Ṭāhir said:

I asked Abū Tammām, "Did you mean anyone specific with your words:

All night long I was like a blind man, broken-hearted,
in love with beauties he cannot see."

"Yes," Abū Tammām replied, "I meant Bashshār ibn Burd the Blind."

I think Abū Tammām intended Bashshār's couplet:

Folks, my ear loves someone in this quarter,
sometimes the ear falls in love before the eye.
"Are you mad for someone you cannot see?" they asked.
"The ear, like the eye," I replied, "informs the heart what's there."

101.1 We cite al-Mubarrad, who said:

ʿAbd Allāh ibn Ṭāhir lost two young sons on the same day. Abū Tammām was given an audience and recited the following:

The days never fail to tell any questioner
that they will assail open land and fortress alike.

Then he reached the words:

Glory arrived seeking shelter in the night, and
when we said, "It is here to stay," it moved on in the morning—
God willed that two stars would rise
for the blink of an eye before they set.
The loss of lush gardens is worse
than the loss of withered ones.
Had they grown up, one son would have been the withers
the other the hump of noble deeds.[368]

Al-Ṣūlī: This is how al-Mubarrad and people in general recite this verse. But Abū Mālik, ʿAwn ibn Muḥammad al-Kindī, with whom I studied it, said, "I recited this to Abū Tammām as 'had they been given more time,' meaning, 'if only their death had been postponed,'" which I think is better.

How I grieve for their signs of promise,
if only they had been given time to grow up
Their poise would have become astuteness,
their youthful love generosity, and joyfulness bounteous gifts . . .
When you see the crescent moon grow,
you know for sure it will become a full moon.

Al-Mubarrad recited it thus. However the correct version is "their youthful love would have become insight," which is better for several reasons. One is that "bounteous gifts" already stands for "generosity," so Abū Tammām provides "insight" instead in order to bring together all the aspects of praise. Another is that "insight" is a better match for "astuteness," that is, intellect, than generosity. Yet another is that he turned their "poise" into "astuteness," and their "joyfulness" into "bounteous gifts." "Youthful love" must therefore become "insight," so that this kind of behavior is only included because of "insight."

101.2 Whoever judges fairly when reading this commentary and others like it by us knows that such things can only be accomplished, and speech understood properly (as we understand it) by intelligent and perceptive people who study and learn this kind of approach. Such commentary proves Abū Tammām's skill and people's lack of knowledge about the transmission of poetry, which is an old affliction.

101.3 For example, Jarīr questioned a transmitter, "By God, I ask you, who do you think is a better poet, me or al-Farazdaq?"

"By God, I will tell you the truth: the elite and the scholars find him a better poet than you, but the crowds and the general public find you better."

"I have won—by the Lord of the Kaaba, I am first! The elite are nothing compared to the public."

101.4 Al-Mubarrad: When ʿAbd Allāh heard this section of the lament, he was greatly vexed, and responded, "You have done a good job, but you're making me grieve, not providing consolation."[369] Abū Tammām went on:

Say to the commander, even though you meet him
grave and dignified, wounded by fate's blows:
"If you were struck twice at the beginning and end of a single day,
two blows that consume your heart with the sting of grief,
It is because only the strong, fully grown camel is given a double load . . .
Your are too lofty by nature to be consoled or to need reminding by anyone—
should you ever forget or be distracted—

Other than by admonitions that your own gentle mind
leads obediently to you, whatever you are doing, listening or speaking."[370]

ʿAbd Allāh said, "Now you have given me comfort." He ordered that the poem be written down and the poet be given a reward.

Here Abū Tammām composed in the style of al-Farazdaq when a pregnant slave had died and the dead child was found inside her womb: 101.5

I lost the sheath of a weapon,
but I did not weep nor summon the mourners.
Inside it was a plump child, to cherish and protect
if death had only given him a few nights' respite.

There are no better words than al-Farazdaq's composition "I lost the sheath of a weapon" and this comparison by him.

I cite Abū Bakr ʿAbd al-Raḥmān ibn Aḥmad, who heard Abū ʿAlī l-Ḥusayn say: 102

No one was more taken with the poetry of Abū Tammām than Isḥāq ibn Ibrāhīm al-Muṣʿabī, who would give him many gifts.

We cite Abū Aḥmad Yaḥyā ibn ʿAlī ibn Yaḥyā l-Munajjim, who cites his father as follows: 103

Abū Tammām appeared before Isḥāq ibn Ibrāhīm and recited a praise poem to him. Then Isḥāq ibn Ibrāhīm al-Mawṣilī arrived to pay the commander his respects. When he asked to be admitted, Abū Tammām said, "Commander, I beg you to order Isḥāq to listen to some of my odes about you." When Isḥāq entered the commander told him this. Isḥāq sat down and Abū Tammām recited several odes.[371] Then Isḥāq turned to Abū Tammām and said, "You are a brilliant and excellent poet and you rely on your own powers."

He meant that Abū Tammām coined motifs. Isḥāq was a fervent champion of the ancient poets whom he supported.

104 It is said that ʿAbd Allāh ibn Ṭāhir kept Abū Tammām waiting at his door, so the poet wrote a note to the commander:

Bear the delay with patience, as long as no lie follows it,
because events end well, if borne with grace.
To destiny belongs blame, when a mighty man like you is their target,
but to me belong effort and pursuit.
O Prince, you are so hard to get to see,
but your generosity is so near for the petitioner,
I have not abandoned my hopes just because a veil hides you:
one has hopes for a sky veiled with clouds.[372]

Abū Tammām is also said to have written these lines to Abū Dulaf or Ibn Abī Duʾād, but they were actually said about Isḥāq ibn Ibrāhīm al-Muṣʿabī.

105 I cite Aḥmad ibn Muḥammad al-Baṣrī, who cites Faḍl al-Yazīdī as follows:

When Abū Tammām traveled to Khurasan to praise ʿAbd Allāh ibn Ṭāhir, he hated being in the country, because winter had arrived and he suffered in the intense cold. So he composed the following verses, blaming winter and praising summer:

No trace, no remnant of summer is left,
I have no clothes to wear, worn out or new!
Tears rightly mourn the passing of summer
as one weeps for lost youth, for dalliance, for love.
Time's right hand has withdrawn its gift—
its left hand now takes its place.[373]

(We will be citing this ode in the *Collected Poems.*) ʿAbd Allāh ibn Ṭāhir learned of these verses and immediately sent Abū Tammām a reward and dismissed him.

I cite Aḥmad ibn Ismāʿīl ibn al-Khaṣīb, who cites ʿAbd Allāh ibn Aḥmad al-Naysābūrī, a man of culture and a poet, who said: **106.1**

Abū Tammām was kept waiting for a gift from ʿAbd Allāh ibn Ṭāhir and wrote the following verses to Abū l-ʿAmaythal, ʿAbd Allāh's poet laureate, as Abū Tammām had previously given him a note with a poem for ʿAbd Allāh:

Abū l-ʿAmaythal, if only the oryxes had brought tidings
to quench the thirsty owls![374]
When fate spreads darkness,
the commander is the light of time and the face[375] of Islam.
By God, the one he protects does not know
which circumstance to praise time for:
The riches with which ʿAbd Allāh united him,
or the poverty from which he separates him?
I think my composition has been delayed for quite some time,
a delay that wearies the souls in our bodies.[376]
When craft commands[377] excellence
it delights men of culture and insight,
Provides room for repeated scrutiny
and receives the adulation of the audience.
Were it not for the commander, were it not that his discerning judgment
is poetry's fairest judge,
I would be bereft of all hope's children,
and recitation would be the sole guardian of my speech.[378]
But because he keeps us apart
I fear the fate people say ʿAmr suffered with his sword Ṣamṣām.[379]

106.2 Thereupon Abū l-ʿAmaythal wrote back in verse:

You sent us a message loud and clear,
Abū Tammām, hear then the answer:
Whether the oryxes cross a path from the right or the left is of no consequence:
they are oblivious to human affairs.
Long ago ink dried
on the tablet with the account of man's deeds and gains.
I was present when the firm verdict was pronounced
on the speech you embellished so well,[380]
Full of intricacies in pleasing verse
that nimbly trip on the tongues of rulers,
Texts smooth to listen to,
like the faces[381] of smooth hard stones we can see and touch.
I was there when the commander said afterward
that it was honey mixed with fresh rainwater.
I was there when the comeliest assembly
bestowed on noble speech the reward of men of noble origin.
Show patience—it is laudable;
it is teamed with success against time.
You mention ʿAmr from days of old
and his parting from the Ṣamṣām of battle and attack.
But through the commander's power and long reign
God has set us together on the most perfect necklace.[382]

Abū Tammām wrote many poems about his unhappy stay in Khurasan and his dislike of the region. We will cite them in his *Collected Poems*, God willing.

Abū Tammām and Abū Sa'īd Muḥammad ibn Yūsuf al-Thaghrī l-Ṭā'ī l-Ḥumaydī

I cite 'Abd Allāh ibn al-Ḥusayn ibn Sa'd, who cites al-Buḥturī as follows: 107

Abū Sa'īd al-Thaghrī was a Ṭayyite from Marw and one of the generals of Ḥumayd al-Ṭūsī. One of Abū Tammām's first poems in his praise is the one which begins:

> It is natural for ruined encampments not to respond,
> and it is right for my eye to shed tears.[383]

Abū Tammām received from Abū Sa'īd more benefactions than he did from anyone else—not that the general was lavish to him, but he gave to him regularly.

I cite 'Abd al-Raḥmān ibn Aḥmad ibn al-Walīd, who cites Abū Aḥmad Muḥammad ibn Mūsā ibn Ḥammād al-Barbarī, who cites Ṣāliḥ ibn Muḥammad al-Hāshimī, who said: 108

I appeared before Abū Sa'īd al-Thaghrī and he took out a letter addressed to him from Abū Tammām. I opened it and it read:

> I received a composition from you,
> which conquered my heart's all-conquering sorrows.

You sought my affections when deserts lay between us.
Thus is your generosity sought, while your glory seeks its goals.[384]

(He cited further verses of this letter, which we will reproduce in full in the *Collected Poems*.)

"I wrote a letter to Abū Tammām," Abū Saʿīd then explained, "and sent it to him along with a favor, and Abū Tammām answered me with these verses. Otherwise he never addressed me directly."

109 I cite ʿAwn ibn Muḥammad al-Kindī for the following:

Abū Tammām was approached by one of his close friends. The friend had heard that the poet was doing well and had become wealthy and asked him for a gift. "If I kept everything I received," Abū Tammām said, "I would need no one, but I spend what I get. However, I will come up with a solution for you."[385] He then wrote a poem to Abū Saʿīd which contained the following verses:

May you always be clothed in my gratitude
that graces its wearer with sumptuous attire.
Those who hear the poem say,
"The ancient poet has left so much for the modern!"
I have a friend who was my confidant and companion
in former times . . .
Red camels bring him,
a marvel that will give the mocker much to mock:
A wealthy man who begs from a beggar,
a man who cannot write poetry but borrows from a poet.
His arrival, hope's stray arrow,
spelled death for my wealth.
Play alongside the loser,
don't side with the winner!

Glory comes from the gifts you give to visitors
but is nothing compared to giving gifts to your visitor's
visitor.[386]

The general sent Abū Tammām three hundred dinars and his visitor two hundred dinars. Abū Tammām gave the man fifty dinars so that the split was even.

Abū Tammām and Aḥmad ibn al-Muʿtaṣim

110.1 I cite Muḥammad ibn Yaḥyā ibn Abī ʿAbbād, who cites his father:

I was present when Abū Tammām recited to Aḥmad ibn al-Muʿtaṣim the following ode in praise of the prince:

> There is no harm in stopping for a moment
> to pay homage to deserted spring encampments.
> Perhaps your eyes will help you with their water
> though tears may fail you or soothe.

Al-Ṣūlī: Some people transmit this as "will flow with their water," which is a misspelling.

Then he said:

> You displayed glory at its furthest reaches,
> in its noblest character and origin—
> ʿAmr's bold advance, Ḥātim's munificence,
> Aḥnaf's insight, and Iyās's wit.[387]

Al-Kindī was present and wanted to insult the poet. He said, "Your description is beneath the prince." Abū Tammām looked down for a moment and added two verses that had not been part of the ode:

Do not blame me for applying analogies
that are beneath one peerless in generosity and courage.
For His own light God uses a lesser example
—the lantern and the niche.[388]

We were astounded by the quickness of his wit.

This account is also transmitted differently, but it is incorrect. This is the correct version.

It is said that Abū Tammām was faulted for the words contained in the following poem he recited: 110.2

My hair turned white: I think that its whiteness
springs from the whiteness of the heart.

He then added instantly:

Hearts precede bodies
in both comfort and misfortune.[389]

I cite Aḥmad ibn Ismāʿīl, who cites ʿAbd Allāh ibn al-Ḥusayn (though I don't know who this ʿAbd Allāh is): 111

I heard Abū Tammām recite the following verses to Aḥmad ibn al-Muʿtaṣim during the prince's illness:

My eyes could not sleep for sorrow,
my insides were filled with pain
In sorrow for what weighs on Prince Abū l-ʿAbbas
struck low by a sudden ailment . . .
He is a man whose protection we seek
when fate chokes and throttles us.
The Mighty One forged them from glory's essence,
and fashioned mankind from its accident . . .[390]
A king like an arrow its Maker fires
that quivers in the target.

The following lines contain the best metonymical allusion to the caliphate:

His well-being is the well-being of hope
    at the moment when it holds or breaks.
His illness affects us all:
    it is we who receive the bedside visit, when he is ill.[391]

"How ill you look!" Aḥmad ibn al-Muʿtaṣim said.

"It is a sickness of the heart that deadens thought, blinds the eyes, and confounds talent," Abū Tammām replied.

Abū Tammām and Mukhallad ibn Bakkār al-Mawṣilī

I cite Aḥmad ibn Ibrāhīm, who cites Mukhallad's servant Badr as follows: 112

Abū Tammām entered the baths. Mukhallad was there. He had so much body hair that he looked as if he were wearing a haircloth.

"What's this?" Abū Tammām asked.

"Protection against your tongue making me the son of a whore," Mukhallad retorted.[392]

I cite Abū Sulaymān al-Nābulusī for the following: 113

"Mukhallad lampooned you," Abū Tammām was told. "Why don't you lampoon him back?"

"Lampooning is too good for him."

"Isn't he a poet?"

"If he were really a poet, he wouldn't be from Mosul."

Abū Tammām meant that Mosul had never produced a single poet.

Abū Sulaymān added: Mukhallad was originally from al-Ruḥbah and later lived in Mosul.

I cite Aḥmad ibn Muḥammad al-Baṣrī, the poet Khālid al-Ḥadhdhā''s servant and transmitter, who cites the Qurashī poet al-Khalīʿ as follows: 114

The first lampoon Mukhallad composed about Abū Tammām was the following:

For me you are Bedouin,
    no bones about it,
Bedouin, swarthy brown Bedouin,
    whatever turns you on!
The hair on your thighs and shins:
    basil and garlic.
The ribs in your chest:
    hard bow wood and balsam tooth sticks.
The mote in your eye: gum arabic,
    your forelocks: dried white wormwood.
If you were to budge,
    ostriches would take flight in panic,
Grazing gazelles
    and giant jerboas too.
Is it my fault if humanity
    disagrees with me about you?
Your Nabatean peasant roots
    show through,
The back of your head declares[393]
    that you inherited no single noble trait.
"Of Jāsim,"[394] they say,
    "A branch of the Nabatean tribe."
They lied! You are a Bedouin through and through,
    you shall not be wronged,
Your dwelling by the white stones
    between Salmā's abode and its surroundings.
Your inheritance from your fathers:
    bows and arrows,
And tall palm trees
    ripe for the harvest.
Bedouin, Bedouin you are to me.
    Farewell!

Abū Ja'far, a freed slave of the House of Sulaymān ibn 'Alī, recited to me the following verses by Mukhallad about Abū Tammām: 115

Look at him, rotten as he is,
how could his filth be covered up, when it is so well known?
Look at his pedigree, a flimsily woven garb,
whereas his low birth is a tightly twisted rope.
Woe to you! Whoever tricked you to adopt an ancestry
that permanently fills your heart with fear?
When Ṭayy is mentioned a league away,
the light in your eyes goes out.

Abū Sulaymān the Blind recited to me further verses by Mukhallad about Abū Tammām: 116.1

Were you to grab a hyrax and a lizard,
Suck the bone marrow raw from a tough jerboa,[395]
Chew on a fresh juicy colocynth,
And taste no cool sweet water,
Pee like a camel stallion after running,
And care only about the camel trade,
Were you to sit hunched and cross-legged,
Aping a true desert Arab
Who would scream with fear if he walked beneath an arch,
Desperate to be back in the plain's droughty expanse
And to fuck Ḥimyar, Kalb, and Qays 'Aylān,
Who carry their heads high with pride
In Syria where their rallying call is heard
But not where pedigree comes through upbringing,
Where a slave at dawn becomes a lord by dusk;
Were you then to choose al-Lāt as our Lady,
And call cotton "wool,"
And chide[396] a stupid ass as if it were a camel,
You would still be a pure Nabatean peasant,
One who would weep buckets of tears when hoeing rocky ground,

To give his plants fresh water
And tend his grain and hardwood trees.
You have stirred me up, a resolute poet who
Wields a sharp sword in his mouth,[397]
An Indian blade that doles out praise and blame
And slices up the honor of the dishonorable.

116.2 Mukhallad had a precedent for this type of verse.[398] Abū Nuwās said the following verses about Abū Khālid, a Persian who went to live in the desert for two months, became a Numayrī Bedouin, and who, when he came back, no longer knew what water pipes were. "What are these elephant trunks? I don't know them," he said. Abū Nuwās then said about him:

Rider, arriving from Thahmad,
how were the camels and the sheep when you left them?
How was the sandy slope where the *qaʿnab* grows,
amid castor beans and meru berries?[399]
Abū Khālid came from the desert,
though he never stopped living in the city.
Abū Khālid knows many nouns for fire
but does not know the noun people use.[400]
When he calls to a friend he hollers
as if he were hollering again and again to a camel.
If you were a fruit relished for its sweetness
you would be a sour berry
That can only be swallowed
with water.[401]

116.3 Abū Nuwās too had a precedent in this. I cite Musabbiḥ ibn Ḥātim al-ʿUklī, who cites Yaʿqūb ibn Jaʿfar as follows:

Ismāʿīl ibn ʿAlī ordered that the poet Ḥammād ʿAjrad be given five thousand dirhams, but Ismāʿīl's scribe Muḥammad ibn Nūḥ delayed the payment. Ḥammād delivered the following poem about him:

Noah's son[402] said to me,
with a flash of anger,
"Was it your poetry that cut me off
from my ancestor Noah?"
"No," I protested, "don't accuse me
of blatant lies!
Woe to you, I did no such thing,
even if your deeds are foul.
I am a man
versed in genealogy:
You said to me, 'Noah is my father,'
and I replied, 'Go back further: who was his father?'
But you couldn't go beyond him,
and this raises just a little bit of doubt.
Son of Noah, brother of the saddle blanket,[403]
son of the pack saddle,
Your father grew up amid hills and dunes,
Bedouin, Bedouin, Bedouin, Bedouin!"

When Abū Tammām died Mukhallad composed a satirical lament: 117

Ṭayyite, may the rim[404] of your shitty grave be watered
by a morning downpour of semen and flocks of dicks![405]
No doubt your anus desires a prick's watering[406]
more than your grave desires the watering of two rainstars.
Worn out by the heat of buggery and the chill[407] of his poetry,
he died from both heat and icy cold.

Abū Tammām did not lampoon him back. He did not consider him an equal and preferred to ignore him. I cite the poet Abū l-ʿAshāʾir al-Azdī, who cites his father as follows: 118

I said to Abū Tammām, "This Mosuli has dishonored us with his lampoon of you. Give him a taste of his own medicine!"

“My answer,” Abū Tammām replied, “would elevate him and draw out more insults. If I leave him alone, he will stop puffing out his cheeks like a rutting camel. Anyway, I am far too busy praising people and making a living.”

119 Mukhallad composed the following verses about Abū Tammām:

> God’s emissary in poetry
> Jesus, son of Mary,[408]
> You are the best poet among God’s creatures—
> as long as you keep your mouth shut.

120 Better poets than Mukhallad lampooned Abū Tammām. I cite both Muḥammad ibn Mūsā l-Hāshimī and Abū l-Rabīʿ al-Minqarī as follows:

Abū Tammām decided to go down to Basra and Ahwāz to praise people there. News of this reached ʿAbd al-Ṣamad ibn al-Muʿadhdhal, who wrote the following verses to Abū Tammām:

> You are between two things that happen to people,
> both contemptible:
> You never stop asking for
> either a lover’s rendezvous or gifts.
> Has your face not run out of water
> after the humiliation of desire and beggary?[409]

“That takes care of it,” Abū Tammām said when he read the poem, “we don’t need this,” and abandoned his travel plans.

121 I came across a long lampoon of Abū Tammām by al-Walīd[410] in my books. Here is a selection of verses:

> Leave off lampooning, God forbids it,
> and stick to well-known truth!

Remember Ḥabīb, son of Awshūnā,[411] and his pretended pedigree!
The Ṭayy grow scared when insulted because of him.
If they accept you, Father of Imperfection,[412] they are burdened with shame,
because you lower everything they hold high.
Were the ʿAbd Manāf to accept you among their stock,
it would do them neither harm nor benefit
But if they chased you away like a dog
they would be right and be much better off.
If they used you to patch a hole in their water skin[413]
all God's people would say "What a poor patch!"
Church bell and psalmody your people's booty,[414]
remember where they would strike camp for the spring!
Should every dishonor be attached to Ṭayy,
you would still be the worst of the bunch.
I lampooned you in the knowledge
that fear has killed your poetry.
When prize stallions in rut puff out their throats and bray
newborn camels do not approach.

Criticisms of Abū Tammām

122.1 I cite Hārūn ibn ʿAbd Allāh al-Muhallabī, who said:

When asked about Abū Tammām, Diʿbil replied, "A third of his poetry is stolen, another third is bad, and only one third is good."

122.2 I cite Muḥammad ibn Dāwūd, who cites Ibn Abī Khaythamah as saying:

"Abū Tammām was no poet," I heard Diʿbil say, "he was an orator. His poetry is closer to prose[415] than verse."

Diʿbil was prejudiced against Abū Tammām and did not include him in his *Book of Poets*.

123 When a poem by Abū Tammām was recited to Ibn al-Aʿrābī, he is said to have remarked:

"If this is poetry, then what the Arabs have composed is worthless."

124 I cite Muḥammad ibn al-Ḥasan al-Yashkurī as follows:

A poem by Abū Tammām was recited to Abū Ḥātim al-Sijistānī, who found some of it beautiful and some of it ugly. The reciter then began to ask about its motifs, but Abū Ḥātim was not familiar with them.

"The only thing I can compare this poetry to is thin flimsy garments," he remarked. "They are beautiful but have no substance."

I cite al-Qāsim ibn Ismāʿīl, who said: 125

We were at al-Tawwajī's place, and one of Abū Ruhm al-Sadūsī's sons came and recited an ode by Abū Tammām in praise of Khālid ibn Yazīd. It begins:

> Decayed remnants of the assembled tribe, you are effaced,
> though once praised! This is witness enough to my loss.[416]

Then the reciter got confused, but I knew Abū Tammām's poetry and proceeded to correct him.

When he had finished, the reciter asked, "Abū Muḥammad,[417] what do you think about this poetry?"

"Some of it I find beautiful, and some of it I don't recognize and have heard nothing like it. Either this man is the best poet of all, or all others are better poets than him."

The following remark is related from Ibn Mihrawayh, who cites Abū 126
Hiffān as his authority:

I said to Abū Tammām, "You find a pearl and then throw it into an ocean of shit from which none but you could retrieve it."

I cite the scribe Abū Ṣāliḥ ibn Yazdād, who heard his neighbor Abū 127.1
l-ʿAnbas al-Ṣaymarī say:

Abū Tammām wrote a letter to al-Buḥturī's mother asking her to marry him. She agreed, saying, "Assemble the people for the marriage contract."

"God is too great to be invoked for us," Abū Tammām replied, "Let's shack up." So they lived together out of wedlock.

But Abū l-ʿAnbas made this up, modeling it on a story al-Kudaymī 127.2
told him, citing al-Aṣmaʿī as his authority:

A black man and a black woman came to Abū Mahdiyyah. "We want to marry," they said. "Pronounce the marriage contract between us."

"God is too great to be invoked for you two," he replied. "Go ahead and fuck,[418] God curse you!"

128 According to some, his name was Ḥabīb ibn Tadūs the Christian, then it was changed into Aws.[419]

129 I cite a group of people, who cite Ibn al-Daqqāq as their authority:

We recited to Abū Tammām Abū Nuwās's *rajaz* poem in praise of al-Faḍl ibn al-Rabīʿ that opens:

> A country that bends . . .[420]

and he found it beautiful. "I will practice composing in this style," he said. He would go into a small garden and would sit busily composing on the banks of a stream. Then he would leave in the afternoon. He did this for three days, only to tear up what he had composed. "I am not satisfied with what I came up with," he admitted.

130 I cite Aḥmad ibn Saʿīd, who cites Muḥammad ibn ʿAmr:

The poet Ibn al-Khathʿamī claimed, "Abū Tammām was mad to compose the following verse:

> Day by day, from morning to night,
> events come to pass that nearly strike Fate down.[421]

"Can Fate ever be struck down?" he nitpicked.

"The great Bashshār," I challenged him, "said:

> I am just like Fate: when it is sober I am sober,
> and when it is foolish, I am foolish too."[422]

Ibn al-Khathʿamī was silent.

"And your own father," I went on, "said:

> He so softened Fate for me with frequent tokens of his generosity,
> that it became so pliable I could almost tie knots with it.

"Can Fate be tied into knots?" Ibn al-Khathʿamī was silent.

Muḥammad ibn ʿAbd al-Malik ibn Ṣāliḥ composed a lampoon of Abū Tammām containing the following verses: 131

> The poetry of Imperfection's Father[423] came to me from far
> away.
> Talk gets around.[424]
> It was like an arrow that swerved from
> soundness, and intent from its goal.[425]

Abū Tammām as a Source

132 We cite al-Ḥasan ibn ʿUlayl al-ʿAnazī, who cites Abū Bakr Muḥammad ibn Ibrāhīm ibn ʿAttāb, who cites Abū Tammām as follows:

Al-Ṭirimmāḥ swaggered past the mosque of Basra. "Who is this strutting by?" a man asked.

"I am the one who said:

> I love myself more for being hated
> by anyone of no consequence,
> When he sees me, he looks away
> like one who knows but pretends not to.
> I blocked his every move, like a hunter tightening the net
> to judge from the panic in his eyes."[426]

133 I cite Aḥmad ibn Yazīd al-Muhallabī, who cites Abū l-Faḍl Aḥmad ibn Abī Ṭāhir, who cites Abū Tammām, who cites al-ʿAttāf ibn Hārūn, who in turn cites as his authority the judge of Damascus, Yaḥyā ibn Ḥamzah (one of those responsible for killing al-Walīd ibn Yazīd) as follows:

I was at a gathering held by Yazīd ibn al-Walīd the Reducer,[427] when a man lied to him. Yazīd knew he was lying. "You lie to yourself before you lie to your companion," he said.

Afterward we noticed that this man was always on his guard.

We cite Aḥmad ibn Yazīd, who cites Aḥmad ibn Abī Ṭāhir, who cites Abū Tammām, who cites an old man from the quarter, who said: 134.1

A nobleman lived among us. He spent all his wealth on acts of generosity and then could no longer honor his promises. "Have you turned into a liar?" he was asked.

"Devotion to truth has reduced me to lying," he replied.

Al-Ṣūlī: Ibn Abī Ṭāhir turned this into verse: 134.2

> For a long time I kept all my promises
> until Fate[428] destroyed the property I had amassed.
> If I have become a liar in my promises,
> devotion to the truth has reduced me to lying.

We cite Aḥmad ibn Yazīd, who cites Ibn Abī Ṭāhir, who cites Abū Tammām, who cites Karāmah ibn Abān al-ʿAdawī, who in turn cites a man from the ʿĀmilah clan of the Zahdam tribe, who said: 135

ʿAdī ibn al-Riqāʿ said, "I never made ʿUmar ibn al-Walīd ibn ʿAbd al-Malik listen to one of my praise poems without literally hearing him determine my gift."

The man continued: Later, after ʿAdī had made this statement, I was at a gathering held by ʿUmar when ʿAdī entered and recited a poem about him. ʿUmar called one of his freed slaves. "Produce the flyting to counter this ode!" he ordered. I thought the freed slave was going to recite a poem, but instead he brought a bag with ten thousand dirhams in it and gave it to ʿAdī.

We cite Aḥmad ibn Yazīd al-Muhallabī, who cites Aḥmad ibn Abī Ṭāhir, who cites Abū Tammām, who cites Abū ʿAbd al-Raḥmān al-Umawī, who said: 136

Ibn Lisān al-Ḥummarah, that is, Rabīʿah ibn Ḥiṣn of the tribe of Taym al-Lāt ibn Thaʿlabah, described inarticulate people as follows:

"The speech of one person does not reach his tongue, the speech of another does not reach his companion's ear, and the speech of yet another forces your ears to overburden your mind."

137 I further cite Aḥmad, citing Aḥmad,[429] citing Abū Tammām:

Usually Yazīd ibn al-Ḥuṣayn ibn Tamīm al-Sakūnī gave no gifts, but when he did, he gave lavishly, saying, "I like to give presents in rows, like cavalry lined up for battle not like scattered troops of horsemen."

138 We cite Aḥmad, citing Aḥmad, citing Abū Tammām, citing as his authority a man of Kalb, who said:

I was with Yazīd ibn Ḥātim in Ifrīqiyah. He examined some body armor very carefully and paid a great amount of money for it, as it was of very high craftsmanship. I asked about this. "I am purchasing lives, not armor," he retorted.

139 I cite Aḥmad ibn Yazīd, who cites his father, who cites as his authority his paternal uncle Ḥabīb ibn al-Muhallab, who said:

When I saw a man wearing a breastplate in battle I would count him as two men, and when I saw two men with no helmets I would count them as one.

140.1 We cite Aḥmad, citing Aḥmad, citing Abū Tammām, citing Karāmah, who said:

A descendant of Maʿdān ibn ʿUbayd al-Maʿnī arrived from the Barmakids. "How were they when you left?" I asked him.

"When I left them Grace kept them such close company that she was like a member of the family," he replied.

140.2 Abū Tammām then said that Karāmah added:

I told this to Thaʿlabah ibn al-Ḍaḥḥāk al-ʿĀmilī. "I heard something similar from one of your Bedouins," he replied. "Ghassān ibn ʿAbd Allāh ibn Khaybarī came to us in the heyday of Hishām's caliphate. He saw the House of Khālid al-Qasrī and declared, 'I see Grace cling to these people like clothes.'"

I said, "As I see it, this speaker is the paternal cousin of the man who made the other statement. Don't you think that both these speeches are cousins?"

We cite Aḥmad, citing Aḥmad, citing Abū Tammām, citing Karāmah, who said: 141

A man spoke in the gathering of al-Haytham ibn Ṣāliḥ and rambled on without getting to the point. "You there," al-Haytham interrupted, "speech like yours makes silence precious."

We cite Aḥmad, citing Aḥmad, citing Abū Tammām, citing Salāmah ibn Jābir al-Nahdī, who said: 142

I heard a Bedouin describe people who had been clothed in grace but later stripped of it. "The grace of the House of So-and-so," he declared, "was but a figment that fled when they awoke."

We cite Aḥmad, citing Aḥmad, citing Abū Tammām, citing Salāmah ibn Jābir as his authority, for the following: 143

Hishām asked Asad ibn ʿAbd Allāh al-Qasrī about his enemy Naṣr ibn Sayyār. Asad replied, "He is a man whose virtues outnumber his faults, who attacks no one, no matter whom, without obtaining satisfaction, who does nothing that needs an apology. He divides his behavior evenly among days ever virtuous, giving each trait its turn, oblivious to which occasion to prefer: that to which his intellect guides him or to which his refinement brings him."

"You praise him," Hishām said, "despite your low opinion of him."

“Yes, indeed,” Asad replied, “because, in terms of the question the Commander of the Faithful asked me, I am as the poet says:

The right way to pay back what you’ve given me
    is for me to tell you the truth about friend and foe,
And when you charge me with a task
    for your wish to mean more to me than my own.”

“This is exactly how I think of you,” Hishām agreed.

144 We cite Aḥmad, citing Aḥmad, citing Abū Tammām, citing Muḥammad ibn Khālid al-Shaybānī as saying:

Raqabah ibn Maṣqalah al-ʿAbdī was asked one day, “Where do your doubts come from?”

“From my defense of certitude.”

145 We cite Aḥmad ibn Yazīd, citing Aḥmad ibn Abī Ṭāhir, citing Abū Tammām, citing Abū ʿAbd al-Raḥmān al-Umawī, who said:

Speech was the topic of conversation at a gathering held by Sulaymān ibn ʿAbd al-Malik, and some of those present criticized it. “Give me a break!” Sulayman protested, “Whoever is good at speaking is good at keeping silent. But not everyone who is good at keeping silent is good at speaking.”

146 We cite Aḥmad, citing Aḥmad ibn Abī Ṭāhir, citing Abū Tammām, citing an old man from the tribe of ʿAdī ibn ʿAmr as follows:

Members of the Ṭayy pitched tents near us, and I used to speak to one of their young men. He in turn often conversed with a paternal cousin of his who had broken his heart. Her clan moved away to the lowlands around Damascus, while he, deeply distraught, stayed behind with his own relatives.

“Cousin,” he said to me, “it is harder not to be with someone you love than it is to be with someone you hate.”

We cite Aḥmad, citing Aḥmad ibn Abī Ṭāhir, citing Abū Tammām, citing Qilābah al-Jarmī, who said: 147

Yazīd ibn al-Muhallab said to his companions one day, "I see you reproach me for my boldness in battle."

"Yes," they replied, "you expose yourself to mortal danger."

"Leave me alone!" he said. "If I didn't seek death at my own pace, it would be in hot pursuit of me. I don't seek death because I love it but because I hate it. Al-Ḥuṣayn ibn al-Ḥumām al-Murrī excelled when he said:

> I was slow to ask life to stay,
> because I saw no point in life if I am not first."[430]

We cite Aḥmad, citing Aḥmad, citing Abū Tammām as his authority as follows: 148

A man from the ʿAmr ibn Tamīm said, "People say that, when ordered to,[431] swords will strike till they become blunt but, by God, I never saw Yazīd ibn al-Muhallab's sword miss."

"By God," Thābit Quṭnah replied, "if swords were not ordered to strike, Yazīd's hand would give them the order."

We cite Aḥmad, citing Aḥmad ibn Abī Ṭāhir, citing Abū Tammām as his authority, citing Mālik ibn Dalham, who in turn cites Ibn al-Kalbī as his authority as follows: 149

Arṭāh ibn Suhayyah al-Murrī (Suhayyah was Arṭāh's mother and his father Ẓufar belonged to the Murrah tribe and lived during the reign of Muʿāwiyah) lost a son called ʿAmr, and Arṭāh nearly went mad with grief for him. He pronounced the following verses at his son's grave:

> I stood over the tomb of Ibn Salmā,
> all tears and grief,
> Forgive Fate, it will not mend its ways,[432]
> and long for someone else, not covered by earth.

If I wait for you, Ibn Salmā, will you come back with our people
or follow me early tomorrow?[433]

150 We cite Aḥmad, citing Aḥmad, citing Abū Tammām as follows:

We were discussing the beauty of speech and the nobility of silence at a gathering held by ʿAbd al-ʿAzīz al-Tanūkhī. "Stars are not like the moon," he remarked. "Silence can be praised by speech, but speech cannot be praised by silence. The thing that provides information about another thing is the greater of the two."

151 We cite Aḥmad, citing Aḥmad, citing Abū Tammām, who cites Abū ʿAbd al-Raḥmān al-Umawī as follows:

A man who was at Hishām's place spoke eloquently. "The best speech," Hishām said, "is that which wins the heart's commitment."

152 We cite Aḥmad, citing Aḥmad, citing Abū Tammām, who cites ʿAmr ibn Hāshim al-Sarawī as follows:

We were talking at Muḥammad ibn ʿAmr al-Awzāʿī's place (the Awzāʿ belong to Ḥimyar). A Bedouin from the tribe of ʿUlaym ibn Janāb was present but did not say a word. "You have rightly been called the most taciturn of Bedouins," we said to him. "Will you not talk to the group?"

"One man profits from his ear," the Bedouin replied. "The others profit from their tongue."

"My goodness, how brilliant!" al-Awzāʿī exclaimed.

153 We cite Aḥmad, who cites Aḥmad, who cites Abū Tammām as follows:

One man said to another, "How beautiful your speech is!"

"You make it so by listening so beautifully."

We cite Aḥmad, citing Aḥmad ibn Abī Ṭāhir, citing Yaḥyā ibn Ismāʿīl al-Umawī, who cites Ismāʿīl ibn ʿAbd Allāh as follows: 154

My grandfather said, "Silence is the sleep of the mind. Speech awakens it. There is no sleep without awakening and no awakening without sleep."

Abū Tammām Described; Stories Told of His Family

155 I cite ʿAwn ibn Muḥammad al-Kindī, who said:

Abū Tammām was tall and had a slight stammer. He spoke smoothly and eloquently like the Bedouin.

156 I cite ʿAlī ibn al-Ḥasan al-Kātib, who said:

When I was a boy, I saw Abū Tammām—he was dark-skinned and tall.

157 I cite Aḥmad ibn Yazīd al-Muhallabī, who said:

I was sitting with Ibn ʿAttāb when a scribe passed by and joined us. He was articulate, his conversation delightful. He stayed for quite a while, and then got up and left.

"I have never before met anyone who speaks more like Abū Tammām," Ibn ʿAttāb said to me, "though he does not have Abū Tammām's slight stammer."

158 I cite ʿAbd Allāh ibn ʿAbd Allāh, who said:

Abū Tammām had a brother by the name of Sahm, who also composed poetry. This is an example:

> I vied with him for something he had been taught to abhor,
> but when he saw my passion for him[434] he came to love it.

Let him be! Don't grieve with envy should someone else win him:
he will be worn out by the ever-changing nights.

I cite Sawwār ibn Abī Shurāʿah, who cites al-Buḥturī as follows: 159

Abū Tammām had a brother called Sahm who composed mediocre verse. He came to Abū Tammām and asked him for a gift. "By God," Abū Tammām said, "I have nothing to spare, but I will come up with a plan."[435] He wrote a poem to Yaḥyā ibn ʿAbd Allāh.[436] It begins:

A woman of the tribe of Bakr ibn ʿAbd Manāt[437]
between the single dune and the watering holes . . .

In the poem he said:

Sahm ibn Aws trusts that you vouch
not to overlook or forget anyone.
Lavish on him both your fortunes,
be his unyielding defence against Time
In both your spheres of power: one your territory,
which all acknowledge, the other conferred by your high rank.
In wealth Sahm is my protégé, and in high station yours.
Whatever you decide, you are the protégé of God.[438]

I cite Aḥmad ibn Ismāʿīl, who cites Abū Sahl al-Rāzī, who said: 160

The people came to congratulate Muḥammad ibn Ṭāhir when he was appointed governor of Khurasan. Abū Tammām's son, Tammām, was one of them and he recited these verses to Muḥammad:

May the Lord of Mankind[439] let you enjoy, let you enjoy
the bountiful realm He has given you!
May what you have been given be pleasing to your eyes,
you sagacious, brave, and generous man!
May the earth shine with your achievements,
and may your whispered secrets make the wood of the pulpit
sprout leaves.[440]

The assembled company thought Tammām's poem weak. "A far cry from his father!" they said. ʿAbd Allāh ibn Isḥāq, who was in the governor's service, had told him who everyone was. "Tell one of our poets to respond to him!" Muḥammad instructed him. ʿAbd Allāh winked at one of the men present. He stepped forward and delivered the following verses to Tammām:

May the Lord of Mankind greet you, greet you!
Your expectations have failed you.
You praised a leader who gives his wealth as spoils
and would give you a share of it, if he could spot any praise.
Take this as your praise if you like;
he has given you what you gave him.

"God support the Commander," Tammām said. "This poem is payment of interest on my poem. Throw in a few dirhams, so that the interest becomes lawful[441] for both of us."

"He may not have his father's gift for poetry, but he certainly has his panache," Muḥammad laughed and gave him three thousand dirhams. ʿAbd Allāh ibn Isḥāq chimed in, "And another three thousand dirhams for this verse by his father about Commander ʿAbd Allāh ibn Ṭāhir:

'Are you taking us to where the sun rises?'
'No,' I replied, 'to the place where generosity rises.'"[442]

Tammām received it all.[443]

Diverse Information about Abū Tammām

I cite Abū Jaʿfar Aḥmad ibn Yazīd al-Muhallabī, who cites Muḥammad ibn al-Qāsim ibn Mihrawayhi (this Ibn Mihrawayhi studied with us under al-Mughīrah ibn Muḥammad al-Muhallabī and others in Basra, though I never heard him transmit anything from al-Ḥamdawī) as follows: 161.1

I heard Abū Tammām say, "I am like the poem I composed: 161.2

Move your heart to every desire,
love belongs to your first love alone.
No matter how many places a man lives in on earth
he always longs for his first home."[444]

Muḥammad ibn Dāwūd ibn al-Jarrāḥ reproduced this poetry in his 161.3
book,[445] adding the comment:

Abū Tammām took this from the words of Ibn al-Ṭathriyyah:

Love for her came to me before I knew love,
and thus took possession of an empty heart.

But I think it is closer to the following lines by Kuthayyir, and this rather is where Abū Tammām took it from:

When a sweetheart comes along to replace her,
we refuse, saying, "The Ḥājibī girl came first."[446]

161.4 Kuthayyir's line also relates to the following verse.[447] I cite Muḥammad ibn Yazīd al-Muhallabī, who cites his father as saying:

One day I recited Jarīr's verse:

> ʿIqāl is ever restrained from generosity,
> Ḥābis permanently prevented from doing good.[448]

162 Muḥammad ibn Dāwūd recounted that when Abū ʿAbd Allāh Aḥmad ibn Muḥammad al-Khathʿamī l-Kūfī and Abū Tammām met and Abū Tammām rose to go to the privy, Abū ʿAbd Allāh said, "Do I stick in your stomach?"

"Yes," Abū Tammām replied, "but I am not going to carry you around any longer."[449]

163 I cite Aḥmad ibn Mūsā, who was informed by Abū l-Ghamr al-Anṣārī, who cites ʿAmr ibn Abī Qaṭīfah as his authority, saying:

I saw Abū Tammām in a dream and asked him, "Why did you begin a poem like this:

> So! Great be the blow and crushing the matter!"

"The preceding verse has been left out," Abū Tammām replied. "What I said was:

> Eyes are forbidden to taste sleep
> and leave their lashes dry for the rest of time.
> So! Great be . . ."[450]

164 I cite ʿAlī ibn al-Ḥasan al-Kātib, who said:

The man about whom Abū Tammām said the following line:

> O namesake of the Prophet in the sura of the jinn,
> O second ruler of Egypt[451]

was ʿAbd Allāh ibn Yazīd ibn al-Muhallab al-Ṭurhubānī from al-Anbār,[452] who served as secretary to Abū Saʿīd al-Thaghrī and then his son Yūsuf.

I cite Ibn al-Mutawakkil al-Qanṭarī who said: 165

Abū Tammām appeared before Naṣr ibn Manṣūr and recited a praise poem. When he reached the words:

> You who ask Naṣr's favor, refrain!
> He cares more about giving than you do about his gifts[453]

Naṣr said to him, "By God, I care too much for your praise for you to misapply it. If I survive I will deny it to all but those who deserve it." He ordered Abū Tammām be given a handsome prize and a robe.

Naṣr died soon thereafter in the month of Shawwal 227 [July 842].

We cite Aḥmad ibn Ismāʿīl, who cites someone else who asked Abū 166
Tammām about this verse:

> An exile like that of Qays ibn Zuhayr
> and al-Ḥārith ibn Muḍāḍ.[454]

He replied, "The exile of Qays ibn Zuhayr al-ʿAbsī is well known, and this al-Ḥārith ibn Muḍāḍ al-Jurhumī was married to a lady from the line of Ismāʿīl ibn Ibrāhīm."[455] Then he provided a long account. We will reproduce it at this verse in Abū Tammām's *Collected Poems*.[456]

I cite Muḥammad ibn al-Barbarī, who cites al-Ḥasan ibn Wahb, who 167
said:

"Did al-Muʿtaṣim understand any of your poetry?" I asked Abū Tammām.

Abū Tammām replied, "He asked me three times to repeat this verse he admired:[457]

The ugliest recipient of a lover's complaint
is the one who thinks blame has great beauty.[458]

"Then he said to Ibn Abī Du'ād, 'The Ṭayyite resembles the Basrans more than the Syrians.'"[459]

168 We cite Abū ʿAbd Allāh al-Alūsī, who was informed by Abū Muḥammad al-Khuzāʿī l-Makkī, the author of the *Book of Mecca*, who cites al-Azraqī as his authority for the following:

Diʿbil heard that Abū Tammām had lampooned him when Diʿbil composed his poem in response to al-Kumayt's ode, which runs:

Quit the censure, woman, as you go on your way,
forty years should be blame enough.[460]

Abū Tammām then said:

We wrecked a thousand verses of al-Ḥuṭay'ah:
thus one man alive can vanquish a thousand dead men.
This Diʿbil holds the idle hope
of matching Kumayt.
When a man defiles a tomb
he is the son of a greasy whore.[461]

When these verses reached Diʿbil he said:

What a poetic genius
whose fathers hail from Ṭayy!
I heard he foolishly insulted my mother—
that didn't worry me—
"Bravo for his mother," I said.
"She, I know, is pure through and through."
But I lie, by God, about his mother
just as he lied about mine.

The first set of verses, those rhyming in *T*, is also attributed to Abū Saʿd al-Makhzūmī, and the second set, those rhyming in *M*, is attributed to another poet's attack on Abū Tammām, not to Diʿbil.[462]

Ibn Dāwūd claims Muḥammad ibn al-Ḥusayn as his authority for the following: 169

Al-Ḥasan ibn Wahb and Abū Tammām visited Abū Nahshal ibn Ḥumayd. When they were seated, Abū Tammām delivered this line:

> Abū Nahshal, may God make you nibble . . .[463]

"Continue the verse!" he challenged al-Ḥasan, who said:

> . . . the cheek of a dark-eyed gazelle fawn!

and in turn challenged Abū Nahshal to continue the poem. Abū Nahshal said:

> He arouses your desire for a rendezvous
> and when you are dying for it, he is as remote as Capella.

We cite Maymūn ibn Hārūn, who cites Abū Tammām's page Ṣāliḥ as saying: 170

Abū Tammām was angry with me so I wrote him this couplet, the very first poetry I ever composed:

> What makes the noble better than the base
> when you punish me for every single sin?
> Calamities may have shaken me—
> but my fortitude blows sorrow away.

Abū Tammām came to find me where I was and we were reconciled.

I came across the following verses in the handwriting of Ibn al-Muʿtazz: 171

In the reign of al-Wāthiq, Abū Tammām visited Aḥmad ibn al-Khaṣīb to request a favor, but Aḥmad made him sit and wait so long that the poet suffered sunstroke. He then pronounced the following couplet:

Aḥmad ignored us, pretending he forgot
to protect the bonds of praise, thanks, and gratitude.
We are dying at his door from brutal heat
while our requests have perished from his icy cold.[464]

172 I cite Abū Dhakwān, who cites my paternal uncle Aḥmad ibn ʿAbd Allāh Ṭimās as follows:

I was with my paternal uncle Ibrāhīm ibn al-ʿAbbās when a man appeared before him. Ibrāhīm brought him forward, made him sit next to him, or close by, and then engaged him in conversation. "Abū Tammām, is there anyone still alive who can be appealed to for shelter and protection?" he eventually asked the man.

"You!" Abū Tammām responded, "May we not be without you!"

Ibrāhīm was a man in full possession of his powers, and Abū Tammām recited the following verses to him:

His sword-belt is so long that when he walks,
he seems mounted on a two-humped camel.
At night he travels to fulfill the needs of those who sleep,
and when he strikes fire, he ignites generosity.
When he dons a Yemeni mantle
you think he's the crescent moon shining brightly on the horizon.
He adds to men's virtues a higher virtue
while the praise of all who praise him falls short.

Ibrāhīm commented, "You really excel in everything: composing, transmitting, and choosing pithy verses."

When Abū Tammām left I followed him. "Dictate these verses to me," I begged.

"Abū l-Juwayriyyah al-ʿAbdī composed them for al-Junayd ibn ʿAbd al-Raḥmān: I excerpted them," Abū Tammām replied.[465]

The Death of Abū Tammām and His Age at the Time

I cite Muḥammad ibn Khalaf, who cites Hārūn ibn Muḥammad ibn 'Abd al-Malik, who said: 173

When Abū Tammām died al-Wāthiq said to my father, "The death of the Ṭayyite poet grieves me."

"The whole of Ṭayy and all humankind give their lives for the Commander of the Faithful!" my father replied. "If anyone could live beyond his term to hear the Commander of the Faithful say this, he wouldn't die at all."

I cite Muḥammad ibn Mūsā l-Barbarī as follows: 174

When he was serving Muḥammad ibn 'Abd al-Malik al-Zayyāt as a scribe, al-Ḥasan ibn Wahb looked out for of Abū Tammām and appointed him head of the postal service in Mosul. Abū Tammām lived there for a year, and then passed away in the month of Jumada al-Awwal in the year 231 [January 846]. He is buried in Mosul.

I cite 'Awn ibn Muḥammad al-Kindī as follows: 175

I studied some of Abū Tammām's poems with him in 227 [842][466] and heard him say, "I was born in the year 190 [806]."

Mukhallad al-Mawṣilī informed me that Abū Tammām died in Mosul in the month of Muharram in the year 232 [September 846].

176 I cite Abū Sulaymān al-Nābulusī, who said:

Abū Tammām's son Tammām said, "My father was born in 188 [804] and died in 231 [845–46]."

Laments Composed for Abū Tammām

Abū l-Ghawth recited to me his father's lament for Abū Tammām and Di'bil:[467] 177

The day when Ḥabīb died, his tomb and that of Di'bil too
burdened me with grief and ignited my pain,
When the likes of al-Khath'amī survive,
talentless, worthless to a man.
In their search for novelty, they created inconceivable motifs
and forbiddingly difficult speech.
My brothers, heaven promises clouds that shall forever
cover both your graves in steady rain:
A tomb in Ahwāz—a death announced far and wide—
and in Mosul bones bleached white.[468]

Al-Ḥasan ibn Wahb composed this lament for Abū Tammām: 178

May the tomb of our far-traveled friend in Mosul
be watered by clouds weeping for him,
As they pass above, they collide and cast rain
as a traveler's water skin spills water.
May lightning bolts slap each other's cheeks,
and thunderclaps tear their shirts in mourning.
This dusty grave holds Ḥabīb,
whom I called "beloved,"[469]

Elegant, inspired,[470] astute, intelligent,
with sound judgment in matters of moment.
When you were with him he would give you
things of delightful refinement and freshness to transmit.
Abū Tammām of Ṭayy, you went away.
We were astonished and amazed:
In you we lost a jewel—we do not think[471] we'll ever find
one like it as long as the world exists.
You were a brother who offered us
pure affection and close kinship.[472]
Madhḥij[473] united us
then made our tribes disperse.
When you left, both our home here and distant lands
were altered beyond recognition by the Nights.
Time showed its ugliest side:
a face, stern, grim, and scowling.
It is a worthy tribute to him
that death is sweet and life is not.

179 ʿAlī ibn al-Jahm lamented him as follows:

The creations of intellect have vanished into thin air,
assailed by Time's catastrophe.
Stately poetry has grown thin and tearfully complains
to the reed pens of its bereavement.
Noble rhymes bemoan his departure,
Time has struck healthy rhymes with sickness.
He who set them straight and tamed difficult ones,
the stream that fed their garden—Abū Tammām—has died.

180 Abū Jaʿfar al-Muhallabī and Abū Muḥammad al-Hadādī recited to me this lament for Abū Tammām by Aḥmad ibn Yaḥyā l-Balādhurī. In it he lampooned Abū Muslim ibn Ḥumayd al-Ṭūsī:

Ḥabīb became the hostage of a solitary tomb.
No hand could defend him against destiny.
Refinement did not save him when life came to its end,
nor could he escape by the power of his wit.
I had hoped that you would find mercy
but I fear for you because of your kinship with Ibn Ḥumayd.

Another lament[474] by al-Ḥasan ibn Wahb for Abū Tammām goes: 181

Stately poetry has lost the Seal of the Poets,
the stream that fed its garden,[475] Ḥabīb of Ṭayy.
They died at the same time and live together in the same tomb
as they did when they were alive.

Muḥammad ibn ʿAbd al-Malik al-Zayyāt, while he was still vizier, lamented Abū Tammām: 182.1

The most momentous news arrived
that troubled my heart.
"A beloved," they said, "is buried in the earth."
"I beseech you," I cried, "let it not be the Ṭayyite!"

Another lament by Muḥammad goes: 182.2

Fate's crime cries out to heaven
Ḥabīb whom we love has been taken from us.
Poetry died after Ibn Aws.
There remains no trace of culture, nor men of culture.
People come in different kinds, with different natures—
you were in a class of your own.
Death may have cut you down—
when you were torn from our hearts they were torn apart.

ʿAbd Allāh ibn Abī l-Shīṣ said: 183

He lies in the dark earth,
larger than the earth itself.
His memory reaches as far and as wide
as the earth.
What a noble man to be buried!
Scions of pure nobility, Abū Tammām's honor comes close to yours![476]
Ibn Aws, I cannot be consoled for a beloved,
my eyelids will not close in sleep.
Men of culture are perplexed—they were stunned
by his loss on a black, joyless day.
When his life was undone, so too was resolve:
yet he was the father of doing and undoing.
A mountain of poetry collapsed,
its rocks tumbling down one upon the other.
His was a roaring sea of poetry,
whose waves clashed but yielded delicate pearls.
Poetry was like a garment next to his skin[477]
or like leaves on a fresh branch.
God fulfilled your hopes
of giving and receiving,
Then death's marksman took aim,
but no bowstring twanged to announce the shot.
If poetry had eyes it would weep
for its fallen star.

184 I came across these verses in the handwriting of Ibn Mihrawayhi:

Tomb of the Ṭayyite, what a man
you house in the dust of the grave!
You are his garment next to his skin!
Don't you realize he was the most poetic soul ever?[478]
How much wisdom you contain,
which only yesterday consoled men's souls!

Here ends *The Life and Times of Abū Tammām.* 185
God be forever praised, and God's blessing and peace be
upon our lord and master, the Emissary
Muḥammad, and his pure progeny.

Notes

1 Damage to the manuscript makes an entire line illegible; the partial reconstruction is by ع.

2 *Ibdāʿ* ("originality") derives from the same root as *badīʿ*, which by this time had become the technical term for the style of modern poets, or *muḥdathūn*.

3 Lit. "the eye of insight made me see."

4 Lit. "to be spat out by the ear."

5 Knowledge about modern poetry was apparently not readily available.

6 Note the contemporary poetic topics for description, including buildings, lakes, and convivial gatherings, as well as the distinction between transmitted and extemporized anecdotes.

7 Lit. "their occurrence cried out with their foreignness there."

8 A constellation consisting of three stars in a triangular shape.

9 Q Yūnus 10:39. All Qur'an translations are taken from Arberry, *The Koran Interpreted*.

10 Abū Nuwās, *Dīwān*, 3:265, 269. Var. v. 2: *fī l-ʿilmi*; v. 3: *min ghalaṭin*.

11 Al-Buḥturī, *Dīwān*, 1:76, no. 27:39–40.

12 The variant "[amulets] were suspended on me" (*nīṭat ʿalayya*), similar to the second of Ibn Mayyādah's following verses, appears in a couplet cited by Ḥammād ibn Isḥāq al-Mawṣilī in al-Kisrawī [attributed to al-Jāḥiẓ], *al-Ḥanīn ilā l-awṭān*, 400, v. 1, and anonymously in Ibn al-Marzubān, *al-Ḥanīn ilā l-awṭān*, 43, no. 16. The variant "youth cut off [my amulets]" (*ʿaqqa shababī*) appears in Ibn ʿAbd al-Barr, *Bahjat*

al-majālis, 1:802, v. 9. It further appears as the last of three verses attributed to a Bedouin by al-Mubarrad, *al-Kāmil*, 1:406 and 2:276, and al-Ḥuṣrī, *Zahr al-ādāb*, 2:682. The verse was a staple in early anthologies on this motif; see Gruendler, "Leaving Home."

13 According to al-Ḥuṣrī, *Zahr al-ādāb*, 2:685, the verses were addressed to al-Walīd ibn Yazīd. The first is modeled on a verse by the Umayyad 'Udhrī love poet Jamīl Buthaynah. The first and second verses appear in Ibn 'Abd al-Barr, *Bahjat al-majālis*, 1:802.

14 See Ibn al-Rūmī, *Dīwān*, 5:1825–27, no. 1375. This passage, to which al-Ṣūlī was the first to draw attention, became a classic example of the motif and is ubiquitous in subsequent anthologies, beginning with al-'Askarī's *Dīwān al-ma'ānī*; see Gruendler, "Leaving Home," n. 17. For the historical context and evaluation of the passage, based on al-Ṣūlī, see al-Marzubānī, *Mu'jam*, 146, and al-Ḥuṣrī, *Zahr al-ādāb*, 2:681–82, 684, 686.

15 Al-Ṣūlī decorously refrains from identifying the genre of *mujūn* (bawdy poetry).

16 Al-Nābighah, *Dīwān*, 99, vv. 3–4. The passage occurs in a description of an unnamed beloved following the *raḥīl* and forms the final part of the poem (ibid., 94, v. 2–99, v. 7).

17 Ibn al-Rūmī, *Dīwān* 4:1656, no. 1286:58–60. Var. v. 58: *lahā hanun tasta'īru*.

18 Burning love has charred the lovers' hearts black.

19 The emendation of the verse is based on al-Iṣbahānī, *Aghānī*, 10:162.

20 The pattern of the rhyme word "penboard" (*miqaṭṭ*) alludes to the female "slit" (*mishaqq*), the unnamed theme.

21 *Shayb*, lit. "gray hair," is a synecdoche for old age.

22 The poet addresses a woman.

23 D 1:40 and 1:69, no. 3:1, 59. For an account on the recitation of this ode, see §§61.1–4.

24 I.e., the caliph's sword will determine the time of the conquest, not the predictions of the Byzantine astrologers.

25 Abū Nuwās, *Dīwān*, 1:144, v. 12.

26 Abu Tammām included the panegyric to which this verse belongs in his shorter anthology, *al-Waḥshiyyāt*, 268, no. 449:3, where he does not give an attribution.

27 Here and in the following examples, water is a metaphor for luster, sheen.

28 For the context of this lampoon verse, see §120.

29 Lit. "water of the face." For Abū Tammām's use of this metaphor, see §49.1.

30 Here, al-Ṣūlī explains the procedure, typical of modern poetry, of combining two separate metaphors by a common term on the level of the image, giving formal unity to a verse; see Heinrichs, "Paired Metaphors."

31 Q Shūrā 42:40.

32 Q Āl ʿImrān 3:54.

33 Q Āl ʿImrān 3:21, Tawbah 9:34, Inshiqāq 84:24.

34 The Arabic word for tidings (*bishārah*) derives from the same root as "cheerful, open face" (*bishr*) and "skin of face and body" (*basharah*).

35 Q Isrāʾ 17:24.

36 Lit. "a contemptible position from which blame is protected at the mention of it, and even the low ground rises above it."

37 The poet puns on "pin [him] down" (*yaḍbaṭuhū*) and "clap in irons" (*yaḍbaṭuhū*).

38 In another account by Muslim the verses are addressed to Diʿbil, nicknamed Mayyās, in the presence of al-Faḍl ibn Sahl; see Muslim, *Sharḥ Dīwān Ṣarīʿ al-Ghawānī*, 334, no. 164:1–2, 4. Var. v. 1: *Mayyāsu*. Elsewhere the verses about Diʿbil are attributed to Abū Tammām.

39 Al-Ḥuṭayʾah, *Dīwān*, 312–13, no. 7:3, 6–7, after the recension of al-Sukkarī; var. v. 3: *wa-man*; v. 6: *wa-antum, fa-ṭāra*; v. 7: *wa-dabībukum bi-aʿrāḍinā fiʿla l-imāʾi*. The first two verses appear in Abū Tammām, *al-Ḥamāsah*, 2:1539–40, no. 666:1–2, attributed to Ziyād al-Aʿjam. Var. v. 1: *wa-antum, fa-ṭāra*.

40 Lit. "with your hands and feet!"

41 The emendation of the name is based on *GAS*, 2:631.

42 Lit. "I made him swallow a stone."

43 Al-Buḥturī, *Dīwān*, 2:954–55, no. 379:12, 10. Var. v. 12: *min maqāṭiʿihā*; v. 10: *allātī*.

44 D 2:186, no. 70:10. Var. *fa'inna jullahum bal kullahum*. For a citation of the verse in the context of criticism, see §53.

45 D 4:571, no. 481:13.

46 This means either their camels, which are as thin as their riders, or the rough ground they sleep on, as a metaphor for life's hardships; D 1:221, no. 16:9–10. For a commentary on this and the following verse and the recitation of the poem in which they appear, see §§64.1–5.

47 Here the term *naqala* ("to copy") implies a reuse of the motif only, and not of its wording (as elsewhere). The terminology for borrowing was not yet consistently used in this early phase of evolving Arabic poetics.

48 The name is incomplete in ا, and the verse unattributed in al-ʿAskarī, *Dīwān al-maʿānī*, 1:317, and other sources.

49 The verses are also discussed under this aspect in §64.5.

50 Lit. "more entitled than [the original poet]."

51 I.e., as an example of such optimized borrowing.

52 D 1:214, no. 15:42–43. For a recitation of the ode, see §§69.1–4.

53 The poet produces a paronomasia between "war" (*ḥarb*) and "spoils" (*ḥarā'ib*, sg., *ḥarab*).

54 D 1:64, no. 3:50. For a recitation of this famous poem on the Battle of Amorium, see §§61.1–4. For the word play, see previous note.

55 See, for example, §§44.8–9.

56 I.e., of Abū Tammām's *Collected Poems*.

57 The currency change implies a twenty- to twenty-five-fold drop in price; see Ashtor, "Essai sur les prix."

58 See §114 and n. 394.

59 D 2:22–23, no. 46:1–4, 5–6, 7–8. Var. v. 1: *sarat*; v. 8: *an laysat*.

60 See §§44.5–7 for al-Buḥturī's borrowing of the verse's motif.

61 D 1:402, no. 39:6–8.

62 Diʿbil, *Dīwān*, 239–40, no. 158, where the beginning is *wa-inna* to restore the *ṭawīl* meter.

63 D 3:60, no. 120:5–6.

64 Al-Buḥturī, *Dīwān*, 1:38, no. 11:7.

65 D 4:99, no. 197:1a.

66 The love described here is devoted to the deceased Caliph al-Wāthiq and his successor, al-Muʿtaṣim, in a panegyric ode.

67 D 3:206, no. 139:22, 28.

68 Al-Buḥturī's correct name is Abū ʿUbādah al-Walīd ibn ʿUbayd.

69 *Lam taẓmaʾ* means both "not tired" and "not thirsty."

70 I.e., thirsty for distance *and* saturated in hue. The horse's forceful gallop is described as embodying opposite qualities.

71 D 4:434, no. 420. Var. v. 3: *wa-l-ḥaṣā filaqun*; v. 4: *ḥalafta*.

72 The poet had received a horse from the patron.

73 The vocalization Quṭrabull is attested in Yāqūt, *Muʿjam al-buldān*, 4:68.

74 Al-Buḥturī, *Dīwān*, 3:1737, 1740, 1743–44, no. 674:1, 12–13, 16–17, 25, 31, 18. Var. v. 17: *turayāni*. The selection not only abbreviates the poem but also changes its verse order.

75 D 3:334–35, no. 168:10, 14–15. Var. v. 35 *abdānunā fī Shaʾāmin*.

76 D 2:418, no. 103: 25–26. Var. v. 25: *bishra l-khamīlati*.

77 *Takmīl* or *tatmīm*, i.e., the completion of a motif with a second verse, later became a figure of speech. See al-ʿAskarī, *Ṣināʿatayn*, 404–6.

78 D 4:448, no. 432:5, a poem reprimanding ʿAyyāsh ibn Lahīʿah al-Ḥaḍramī.

79 Al-Buḥturī, *Dīwān*, 3:2046, no. 780:35–36, a panegyric of Abū Yūsuf Rāfiʿ ibn Harthamah al-Ṭāʾī. Var. v. 36: *ustuʾnifat*.

80 Al-Buḥturī, *Dīwān*, 1:599, no. 248:30–31. Var. v. 30: *bi-l-nadā*.

81 Al-Buḥturī, *Dīwān*, 2:823, no. 328:24–25. Var. v. 24: *bi-mawāhibin*.

82 Al-Buḥturī, *Dīwān*, 3:1643–44, no. 641:13–14.

83 Abū Nuwās, *Dīwān*, 2:322–23. Var. v. 1: *bashsharahum*. A description of pigeons carrying letters to lovers precedes and anticipates the praise motif: the arrival of good tidings before their fulfillment.

84 D 1:119, no. 8:11. Var. *bi-l-qafri*.

85 Al-Buḥturī, *Dīwān*, 3:1750, no. 675:9. Al-Buḥturī reuses the motif in the same context of addressing the abandoned campsite of the beloved.

86 D 1:355, no. 34:40. Var. *fa-anta lā shakka ʿindī*.

87 Al-Buḥturī, *Dīwān*, 2:958, no. 379:41. Var. *yumdaḥu fī aḍʿāfihī*.

88 D 1:397, no. 37:46. For the poem in which the verse appears, see §78.9.

89 Al-Buḥturī, *Dīwān*, 1:625, no. 257:25.

90 D 4:345, no. 366:3. Var. *lu'mun*.

91 Al-Buḥturī, *Dīwān*, 1:631, no. 258:33. Var. *wa-tamāḥakū fī*; *dīnan*.

92 D 1:402, no. 39:7, a farewell poem for the poet ʿAlī ibn al-Jahm. See §31 for the occasion of this verse.

93 In al-Farazdaq's *Dīwān*, the verse begins *yā Naṣru*, addressing the governor of Khurasan, Naṣr ibn Sayyār al-Laythī.

94 Al-Buḥturī, *Dīwān*, 1:552, no. 230:27.

95 Lit. "in the two easts" and "in the two wests," referring to the endpoints of the seasonally changing places of sunrise and sunset. D 3:299, no. 162:15.

96 Al-Buḥturī, *Dīwān*, 1:177, no. 61:7. Var. *wa-ghadwati tinnīni l-mashāriqi* ("on the morning of the Hydra of the east"), a hyperbole for the commander Muḥammad ibn Yūsuf al-Thaghrī, praised with this ode.

97 Al-Buḥturī, *Dīwān*, 1:178, no. 61:11. See this account also in al-Ṣūlī, *Akhbār al-Buḥturī*, 151–52, no. 100.

98 Lit. "deflower."

99 D 4:140, no. 206:9.

100 The author creates assonance between "abstain" (*ajtanibu*) and "appropriating" (*ajtadhibu*). It is likely al-Ṣūlī was referring to the work of Abū l-Ḍiyā' Bishr ibn Yaḥyā the Scribe, cited and critiqued in al-Āmidī, *Muwāzanah*, 1:324–70. Al-Āmidī divides Bishr's 105 items into four lists: a first list of those he accepts (64 items, *Muwāzanah*, 1:324–45), and three lists of those he rejects. The second list contains common motifs of which no one could claim ownership, i.e., authorship (20 items, ibid., 1:346–58); the third, meanings that are unrelated (17 items, ibid., 1:358–630); and the fourth, accidental overlaps in the wording of different meanings (14 items, ibid., 1:363–70). Al-Ṣūlī identifies twenty-six borrowings, which he divides into those of general reliance (*lawdh*) on and emulation (*iḥtidhā'*) of Abū Tammām

(§§44.1–10), borrowing (*akhdh*) (§§46.1–6), copying of meaning and wording (*naql*) (§§47.1–11), and matching of Abū Tammām's style (*taqdīr*) (§§48.1–4). Half of these (or 14 cases) concur with Bishr, and they largely refer to what al-Ṣūlī calls "copying." Eight appear in al-Āmidī's first list of the things he accepts, but al-Āmidī rejects six of al-Ṣūlī's cases, as he discounts common motifs as potential objects of theft (the second list).

101 I.e., his actions speak for themselves, making him superfluous. D 1:142, no. 10:14.

102 Al-Buḥturī, *Dīwān*, 1:182, no. 61:42. Var. *li-l-nuṣḥi mawḍiʿun ladā sāmiʿin*. See this account also in al-Ṣūlī, *Akhbār al-Buḥturī*, 152–54, no. 101.

103 D 2:77, no. 49:44.

104 Al-Buḥturī, *Dīwān*, 1:22, no. 3:16. Var. *rakbu shiʿrin*.

105 D 2:339, no. 92:22. Var. *muʿtafin yarjūhu*.

106 Al-Buḥturī, *Dīwān*, 1:629, no. 258:23.

107 D 2:178, no. 68:46. Var. *mujarribūna*; *luqū*.

108 Al-Buḥturī, *Dīwān*, 1:81, no. 28:24.

109 The notion of copied wording included similar syntax, even if no words were reused. For this account, see also al-Ṣūlī, *Akhbār al-Buḥturī*, 155–58, no. 101.

110 D 1:382, no. 35:49. Var. *munazzahatan*; *mukarramatan*. For the occasion of the poem in which the verse appears, see §78.4.

111 Al-Buḥturī, *Dīwān*, 1:606, no. 250:19. Var. *yuʿmilu*; *wa-l-ra'ya l-muraddad*.

112 D 3:338, no. 170:9. Var. *al-ʿīsu wa-l-hammu*.

113 Al-Buḥturī, *Dīwān*, 1:633, no. 259:10.

114 D 1:284, no. 22:9.

115 Al-Buḥturī, *Dīwān*, 1:85, no. 29:29.

116 D 3:70, no. 123:20.

117 Al-Buḥturī, *Dīwān*, 2:990, no. 388:30. The rhyme word *jalīli* in ا is influenced by Abū Tammām's preceding verse, ending in *jalīla*, and changes the type of borrowing to a taking over of both meaning and wording.

118 D 3:200, no. 138:41. Var. *wa-laqad jahadtum an tuzīlū ʿizzahū*. The rhyme word *Mutāliʿu* in ا is influenced by al-Buḥturī's following verse, ending likewise in *Mutāliʿu*, and makes the wording of both verses more similar.

119 Al-Buḥturī, *Dīwān*, 2:1305, no. 517:31.

120 D 3:202, no. 138:58. Var. *wa-hal bika madhhabun*; *ʿalā l-makārimi*.

121 Here both meaning and exact wording are reused. Al-Buḥturī, *Dīwān*, 3:1956, no. 756:18. Var. *ʿalā l-makārimi*.

122 D 4:96, no. 196:23. Var. *talbasu*.

123 Al-Buḥturī, *Dīwān*, 2:255, no. 502:23. Var. *al-aʿrāḍu*.

124 D 4:80, no. 192:9. For a recitation of the ode, see §69.4.

125 Al-Buḥturī, *Dīwān*, 1:291, no. 102:15. Var. *law annahū stāma l-najāta*; *wajada l-najāta*.

126 D 4:461, no. 435:7.

127 Al-Buḥturī, *Dīwān*, 3:1864, no. 717:3. The poem is a lampoon of Murr ibn ʿAlī l-Ṭāʾī composed when the poet's horse was stolen during his stay with him.

128 D 2:289, no. 86:7. For this account, see also al-Ṣūlī, *Akhbār al-Buḥturī*, 158–59, no. 101.

129 Al-Buḥturī, *Dīwān*, 1:507, no. 211:4.

130 D 3:158, no. 133:54.

131 Al-Buḥturī, *Dīwān*, 3:1948, no. 754:9.

132 D 2:181, no. 68:59. For a recitation of the ode, see §52.3.

133 Al-Buḥturī, *Dīwān*, 3:1746, no. 674:39. Var. *mutakaffilun ʿanhum*.

134 D 2:6, no. 48:10. Var. *bi-ḥūri ʿīnin*.

135 Al-Buḥturī, *Dīwān*, 2:1123, no. 454:2. Var. *bi-bīḍin; nujūmu dujan*.

136 See the parallel in al-Masʿūdī, *Murūj*, 4:364–66, no. 2833–36. Var. *kayfa ʿilmuka bi-ʿaskar amīr al-muʾminīn* (ibid., 4:365). Since the army is dealt with in the last question, this redundancy seems to be a corruption. Other *Murūj* variations are misreadings (*taṣḥīf*), *lectiones faciliores*, and explanatory paraphrases of which only major ones are referenced. The present version thus appears to be prior. In an appended comment, al-Masʿūdī questions the account's historicity.

137 Lit. "One who knows a land kills it," a proverb meaning that knowledge of a thing conveys control over it. See al-Maydānī, *Majmaʿ al-amthāl*, 2:108, no. 2908.

138 See also al-Masʿūdī, *Murūj*, 4:365: *raghiba ʿan kulli dhī jināyah*. This refers to al-Wāthiq's imprisonment of and extortion of large sums of money from a number of secretaries in 229/843, namely Aḥmad ibn Isrāʾīl, Sulaymān and al-Ḥasan ibn Wahb, Aḥmad ibn al-Khaṣīb, Ibrāhīm ibn Rabāḥ, Najāḥ ibn Salamah, Abū l-Wazīr, and Ibn al-Zayyāt; see al-Ṭabarī, *Taʾrīkh*, 9:125–28, year 229; Sourdel, *Vizirat*, 1:262–63; Boustany, *Ibn al-Rūmī*, 43. Abū Tammām's death in 231/845 or 232/846, before which he served as postmaster in Mawṣil for a year, calls the account's historicity further into question.

139 For the correction of his name, ʿUmar ibn Faraj al-Rukhkhajī, see Sourdel, *Vizirat*, 1:237, 280, n. 1.

140 Al-Masʿūdī, *Murūj* 4:365: *ḍakhmun nahimun istaʿdhaba l-dama wa-yunṣibuhu l-qawmu tirsan li-l-waghā*. The translation of *ḍakhmun* follows the meaning attested in a parallel, slightly expanded description of another man, *ḍakhmi l-dasīʿi mifḍalin lihammin* (*WKAS*, 2:1553b).

141 Al-Masʿūdī, *Murūj* 4:365: *rajulun nubisha baʿda mā qubira, laysat tuʿaddu lahu ḥayātun fī l-aḥyāʾi wa-ʿalayhi khaftatu l-mawtā*.

142 Q Naḥl 16:21. The verse describes the powerless idols that people pray to instead of God.

143 Al-Masʿūdī, *Murūj*, 4:365, has a different answer, then adds a question and answer about Sulaymān ibn Wahb, and a further question about his brother al-Ḥasan, the answer to which is here applied to Aḥmad ibn Isrāʾīl. Al-Ḥasan's death ca. 248/862 appears to make the answer fit him better. Aḥmad ibn Isrāʾīl served as vizier to al-Muʿtazz.

144 The poet puns on "[glorious deeds] ruled him" (*aslamahu*) and "he does not surrender [his kindness]" (*lā yuslimu*).

145 Al-Masʿūdī, *Murūj*, 4:366: *in aʿṭūnī lam aḥmadhum wa-in manaʿūnī lam adhummahum*.

146 D 3:218, no. 142:6. Lit. "water of the face," i.e., the sheen or luster of the face stands for pride. See §§22.1–10 for water metaphors.

147 The sentence up to here is missing in al-Masʿūdī, *Murūj*, 4:366.

148 D 4:465, no. 438:2. Var. *māʾu kaffika*.

149 Lit. "of the people of this age."

150 Al-Masʿūdī, *Murūj*, 4:366, gives the sum as one thousand dinars, changes the remainder of the sentence to *wa-akhadha lahu min sāʾiri l-kuttābi wa-ahli l-dawlati mā aghnāhu bihī wa-aghnā ʿaqabahu baʿdahu*, and lacks the Bedouin's closing statement.

151 Q Qiyāmah 75:25.

152 Abridgment of poem D 2:198, 203–4, 208, no. 72:1, 20–22, 25, 28, 47–49, 51. Var. v. 21: *shiqqa izāri*; v. 47: *sūdu l-thiyābi, aydī l-samūmi*. The last line's translation is tentative and follows al-Tibrīzī's commentary.

153 Cf. Ibn Qutaybah, *al-Shiʿr wa-l-shuʿarāʾ*, 160.

154 *Zawr* also means visitor.

155 D 2:324, no. 91:12–14. For another passage of this poem used for similar practical criticism, see §90.

156 The end of life is personified as an archer taking aim at the poet.

157 D 4:100, no. 197:9–10.

158 D 2:170–71, 181, no. 68:18, 23, 58–59. For al-Buḥturī's borrowing of this motif, see §48.3.

159 Lit. "It was as if I made him swallow a stone."

160 D 2:186, no. 70:10. The verse is cited for its motif in §25.1.

161 See Isḥāq ibn Ibrāhīm, *al-Burhān fī wujūh al-bayān*, 128, where the two statements are in reverse order and the second slightly reformulated: *fa-kānat maʿāqiluhū taʿqiluhū wa-mā yuḥrizihū yubrizuhū*.

162 The verse describes a traitor fleeing from the caliph praised with this ode.

163 See Isḥāq ibn Ibrāhīm, *al-Burhān fī wujūh al-bayān*, 128.

164 Teknonym of the Abbasid caliph al-Muʿtaṣim (r. 218–27/833–42), to whom this panegyric is addressed.

165 D 3:28–29, no. 112:31–36. For a discussion of the poem as typical for modern poetry, see Heinrichs, "Muslim ibn al-Walīd und *badīʿ*."

166 Lit. "well rope," continuing the preceding image of a well.

167 I.e., obey a friend who advises against the love. Al-Buḥturī, *Dīwān*, 3:1446, no. 571:1.

168 The variant "cheek" in ا changes the verse's subject from desert travel to a nocturnal visit by the beloved's dream apparition.

169 The correction of the tribal name is based in the addressee's descent from Dhuhl.

170 Clan names (in reverse chronological order by poetic license) forming the genealogy of the commander Khālid ibn Yazīd al-Shaybānī, praised with this ode.

171 The double sense of "beam," meaning "rafter" and "ray of light," translates both the literal meaning of *ʿamūd*, "rafter, pillar", and its metaphorical meaning as the horizontal strip of light at dawn.

172 The tribal confederacy to which Khālid's tribe belongs.

173 Abridgment of poem D 1:410–15, 421, no. 40: 11–13, 16, 18–21, 23, 26, 45–46. For acclaim of verses 45–46 in a literary gathering as the perfect description of poetry by a modern poet, see al-ʿAskarī, *Dīwān al-maʿānī*, 1:102, discussed in Gruendler, "Motif vs. Genre," 76–77. For a contemporary philologist's view of the ode, see §125.

174 Both variants, *taʿālā* and *al-muʿallā*, are recorded in D.

175 A woman's taking off her face-veil here implies coquetry.

176 A legendary South Arabian hero and king.

177 In D this verse appears after the next following and does not break up the extended metaphor of the city as woman.

178 The city of Ankara, conquered prior to the conquest of Amorium, is meant. The poet compares the two cities' subsequent destruction to mange passing from one camel to another.

179 The destroyed city is compared to the poetic motif of the deserted campsite, exemplified here by the verses the Umayyad poet Dhū l-Rummah composed about his beloved Mayyah.

180 Literal translation of the caliph's name, al-Muʿtaṣim.

181 The poet plays on "war" (*ḥarb*) and "spoils" (*ḥarab*), which derive from the same root. For an account on this motif, see §26.2.

182 Abridgment of poem D 1:45–73, no. 3:11–16, 18, 17, 21–22, 25–29, 32–35, 37, 39–40, 50, 55, 68–70. Var. v. 11: *fatḥa*; v. 12: *fī athwābihā*; v. 13: *minka*; v. 16: *Abī Karibi* (correct and adopted here); v. 21: *wa-l-riḥabi*; v. 33: *wa-qad udmīna*; v. 34: *samājatan, ghaniyat minnā*; v. 35:

tabdū; v. 39: *lam yaghzu*; v. 50: *Tūfalisu*; v. 69: *ṣurūfi*; v. 70: *allātī*. For the motive and method of al-Ḥasan's selections from this ode, see Gruendler, "Abstract Aesthetics," 213–20.

183 He seems to have left no trace in the biographical sources.

184 D 2:294, no. 87:1a.

185 This and the following verse are discussed for their motif in §25.4.

186 D 1:216, 220–22, no. 16:1, 8–12. Var. v. 1: *a-hunna*, correcting the meter. For a discussion of the account, see Gruendler, "*Qaṣīda*," 332–33.

187 The variant is identical to the verse cited and indicates a corruption in the text. Al-Ṣūlī explains in his commentary that *al-fayāfī* is the plural of *fayfāh*.

188 The sums of one thousand dinars or ten thousand dirhams are standard in accounts, so the governor was rightly offended; see Gruendler, *Verse and Taxes*. For a parallel account of this event, see §99.2.

189 This and the following verse are discussed for their motif in §25.5.

190 Lit. "is unarmed in the evening when he meets the events"; see D 3:98, 102–3, no. 128:1a, 21–24. For a discussion of the account, see Gruendler, *Qaṣīda*, 331–32.

191 Lit. "Tied is the tongue of excuse, even though it were eloquent."

192 D 1:146, no. 11:1a.

193 Black and white metaphorically contrast the sorrow of having to plead for gifts with the joy of receiving them.

194 A brother tribe of the ʿIjl, the commander's tribe, both belonging to the Bakr ibn Wāʾil confederacy. See also n. 196.

195 According to legend, Ḥājib ibn Zurārah of Tamīm refused to surrender the hostage demanded by a Sasanian king and pledged his bow instead as security in return for the permission to establish a cloister in al-Ḥīrah (or sell perfume in the market of Mecca). The monarch accepted.

196 In the famous battle of Dhū Qār against the Sasanians, ʿIjl (whose leader, Ḥanẓalah ibn Thaʿlabah, was instrumental to the victory), Thaʿlabah, and Ḥanīfah ibn Lujaym participated among the clans of Bakr; see *EI2*, s.vv. "Bakr ibn Wāʾil," "D̲h̲ū Ḳār," and "ʿIdjl."

197 Lit. "A fountain whose revenge is in the skies and it does not miss its revenge." ʿAlī ibn al-Jahm, *Dīwān*, 30, no. 9:19.

198 Abridgment of poem D 1:198, 201, 203, 205–10, 214, no. 15:1, 7, 14, 19, 21–23, 27–30, 42–43. Var. v. 21: *tufattiḥuhū l-ṣabā*; v. 29: *taqrinū*; v. 30: *ka'annahā*; v. 43: *idhā njalat*. For a discussion of the account, see Gruendler, "*Qaṣīda*," 330–31. The ode's last cited verses (42–43) are discussed in §26.1 for the innovative borrowing of the motif.

199 This was an inordinately high figure, ten thousand dirhams (or five hundred or a thousand dinars) being more common sums of reward in literary accounts. For a comparative survey, see Gruendler, "Verse and Taxes."

200 Lit. "died" (*māta*), punning with the preceding "he did not die" (*mā māta*).

201 For a borrowing of this motif by al-Buḥturī, see §47.9.

202 ʿUmānī tribe with several independent branches (*EI2*, s.v. "Nabhān," "Banū"), presumably ancestors of the commander. His genealogy is not given in the Arabic sources.

203 D 4:80–82, no. 192:8–9, 11–12, 14–15, and without any variants from D. For an account of the ode's much-criticized opening verse, see §163.

204 The statement emulates Abū Tammām's verse, addressing the deceased general in another lament, "'Did you not die, brother of my soul, some time ago?' He answered, 'The man whose magnanimity has not died is not dead.'" D 4:137, no. 204:6.

205 For an allegation that Abū Tammām plagiarized this verse, see §§94.1–2.

206 Play on the double meaning of "shaykh": "respected scholar" and "old man."

207 I.e., that ignorance leads people to false accusations.

208 Having exposed the incompetence of Abū Tammām's critics, al-Ṣūlī now responds to their criticism of the fallen moon motif quoted in §69.5.

209 Lit. "does not shed light."

210 Bashshār, *Dīwān*, 4:42. Var. v. 1: *minki qurāḥā*; v. 2: *wa-kāna*. See also al-Sharīf al-Murtaḍā, *Āmālī*, 4:53. Var. v. 2: *wa-kāna*.

211 Of the preceding anonymous verse of poetry.

212 Abū Tammām does indeed reuse the words "sun" and "rising" and the conditional clause (*idhā . . . lam*) in addition to the underlying motif, but the distinction between (verbatim) *naql* and (more general) *sariqah* is not consistently applied in this early phase of evolving Arabic poetics and its assessment of plagiarism.

213 D 4:568, no. 481:3. "Full moon" is a metaphor for a beautiful face; she implies: "Will you forget me?" The verse appears in the morning-of-departure motif within the *nasīb* section of a boast. The distinction between *nasīb* as part of a poem and *ghazal* as independent love lyric is a modern one.

214 I.e., the distinction between bright and dim heavenly bodies in the foregoing lament of Muḥammad ibn Ḥumayd al-Ṭūsī.

215 The version of ا reappears in al-Āmidī, *Muwāzanah*, 1:72; the emendation in ج is based on al-Marzūqī, *Sharḥ Dīwān al-Ḥamāsah*, 1:949, no. 326:4.

216 See also Abū Tammām, *al-Ḥamāsah*, 1:949, no. 326: 3–4. (var. v. 3: *ʿalā Wāhidin*; *wa-mā yubqī, wa-mā yadharu*; v. 4: *baynahā qamaru; min baynihā l-qamaru*), and Ibn Qutaybah, *ʿUyūn al-akhbār*, 3:75. The verses are also attributed to Maryam bint Ṭāriq lamenting her brother (al-Āmidī, *Muwāzanah*, 1:72), to an unnamed female Bedouin poet mourning her husband (Ibn ʿAbd Rabbih, *ʿIqd al-farīd*, 3:204), and to al-Khansāʾ (*Dīwān*, 67 (var. *wasṭahā*). Abū Tammām's reusing of an ancient verse from his *al-Ḥamāsah* anthology confirms in this case the accusation made against him that he compiled the anthology as a source for his own compositions. It is further noteworthy that the motif of the fallen moon, for which he was criticized (§§69.5–28), was already copied before him (§69.19) and ultimately goes back to a female poet. Both Ibn Qutaybah and al-Āmidī note Abū Tammām's reliance on this earlier verse. See also §§94.1–2 for Diʿbil's accusation that Abū Tammām stole this very verse from Muknif Abū Sulmā.

217 Abū Tammām's controversial verse *kharra min baynihā l-badru* (§§69.4–5) indeed repeats Ṣafiyyah's words *fa-hawā min bayninā l-qamaru* except for replacing two words with synonyms.

218 Al-Ṣūlī now addresses the second part of the detractors' previous argument, proposing a "better" rendition of Abū Tammām's intention (§69.5).

219 *Incipit* of the "Great Ode" (*muʿallaqah*) by Labīd, and a *locus classicus* for the motif of the abandoned campsite. Of the numerous commentaries written on this and the following quotations, the most comprehensive is by al-Anbārī, *Sharḥ al-qaṣāʾid al-sabʿ al-ṭiwāl.*

220 *Incipit* of the "Great Ode" by ʿAmr ibn Kulthūm, a wine song (*khamriyyah*).

221 *Incipit* of Imruʾ al-Qays's "Great Ode" on the motif of the lover's grief and one of the most famous lines of pre-Islamic poetry.

222 *Incipit* of Ṭarafah's "Great Ode" on the motif of the abandoned campsite.

223 *Muqram*, a noble camel stallion reserved for breeding, is a metaphor for a great tribal chief.

224 Lit. "then the tooth of another noble stallion roars."

225 Abu Tammām included verses from the same poem in his major anthology, *al-Ḥamāsah*, 2:1598, no. 694, but only the last verse overlaps.

226 Abu Tammām included the lament to which this verse belongs in his minor anthology, *al-Waḥshiyyāt*, 126, no. 201:4.

227 I.e., misjudgments.

228 Lit. "thrown off the garb of partisanship."

229 Bashshār was blind. He initiated the motif of falling in love through sound rather than sight.

230 A fixed star in the Auriga constellation. D 4:90, no. 195:6.

231 The word also means shooting stars.

232 Abū ʿUbaydah, the eminent historian of pre-Islamic history, gives the man's full pedigree; see *Kitāb al-Dībāj*, 123.

233 Lit. "I am the most ancient among people in murder."

234 The Umayyads are typecast as hedonists and halfhearted Muslims in later Abbasid historiography so as to legitimize the latter dynasty as bastions of Muslim doctrine and morality.

235 I.e., he combines cowardice and hypocrisy.

236 Lit. "Nor did dew cover the place where one of ours was killed," i.e., his blood was not left there unattended, but revenge was taken. The classic rendition of this motif is the *incipit* of a lament attributed to Ṭa'abbaṭa Sharran, but probably forged by the transmitter Khalaf al-Aḥmar. See Abū Tammām, *al-Ḥamāsah*, 1:827, no. 273:1.

237 *Nabʿah* means both a tree used for bow wood (*Chadara tenax*) and noble origin.

238 D 1:374, no. 35: 16, 20–21. On the occasion for this poem of apology, see §§78.3–4.

239 See the following note for this verse.

240 Abū Nuwās, *Dīwān*, 1:129, 134, and 5:362–63. See this verse also in §78.4.

241 On Ayyūb's father, Sulaymān ibn ʿAbd al-Malik, see also §78.5.

242 This would have multiplied the reward by twenty to twenty-five times.

243 Lit. "I will cut his tongue."

244 The words are addressed to al-Muʿtaṣim's son al-Wāthiq after he had become caliph, whereas in the following poem in praise of his father, he is still referred to as prince.

245 The poet asks the caliph to make his son Hārūn, the later al-Wāthiq, crown prince. The word "wrist" (*miʿṣam*) is a play on his father's name, al-Muʿtaṣim; see D 2:208–9, no. 72:52, 59. For a recitation of the Amorium battle ode, dedicated to al-Muʿtaṣim, see §§61.1–4, and for criticism of a motif in it, see §§20.1–6.

246 This is an allusion to Q Anfāl 8:17.

247 These kings in ancient Arab lore had lifespans of biblical proportions. See D 3:315, no. 165 in 6 verses, with vv. 5 and 6 in reverse order. Var. v. 4: *tajtaththuhā*.

248 Abū Nuwās, *Dīwān*, 1:175. Var. *an yajmaʿu*. The account is reproduced there.

249 The patron is praised by comparison with men who were proverbial for the cited virtues.

250 D 3:47–48, no. 115, addressed to governor Mālik ibn Ṭawq.

251 The poet was to have said, "Muḍar, move from the path of glory!" which does not, however, appear in D; see al-Ṣūlī, *Akhbār*, 154, n. 3.

252 For the occasion of this verse's improvisation, see §110.2

253 This means either that in his youth the poet was ignorant of white hair, and in old age he no longer remembers his youthful black hair, or alternately, he no longer recognizes his own skin darkened by the sun.

254 The validity of a Prophetic tradition (hadith) is typically judged by the soundness of its chain of transmission.

255 Lit. "that your ribs be called." D 1:356–63 no. 34': 1, 7–9, 12–13, 15, 20–26 (no. 34 erroneously appears twice in D). Var. v. 1: *gharbatu l-nawā*.

256 Sending rain is a poetic greeting formula.

257 Iyād is the tribe to which Ibn Abī Du'ād belongs.

258 This and the two verses after the next are cited for a motif in §§72.1–2.

259 See this verse also in §§72.1–2.

260 I.e., "badly repaid your kindness"; on the connotations of black and white, see also n. 193.

261 A reference to Ziyād ibn ʿAmr al-Nābighah, whose dealings with the Lakhmid king Nuʿmān have been mentioned in §§69.13–14.

262 The verse is discussed for its motif in §47.1.

263 Allusion to Q Aḥzāb 33:19, «They flay you with sharp tongues,» referring to people of Yathrib who want to desert the Emissary in battle. D 1:369, 371, 374–78, 380–82, no. 35:1, 8, 15–17, 20–23, 26, 31–32, 34, 38, 44, 47, 49–51 without any variants from D.

264 The poet makes his itinerary in the two main regions of the Arabian Peninsula a metaphor for the record of his deeds. For a similar motif, see n. 348.

265 He later became caliph.

266 Lit. "that my day with their iniquity would be like the day of ʿAbīd." This alludes to the Arabic phrase "day of X," meaning "the battle of X."

267 He carried his own death sentence with him, an Arab version of Uriah's letter in the Bible; on Uriah, see Khoury, *Wahb b. Munabbih*, 72–75, GD 15–16, and for a later example, Gruendler, "Ibn Abī Ḥajala," 120. For Abū Tammām's use of the motif, see §93.1 below.

268 For the motif, see §44.3.

269 D 1:384, 393–97, no. 37:1, 30, 32–40, 42–43, 45–48. Var. v. 30: *ārāʾuhū*; v. 34: *min zuhrin*.

270 A student would read a book aloud to the author, as was common practice in the early days of the Arabic book. Transmission was person to person.

271 He was a better patron than his father, who needed prompting to perform this role with Muslim ibn al-Walīd; for a translation of relevant accounts, see Gruendler, "*Qaṣīda*," 50–61.

272 The poem does not appear in D.

273 See §99.2 for a similar reaction.

274 The verse refers to Khālid's arrival in Armenia upon his appointment as governor in 227/842. The poet puns on "army banner" (*liwāʾ al-khamīs*) and "Thursday" (*yawm al-khamīs*).

275 See §78.5.

276 Al-Tibrīzī comments on the first verse, "He meant to say *tallāhi lā ansā* and elided the negation, because it is implied."

277 D 1:423, 434–35, 439–41, no. 41:1, 26–29, 31, 45–46, 52–53, 55. Var. v. 27: *khilta*; v. 29: *asmara matnan*; v. 52: *tallāhi*; v. 55: *jaʿaltuhu lajaʾan*.

278 Abu Tammām included this couplet in his smaller anthology, *al-Waḥshiyyāt*, 274, no. 463.

279 *Nawāhil* (sg. *nāhilah*) means both "quenched" and "thirsty."

280 D 3:79, 82, no. 126:1, 14–16. Var. v. 1: *munawwira*.

281 Abū Nuwās, *Dīwān*, 1:141, vv. 1–3. Var. v. 2: *tadmā*; v. 3: *tataʾayyā l-ṭayru ghazwatahū*.

282 See §52.8.

283 The poet puns on "squadrons" (*ʿaṣāʾib*) of birds and "troops" (*ʿaṣāʾib*).

284 The poet addresses an imaginary beloved.

285 "Hope" (*rajāʾ*) is a pun on the addressee's father, al-Rajāʾ.

286 See previous note.

287 D 3:76–78, no. 125: 1–2, 4–13. Var. v. 7: *taʿajruf*. For a discussion of the account, see Gruendler, "*Qaṣīda*," 333–34.

288 The emendation of the name is based on the initial *isnād*.

289 Such alternating improvisation (*ijāzah*) had to follow the same rhyme and meter.

290 A play on the literal meaning of the poet's name.

291 As also in the Qur'an, the reckoning of deeds on Judgment Day is expressed with the metaphor of commerce.

292 See the parallel in al-Iṣbahānī, *Aghānī*, 18:335 (transmitted by al-Ḥasan ibn Aḥmad, who cites Ibn Mihrawayh, who cites Aḥmad ibn Saʿīd al-Ḥarīrī), in which the poet memorizes his predecessors' *dīwān*s instead of studying them to compose his own. Al-Lāt and al-ʿUzzā are two pre-Islamic Arabian deities.

293 See §§9.1–10.2.

294 D 4:530, no. 470:1.

295 On this and other proverbs of ʿAlī, see al-Qāḍī l-Quḍāʿī, *A Treasury of Virtues*, 229, §61.

296 On him, see Massé, "Buzurgmihr" and Motlagh, "Bozorgmehr-e Bok̲tagān." For his sayings, see Miskawayh, *Jāvīdān khirad*, 29–41, 45–48; although this collection does not include the saying quoted here, it does contain others with a similar question-and-answer format. See further Zakeri, *Persian Wisdom in Arabic Garb*, 1:73–82 and index.

297 Q Jāthiyah 45:23. The quotation of Ibn al-Muʿatazz ends at this point.

298 D 1:271, no. 20:17. Var. *tarmī*. Ibn al-Aʿrābī meant the musician and composer Isḥāq al-Mawṣilī.

299 *Nawādir* does not mean anecdotes here but randomly assembled snippets on rare vocabulary; the *nawādir* of Ibn al-Aʿrābī survive in Ibn Sīdah's thesaurus, *al-Muḥkam*; see *GAS*, 8:271.

300 ʿUmārah was the great-grandson of Jarīr.

301 See the parallel in al-Jumaḥī, *Ṭabaqāt*, 1:376–77, no. 512.

302 Al-Jumaḥī, *Ṭabaqāt*, 1:376, has the variant *untuqiʿa*.

303 The emendation is based on al-Jumaḥī, *Ṭabaqāt*, 1:376.

304 See the slightly paraphrased parallel in al-Jumaḥī, *Ṭabaqāt*, 2:553–54, no. 744. Var. *al-sabuʿ*; *ṭurida ʿanhā aw sabaqtahū*; *fa-yaftarisuhā al-sabuʿu wa-hiya tashummu*.

305 Lit. "God kill him!" This continues the account of §89.3.

306 The emendation is based on the rhyme letter of Jarīr's preceding verses.

307 Lit. "when he rode it."

308 Of examples of candor about one's enemies, continuing §§89.2–5.

309 For the literal meaning, see n. 305.

310 The poet descended from a Persian family of Ṭukhāristān.

311 I.e., false accusation (§86.2) and not giving someone due credit (§87.2).

312 The image is that of irrigation canals branching off from a large river.

313 D 2:319, 325–26, 328, no. 91:1a, 20, 22–23, 28, without any variants from D. For another passage of this poem used for similar practical criticism, see §52.1. On the paradise motif, see also §78.4, first verse.

314 He was a friend who visited the poet after a long absence. He may be the addressee in §164.

315 D 2:96–97, no. 52:1–5, 7.

316 Deneb, lit. "tail," is Alpha Cygni, the brightest star in this constellation. The name also denotes other stars that represent the tails of animals in constellations. ʿAlī ibn al-Jahm, *Dīwān*, 113, no. 15:2.

317 This implies bad quality. Good wine is described as translucent, and its color as red (grape wine) or yellow (date wine).

318 D 4:483–84, no. 445:1–2, 6, 9–10, abridged but retaining the plot. Var. v. 9: *fa-mā tusʾaluhā ʿumra dhā l-zamāni*; v. 10 *wa-ʿtabarnā*.

319 The poem's occasion was an unannounced visit of the Banū Ḥumayd, so the unprepared poet had to ask a friend for wine; cf. al-Ṣūlī, *Akhbār al-Buḥturī*, 163–64.

320 The poet places the general as from the city of Ṭūs in Khurasan, next to his own tribe of Ṭayy, who settled in the northern ranges of the Najd plateau in the Arabian Peninsula.

321 Lit. "without a rendez-vous" (*waʿd*), which puns with "promise" (*waʿd*).

322 In the earlier Arab solar year, the month of Shaʿban (Shaʿbān) fell in the summer. Roses are a metaphor for the red grape wine harvested later in the fall.

323 Al-Buḥturī, *Dīwān*, 1:491, no. 206:1–7.

324 Lit. "rainy season."

325 Al-Tibrīzī explains *jullilat Uwaysan* in his *Dīwān* commentary (D 2:346, no. 94:15) as follows, "What is meant is really 'Had Uways been graced with it' (*jullilahā Uwaysun*), because it is correct to say "Amr was dressed in a garb' (*ulbisa 'Amrun al-thawba*), but if one says 'the garb has been put on 'Amr' (*ulbisa l-thawbu 'Amran*), this is also permissible, because in reality both nouns refer to objects of the action."

326 A causal hyperbole: the garb makes its wearer so alluring that he attracts the east wind, which in poetry always blows from the direction of the beloved.

327 Al-Tibrīzī gives as a second meaning of *sirr* "a type of fabric embroidered with a pattern of rosettes"; see his commentary to D 2:347, no. 94:15–17.

328 D 2:343, 346–48, no. 94:1, 13, 15–17, 22; the incipit's meter is corrupt. Var. v. 16: *yaltadhdhu malmasuhū sakbun*.

329 D 3:289, no. 160:2. The poet produces a triple paronomasia between "meeting grounds" (*maʿāhid*), "first spring rains" (*ʿihād*, sg. *ʿahd*), and "company" (*ʿahd*).

330 D 2:341–42, no. 93:1–10. Var. v. 4: *min al-hubūbi*.

331 The occasion was the poet's appearance before the commander of Basra when he was drinking sesame oil, perhaps for health reasons; cf. al-Iṣbahānī, *Aghānī*, 13:257–58.

332 The Arabic letters *MDYḤ* spell the word "praise" (*madīḥ*).

333 A reference to the theological notion that fixed bodies receive changing accidents (such as color, taste, etc.) that inhere in them.

334 A reference to the biblical King David's desire for Bathshebah and how he arranged for her husband, General Uriah, to die in battle.

335 D 4:463–64, no. 437, with 3 and 4 in reversed order. Var. v. 2: *fikari*; v. 4: *qad rāqat maḥāsinuhā, mushtaghilu l-aḥshā'i*; v. 5: *nafūr*; v. 6: *jāniban*; v. 9: *taghdū*.

336 The response is in rhymed prose (*sajʿ*).

337 Phlebotomy (*faṣd*), the bleeding of veins, and blood-letting (*ḥijāmah*), the bleeding of other parts of the body, were common procedures in early Islamic medicine. Blood-letting was used for relief of pain and itching. See Bray, "Third and Fourth Century Bleeding Poetry."

338 I.e., al-Ḥasan ibn Wahb.

339 The version of this account cited in al-Marzubānī, *Muwashshaḥ*, 367, gives the name as al-ʿAmrāwī.

340 The Arabic text omits the century.

341 Al-Marzubānī, *Muwashshaḥ*, 367, and another version cited in al-Iṣbahānī, *Aghānī*, 16:315, give the name as Thaqīf.

342 The vocalization is based on *GAS*, 2:601, and al-Iṣbahānī, *Aghānī*, 16:315. In al-Marzubānī, *Muwashshaḥ*, the name is unvocalized.

343 The poet's rhyme word "fart" (*ḍarit*) is a play on the place name's literal meaning of "flatulence" (*ḍurāṭ*), deriving from the same root.

344 See §§69.4–5 and §§69.10–28, especially §§69.18–19 and nn. 216 and 217, for criticism of this motif. There the same verse, with a different name, is attributed to Abū Tammām.

345 The poet produces a paronomasia between "travelers" (*safr*) and "journey" (*safar*). The following variants occur in the versions cited in al-Iṣbahānī, *Aghānī*, 16:315–16, v. 1: *yustaʿdhabu l-shiʿru*; v. 6: *yawma muṣābihi*; in al-Āmidī, *Muwāzanah*, 1:72–73, v. 1: *li-l-dahri ʿutbā*; v. 2: *wa-shallat*; and al-Marzubānī, *al-Muwashshaḥ*, 367–68, v. 1: *yustaʿtabu l-dahru, li-l-dahri ʿutbā*; v. 4: *lā massahā*.

346 For Abū Tammām's poem, see n. 344.

347 D 2:109–10, no. 56:1–2. In the second verse the poet creates a paronomasia between "help me with!" (*anjid*) and the toponym *Najd*.

348 The poet metaphorically equates movement in a landscape with moral action; see n. 264 for a similar image.

349 D 2:109–10, 115–17, no. 56:1–2, 24–25, 27–28, 31–33, 38. Var. v. 27: *nasītu*; v. 32: *a-ulbisu*. The poem's abridgment is discussed as an act of practical criticism in Gruendler, "Abstract Aesthetics," 30. The last verse reads literally, "my excuse is intended."

350 Here the verse is cited as in D (*a-ulbisu*).

351 Here *manqūl* differs from its more common meaning in this book of "copied verbatim."

352 Lit. "By the father of the encampments." Al-Tibrīzī (D 3:323, no. 167: 1) explains, "He swore by their father, even though they do not have one, by semantic extension, and means, 'Dwellings deserted

by their inhabitants are sorrows by which I swear,' using this as an amplification."

353 D 3:323, 328–32, no. 167:1, 39–41, 43–46, 48. Var. v. 40: *ajādahā.*

354 D 1:124–25, no. 8:29, 34. The reciter has combined two verses that are some distance apart in the ode.

355 The "depravity" of the Aws may hint at their feud with the Khazraj (both were leading tribes of Yathrib), which led to negotiations with Muḥammad to move to the city and reinstate peace.

356 Lit. "Are you my lightning? Since I have none." Lightning often acts as a lover's message in the love lyric.

357 The verses are missing in D.

358 A Ṭāhirid patron also appears in the chapter on Abū Tammām's superiority (§§64.1–3).

359 The quatrain's first, second, and fourth verses closely rephrase passages of Q Yūsuf 12:88 in rearranged order, the second verse partly quotes Q 12:78, and the fourth verse ends with a partial quote from Naḥl 16:21. Q 12:78 and 88 refer to Joseph's brothers' second and third journeys to Egypt to implore Joseph (whom they do not recognize as head of the Egyptian storehouses) not to imprison Benjamin for theft and to sell them grain. Abū Tammām's verses are missing in D.

360 The name derives from Khuttal Kaskar, a region of Transoxania.

361 See §79.2. for a similar reaction. For a parallel account on this event, see §§64.1–3.

362 In a different account about this event, Abū l-ʿAmaythal and another poet admit a panegyric by Abū Tammām, after first rejecting it, because they recognize two borrowed motifs; see al-Āmidī, *Muwāzanah*, 1:20–21.

363 D 2:132, no. 59. For an account about the second verse, see §160.

364 Lit. "liver."

365 Verses missing in D.

366 Arabic *ṣawt* means both "voice" and "song, tune."

367 Abu Tammām included the love lyric to which these verses belong in his minor anthology, *al-Waḥshiyyāt*, 193, no. 318:6–7. Verse 7 is augmented to two verses by inserting two hemistichs.

368 The noble deeds are personified as a camel.

369 Here al-Ṣūlī returns to the account begun in §101.1.

370 D 4:113–15, no. 200: 1, 7–12, 14 (first part), and 4:115–16, 118, no. 200:15–17, 23–24 (second part). Var. v. 10: *yunsa'āni*; v. 12: *wa-ṣibāhumā ḥilman*. For a discussion of the patron's reaction, see Gruendler, "*Qaṣīda*," 335–36.

371 These may have been any of nos. 17 (D 1:234–38), 33 (D 1:343), 76 (D 2:219–20), 135 (D 3:165–75), 150 (D 3:261–68), or 162 (D 3:297–307), which Abū Tammām addressed to al-Muṣʿabī.

372 D 4:446, no. 430: 1–4. Var. v. 1; *rumītu*; v. 2: *ʿādilin*; v. 3: *li-murajjī, kathibu*.

373 D 4:526, no. 469:1–3. Var. v. 3: *min baʿdihā*. Since giving, like eating, is done only with the right hand, the left hand stands for withholding gifts.

374 According to ancient Arab lore, the spirit of a killed man lived on as an owl until he was avenged, i.e., the owl drank his killer's blood. Abū Tammām here obliquely refers to the unpaid reward.

375 *Ḥilyah* means both "ornament" and "facial features."

376 The poet produces a paronomasia between "quite some time" (*fatrah*) and "tires" (*fatarat*).

377 "Craft commands [excellence]" (*ʿalathā ṣanʿatun*) puns with "[my writing] has tarried" (*ʿalathā fatratun*) in the preceding verse.

378 Instead of sharing it in writing. Abū Tammām alludes to the fact that he had not recited the earlier poem in person, which would have prompted an immediate reward.

379 D 3:281–82, no. 156. Var. v. 3: *yab'ā*; v. 4: *a-bimā*; v. 7: *bi-ʿināyati*; v. 9: *aw kāna*. Abū Tammām alludes to the legend according to which the famous sword (called Ṣamṣām) of the South Arabian hero ʿAmr ibn Maʿdīkarib (d. after 16/637) lost its power to cut after it had been taken from him. The poet thus suggests that his ode, by being delivered in writing in his absence, had lost its power.

380 "You embellished" (*ḥabbarta*) is an etymological word play on "ink" (*ḥibr*) implied in the previous verse.

381 The poet puns on "texts" (*mutūn*) and "[sur]faces" (*mutūn*).

382 *Niẓām* means both "necklace" and "order, regimen." The poet contrasts the pre-Islamic hero ʿAmr, who lost his power together with his sword, with the commander's lasting God-given power.

383 D 1:157 no. 12:1. Var. *min muqlatin.*

384 D 1:174, no. 13: 1–2.

385 For a similar plot element, see §159.

386 The merit of giving indirectly is greater for letting the intermediary share in the recipient's gratitude. D 2:161–63, no. 66:5–7, 11–15. Var. v. 13: *ʿāthiri.*

387 ʿAmr ibn Maʿdīkarib was a famous South Arabian poet and warrior. The caliph is praised by comparison with men who were proverbial for the cited virtues. See also §77, n. 249 for this motif.

388 D 2:242–3, 249–50, no. 81:1–2, 22–25. Var v. 1: *naqḍī*; v. 24: *min dūnihī.* For a discussion of this event, see Gruendler, "*Qaṣīda*," 348.

389 D 1:357–58, no. 34:7–8 (number 34 erroneously appears twice in D). For the recitation of this ode, see §78.2.

390 See n. 333.

391 D 2:317–18, no. 90:1–2, 4–5, 7–9. Var v. 4: *yustajābu*; v. 7: *bādīhi*; v. 9: *yajid, nuʿammu, ḥattā tarānā.*

392 See §168 for Abū Tammām using this insult for Diʿbil.

393 Lit. "You show a back of the head that swears..." The poet alludes to the Islamic science of physiomancy (*firāsah*), which foretells a person's moral behavior from bodily features, or its ancient Arab precursor of *qiyāfah*, used to recognize physical signs of paternity.

394 The name both of an ancient Arabian tribe and the Syrian village where Abū Tammām was born; see §29.

395 The litany of typecast and comically exaggerated Bedouin behavior is intended to ridicule Abū Tammām's alleged Arab ancestry.

396 Lit. "said to it '*Ḥawb*,'" a word used to chide camels.

397 His tongue is meant.

398 I.e., lampoon of forged ancestry.

399 The olive-shaped fruits, eaten by antelopes and ostriches, of two types of trees growing on wadi slopes. Descriptions of them frequently serve as a poetic motif; see Zuhayr in Ahlwardt, *The Divans*, 76, v. 16,

and Abū Nuwās, *Dīwān*, 2:102, 14. On the castor tree (*tannūm*), see Abū Ḥanīfah al-Dīnawarī, *The Book of Plants*, 25 (Arabic pagination), and on the Meru tree (*Maerua crassifolia*, Ar. *sarḥ*) and its fruit (*ā'*), see Abū Ḥanīfah al-Dīnawarī, *The Book of Plants*, 22 (Arabic pagination) and 21, 38 (Latin pagination), and al-Dīnawarī, *Le dictionnaire botanique*, 35–36.

400 I.e., rather than using the regular word, he imitated the Bedouins' way of using many rare synonyms.

401 Abū Nuwās, *Dīwān*, 2:102–3 (with two additional verses). Var. v. 1: *rajulan*; v. 3: *ji'ta, Abā Khālidin*; v. 6 *ḥaqqan yā Abā Khālidin fākihatan*.

402 The poet plays on the scribe's name, Muḥammad ibn Nūḥ, Nūḥ being the Arabic form of Noah.

403 Epithet for a seasoned rider.

404 *Ḥitār* means also "anus," signaling the obscene content of the poem.

405 Lit. "glandes penis."

406 *Jurdān* is the penis of a hoofed animal. The poet puns on "rising [prick]" (*naw' jurdān*) and "rising/setting [rain stars]" (*naw'ayni mina l-maṭar*).

407 "Cold" is an epithet for bad or trite poetry.

408 This alludes to the fact that Abū Tammām used to be a Christian.

409 "Water" here stands for pride. For varieties of the water motif, see §§22.1–10, and on this verse in particular, §22.3.

410 His identity is uncertain. Al-Buḥturī, whose name is al-Walīd ibn ʿUbayd, is unlikely.

411 Intentional misspelling (or mimicked Nabaṭī pronunciation) of Abū Tammām's adopted Arab tribe, the Aws, a word close to his real patronym, Tadūs (from Greek Thaddeus or Theodosius); see §128.

412 A play on the poet's name Abū Tammām, *tamām* meaning "perfection." See also §131.

413 Lit. "in their skin, hide," which could also refer to any leather object.

414 *Mirbāʿ* "a chief's share of the booty of war" forms a paronomasia with *irtabaʿū* ("they struck camp for the spring.")

415 The account's variant in al-Āmidī, *Muwāzanah*, 19, clarifies this as *al-kalām al-manthūr*.

416 D 1:405, no. 40:1. For al-Buḥturī's comment on this ode, see §60.

417 The teknonym of al-Tawwajī.

418 Lit. "rub against each other!"

419 For a lampoon of this acquired ancestry, see §121.

420 Abū Nuwās, *Dīwān*, 1:161.

421 D 2:324, no. 91:17. Var. *ka-anna*.

422 Abu Tammām included the wine song to which this verse belongs in his minor anthology, *al-Waḥshiyyāt*, 164, no. 261:3.

423 On this mockery of his name, see note 412.

424 An alternate translation of *mukhtalifun* is "[Talk] comes in different kinds."

425 The analogy is between an arrow's straightness, orientation, and reaching of its goal and the correctness, intent, and formulation of speech.

426 Lit. "I filled the earth before him." Abu Tammām included this passage with an additional verse in his major anthology, *al-Ḥamāsah*, 1:227–29, no. 56:1, 3–4.

427 So nicknamed because upon his accession he cut the pay increase his father, Caliph al-Walīd, had granted to the troops; see al-Ṭabarī, *Ta'rīkh*, 7:261–62.

428 The poet puns on "a long time" (*dahran*) and "fate" (*al-dahru*).

429 As the same *isnād* (Aḥmad ibn Yazīd al-Muhallabī - Aḥmad ibn Abī Ṭāhir - Abū Tammām) repeats itself throughout the rest of this chapter, al-Ṣūlī abbreviates to first names.

430 In this context, the interpretation of the verse is "the first to die," and the second instance of "life" means a hero's posthumous fame. Abu Tammām included this and two further verses in his major anthology, *al-Ḥamāsah*, 1:197–99, no. 41.

431 I.e., by the army commander. Another meaning of *ma'mūr* is "prolific, multiplying."

432 I.e., it will not return the dead son, as the poet, mad with grief, requests. The emendation *fa-ṣfaḥ* is based on al-Marzūqī, *Sharḥ Dīwān al-Ḥamāsah*, 2:894, no. 300.

433 The following variants appear in Abū Tammām, *al-Ḥamāsah*, 1:894, no. 300: v. 1: *Ibn Laylā*; v. 2: *'ani l-dahri fa-ṣfaḥ, mu'tibi*; v. 3: *ma'a*

l-rakbi (verse order there 3, 1, 2); see also al-Iṣbahānī, *Aghānī*, 13:39. Var. v. 2: *fa-daʿ dhikra man qad ḥālati l-arḍu dūnahū*; v. 3: *maʿa l-rakbi* (there as verses 1, 8, and 2 of eight verses in different order following a longer version of the account).

434 The Arabic pronoun (*-hu*), meaning both "him" and "it," is ambiguous and either refers to the male beloved or the beloved thing, which in this context is probably anal intercourse.

435 For a similar plot element, see §109.

436 This patron is not otherwise identified and received only this single praise poem (other than a poem of reprimand, D 4:499).

437 Al-Tibrīzī explains the form of Manāh in his *Dīwān* commentary as follows: "Someone criticized Abū Tammām for saying Manāhi, stating that the idol's name was Manāt, and the poet responded, 'You should know that the *hāʾ* of femininity, the *hāʾ* of the personal suffix, and the *hāʾ* of pause are interchangeable to the Bedouin, as they all resemble each other.'"

438 D 3:343, 350, no. 174:1, 31–34. Var. v. 31: *ʿālimun*; v. 33: *madhkūratan mashhūratan*; v. 34: *annā nṣarafta*.

439 Epithet of God; Q Nās 114:1.

440 Lit. "May the wood sprout leaves." Pulpits, made of wood, are frequently thus personified in paneygyrics. Another meaning of *ʿūd* is "lute."

441 The poet refers to putative gifts with a previously fixed buyback price combined with a loan (as nominal countervalue for the interest earned). These served as devices to define in a legal way what really were (illicit) loans with interest. The poet thus suggests a small monetary reward as a nominal countervalue for his "interest-poem" to make it licit.

442 D 2:132, no. 59:2. See §99.2 on the first recitation of this couplet.

443 For a variant of this account, see al-Ḥuṣrī, *Zahr*, 2:376–77.

444 D 4:253, no. 303:3–4.

445 The account does not appear in the edition of Ibn al-Jarrāḥ's *Kitāb al-Waraqah*.

446 The poet plays on the etymology of his beloved's ancestral name ʿAzzah bint Ḥumayl al-Ḥājibiyyah, derived from the root *ḥajaba*,

which means "to prevent from entering, to veil" (hence *ḥijāb al-qalb* ["pericardium"]). He thus implies that her love bars all other women entry to his heart. For the verse, see also Ibn al-Jawzī, *Dhamm al-hawā*, 445; var. *kay nuzīlahā.*

447 In the Cairo edition, ʿAzzām et al. place this sentence with the previous account, in which case it would be translated as "Kuthayyir's line also relates to a specific aspect of Abū Tammām's composition." But the sentence is needed as an introduction to §161.4 to justify its inclusion. The relation to the previous section al-Ṣūlī intends is the correspondence between a person's character and his or her name. The fact that an introductory phrase is set off by a dotted circle also occurs elsewhere (e.g., §167) and thus does not necessarily imply a break with what follows.

448 Jarīr, *Dīwān*, 253–54, v. 6. Var. *fa-mā, ʿani l-ʿulā, ʿani l-majdi.* ʿIqāl ibn Muḥammad ibn Sufyān al-Mujāshiʿī and his son Ḥābis were ancestors of Jarīr's foe al-Farazdaq, whom this verse lampoons. The parallel is between the woman's name, which literally means "gatekeeper" (*ḥājib*), in the preceding verse and the cowardice and stinginess of two men, whose names spell out these traits.

449 Lit. "Am I getting inside you?" The meaning of the dialogue is unclear and the translation is conjectural. It might be a quip that the visitor caused Abū Tammām a sick stomach. Alternately anal intercourse may be alluded to, as described more explicitly in §117.

450 D 4:79, no. 192:1a. For a recitation of this lamentation of Muḥammad ibn Ḥumayd, see §§69.1–4.

451 Verse missing in D. The first hemistich refers to Q Jinn 72:19, which calls the Prophet "servant of God" (*ʿabd Allāh*). The second hemistich means ʿAbd Allāh ibn Saʿd ibn Abī Sarḥ, second governor of Egypt after its conqueror ʿAmr ibn al-ʿĀṣ. *ʿAzīz* ("mighty king") is the Qurʾanic designation for high officials in Egypt (Potiphar and Joseph).

452 He may be identical with Abū Tammām's friend, the scribe ʿAbd Allāh of §91.1.

453 D 2:66, no. 49:17.

454 D 2:309, no. 89:7.

455 According to Arab legend, Ismāʿīl, the son of Ibrāhīm and Hājar, married into Jurhum and became the ancestor of all Arabs.

456 Only a short notice appears in D at this verse. Al-Ṣūlī's commentary (edited by K. R. Nuʿmān, 1:610–11) explains Qays's self-imposed exile and death in ʿUmān by his refusal to participate in the truce between his own tribe, ʿAbs, and Dhubyān after their long feud, and explains the wandering and death in exile of al-Ḥārith after his tribe, Jurhum, had been ousted from Mecca by the tribe of Khuzāʿah.

457 A repetition may be requested for clarification (cf. §91.2), appreciation, or appreciation after clarification; thus Abū Tammām's answer is ambiguous.

458 D 3:5, no. 111:2.

459 The poet's play with logic was more in keeping with the intellectual urban atmosphere of Basra than his native Syrian countryside.

460 Diʿbil, *Dīwān*, 291, no. 220:1, a retort to al-Kumayt ibn Zayd's poetic attack on the southern Arab (Yemeni) tribes to which Diʿbil belonged.

461 The verses are missing in D.

462 Al-Iṣbahānī attributes the former verses to Abū Saʿd al-Makhzūmī, chastising Diʿbil for lampooning the dead Kumayt (*Aghānī*, 20:72), and the latter verses to Diʿbil, lampooning al-Khārikī l-Baṣrī from the tribe of Azd (ibid., 20:81).

463 The hemistich suggests the obscene continuation *ḥirammika* ("your mother's clitoris") with elision of the *hamzah*, which is standard in this phrase. The hemistich and its continuations are missing in D.

464 The verses are missing in D.

465 The verses do not appear in Abū Tammām's *al-Ḥamāsah* or *al-Waḥshiyyāt*, where two other poems of Abū l-Juwayriyyah appear (pp. 261–62, nos. 434, 435). They may have been contained in one of Abū Tammām's anthologies that have not survived.

466 His earlier study with the poet in 258/872 is mentioned in §20.5.

467 With characteristic political savvy, al-Buḥturī mourns with one lament two poets who were enemies.

468 Al-Buḥturī, *Dīwān*, 3:1786–87, no. 685. Var. v. 1: *fī kamadī wa-aḍrama, yawma bāna*; v. 2: *wa-ṣinfihī, makdūdi l-qarīḥati mujbili*; v. 3: *ṭalabū l-barāʿata wa-l-kalāmi l-muqfali*; v. 4: *bi-samāʾi muznin.*

469 A play on the literal meaning of the poet's given name, "beloved." This pun recurs below in §§182.1–3.

470 The line brings out the original meaning of the word for poet (*shāʿir*), "one who knows, or senses, by intuition or inspiration," harking back to the pre-Islamic idea that poets were inspired by *jinn*.

471 Lit. "you don't think," addressing the universal "you," not Abū Tammām.

472 Al-Buḥturī refers to their common Ṭayy ancestry, which was adopted by Abū Tammām (and generally accepted) and true for al-Buḥturī; together they are often referred to as "the two Ṭayyites" (*al-Ṭayyiʾān*).

473 Madhḥij, a South Arabian tribal group, here serves as an umbrella term for all southern Arabs including the Ṭayy, whose ancestry Abū Tammām had adopted.

474 See his earlier lament in §178.

475 Note the reuse of ʿAlī ibn al-Jahm's image from §179.

476 *Wajh* means both "face" and "honor, glory."

477 The poet creates a paronomasia on "poetry" (*shiʿr*) and "undergarment" (*shiʿār*).

478 The poet creates a triple paronomasia on "undergarment" (*shiʿār*) (see also previous poem), "to sense, know by intuition" (*tashʿurī*), and "best poet" (*ashʿaru*).

Glossary of Names and Terms

Abbasids (caliphate) the line of caliphs (q.v.) descended from the Prophet's uncle al-ʿAbbās, established in 132/749 after the overthrow of the Umayyad dynasty. Their rule lasted until the fall of Baghdad to the Mongols in 656/1258.

al-ʿAbbās ibn ʿUbayd Allāh (or ʿAbd Allāh) ibn Jaʿfar ibn Abī Jaʿfar al-Manṣūr (fl. end of the second/eighth century) Abbasid prince and patron of Abū Nuwās (q.v.).

ʿAbd Allāh ibn al-ʿAbbās (d. 68/687) a cousin of the Prophet and ancestor of the Abbasid dynasty (which took its name from him); considered to be one of the earliest Qurʾan exegetes.

ʿAbd Allāh ibn Abī l-Shīṣ (fl. first half of the third/ninth century) minor Abbasid poet and son of the poet Abū l-Shīṣ (q.v.).

ʿAbd Allāh ibn al-Ḥusayn ibn Saʿd, Abū Muḥammad (fl. second half of the third/ninth century) frequently cited source for al-Ṣūlī's accounts and owner of a mansion in the Khuld quarter of Baghdad.

ʿAbd Allāh ibn Muḥammad ibn Jarīr (fl. first half of the fourth/tenth century) son of the famous historian al-Ṭabarī (q.v.).

ʿAbd Allāh ibn Saʿd ibn Abī Sarḥ (d. 36 or 37/656–58) Umayyad statesman and general belonging to the Quraysh. He took part in the conquest of Egypt and was appointed its governor after ʿAmr ibn al-ʿĀṣ in 25/645–46.

ʿAbd Allāh ibn Ṭāhir, Abū l-ʿAbbās (r. 213–30/828–44) capable statesman, poet, and patron of Arabic and Persian culture; governor of Khurasan in northeast Iran; son and successor of al-Maʾmūn's general Ṭāhir ibn al-Ḥusayn, who founded the semi-independent Ṭāhirid dynasty.

ʿAbd Allāh ibn al-Zubayr ibn al-ʿAwwām (d. 73/692) a member of the second generation of Muslim nobility, belonging to the ʿAbd al-ʿUzzā clan of Quraysh; he supported ʿĀʾishah against ʿAlī in the civil war and then set up a counter-caliphate to the Umayyads in 64/683 in Mecca, which ended during the caliphate of ʿAbd al-Malik with a siege of the city in which Ibn al-Zubayr was killed.

ʿAbd al-ʿAzīz ibn al-Walīd (d. 110/728–29) Umayyad prince and son of Caliph al-Walīd I (q.v.).

ʿAbd al-Malik ibn Ṣāliḥ ibn ʿAlī ibn ʿAbd Allāh ibn al-ʿAbbās (d. 196/811–12) member of the Abbasid family, he served as governor of various regions under al-Rashīd and al-Amīn and was known as an eloquent orator.

ʿAbd Manāf subgroup of the Quraysh that comprised several clans including that of the Prophet.

ʿAbd al-Ṣamad see *Ibn al-Muʿadhdhal.*

ʿAbīd ibn al-Abraṣ al-Asadī (fl. first half of the sixth century AD) famous pre-Islamic poet.

Abrashahr see *Nishapur.*

Abū Aḥmad see *Muḥammad ibn Mūsā ibn Ḥammād.*

Abū Aḥmad Yaḥyā see *Yaḥyā ibn ʿAlī l-Munajjim.*

Abū ʿAlī l-Ḥusayn ibn Muḥammad ibn Fahm al-Baghdadi (d. 289/902) Qurʾan reader and leading hadith-transmitter who studied with Yaḥyā ibn Maʿīn and Muṣʿab ibn al-Zubayr, authorities on the subject.

Abū l-ʿAmaythal (d. 240/854) lexicographer, poetic critic, and poet laureate of the Ṭāhirids (q.v.).

Abū ʿAmr ibn al-ʿAlāʾ, Zabbān (or Zayyān, or al-ʿUryān) ibn ʿAmmār (d. 154/771 or 157/774) famous early lexicographer, grammarian, Qurʾan reader, and expert on poetry, active in Basra; he taught most of the subsequent generation of scholars.

Abū l-ʿAnbas Muḥammad ibn Isḥāq al-Ṣaymarī (d. 275/888) an eloquent but foul-mouthed poet, *adīb*, and jester who served al-Mutawakkil as familiar.

Abū l-ʿAtāhiyah (d. 210/825) a poet famous for his ascetic, world-renouncing verse.

Abū l-ʿAynāʾ Muḥammad ibn al-Qāsim ibn Khallād al-Hāshimī, Abū ʿAbd Allāh (d. 283/896) a poet from Yamāmah and client of al-Manṣūr, he studied with major grammarians in Baghdad and became a companion of al-Mutawakkil; he was renowned for his anecdotes and repartee.

Abū Ayyūb ibn Ukht Abī l-Wazīr, Aḥmad ibn Muḥammad ibn Shujāʿ (fl. mid-third/ninth century) tax agent, appointed 258/872 under al-Muʿtamid in Egypt, and patron of al-Buḥturī (q.v.); his name refers to his maternal uncle Abū l-Wazīr Aḥmad ibn Khālid (q.v.).

Abū Dhakwān al-Qāsim ibn Ismāʿīl (d. end of the third/ninth century) transmitter of the poet Ibrāhīm ibn al-ʿAbbās al-Ṣūlī (q.v.) from when he became governor of Ahwāz, and author of a lost book on poetic motifs.

Abū Dulaf al-Qāsim ibn ʿĪsā ibn Idrīs al-ʿIjlī (d. ca. 225–28/840–43) general and governor under several caliphs, and a patron of the arts who hosted a literary circle in Jibāl (northwest Iran); he had Shiʿi leanings and a tribal affiliation to the ʿIjl, belonging to the Bakr ibn Wāʾil confederacy (q.v.) within the Rabīʿah group of tribes.

Abū l-Faḍl Aḥmad ibn Abī Ṭāhir see *Ibn Abī Ṭāhir.*

Abū l-Faraj see *al-Iṣbahānī.*

Abū l-Ghawth Yaḥyā ibn Abī ʿUbādah al-Buḥturī (fl. second half of the third/ninth century), son and transmitter of the poet al-Buḥturī (q.v.) and a minor poet.

Abū Ḥanash al-Fazārī perhaps identical with Ḥanash ibn ʿAmr al-Dhubyānī, who fought with and witnessed the death of the brothers Ḥudhayfah and Ḥamal ibn Badr al-Fazāriyyān of Dhubyān in the Battle at the Well of Habāʾah (q.v.). The battle was part of the long war between the tribes of ʿAbs and Dhubyān.

Abū Ḥanash Khudayr ibn Qays al-Hilālī l-Numayrī (d. 187/803) panegyrist of the Barmakids (not to be confused with the Umayyad poet Abū Ḥayyah [or Abū Numayr] Muḥammad ibn ʿAbd Allāh al-Numayrī).

Abū Ḥātim see *al-Sijistānī.*

Abū Hiffān ʿAbd Allāh ibn Aḥmad al-Mihzamī l-ʿAbdī (d. 255/869) Basran poet who moved to Baghdad and a famous *adīb* and transmitter of literary accounts, notably about the poet Abū Nuwās (q.v.), which are preserved.

Abū l-Juwayriyyah ʿĪsā ibn Aws al-ʿAbdī (fl. first quarter of the second/eighth century) minor Umayyad poet.

Abū Karib Asʿad (d. ca. AD 433) the hero of a legendary saga and the best-known king of the Ḥimyarite dynasty (Ar. Tabābiʿah, sg. Tubbaʿ), which ruled southwest Arabia between the late third and early sixth century AD.

Abū Khalīfah see *al-Faḍl ibn al-Ḥubāb.*

Abū l-Layth see *Muzāḥim ibn Fātik.*

Abū Mālik see *ʿAwn ibn Muhammad al-Kindī.*

Abū Muḥallim Muḥammad ibn Saʿd (or Hishām) ibn ʿAwf al-Shaybānī (d. 248/861) lexicographer and transmitter of poetry from Ahwāz who went to live among the Bedouin.

Abū Nahshal ibn Ḥumayd (fl. mid-third/ninth century) son of general Ḥumayd and brother of general Muhammad ibn Ḥumayd (qq.v.), he served as companion to al-Amīn and was a patron of Abū Tammām, whose tomb he had constructed.

Abū l-Najm al-ʿIjlī (fl. early second/eighth century) one of the best poets of *rajaz* (q.v.), in which meter he also composed panegyrics and hunting poems.

Abū Nuwās al-Ḥasan ibn Hāniʾ al-Ḥakamī (d. ca. 200/814) one of the greatest and most versatile Arabic poets and companion of Caliph al-Amīn, famous especially for his poetry on wine and hunting and his lyrics on love, including love of boys.

Abū Saʿīd Muḥammad ibn Hubayrah al-Asadī (d. ca. 280/893) known as Ṣaʿūdāʾ, lexicographer and *adīb* from Samarra and active in Baghdad; he was a familiar of Ibn al-Muʿtazz (q.v.).

Abū Saʿīd Muḥammad ibn Yūsuf al-Thaghrī l-Ṭāʾī l-Ḥumaydī l-Marwazī (d. 236/851) a Ṭayyite from Marw, he was one of the generals under al-Afshīn (q.v.), instrumental in the defeat of the rebel Bābak (q.v.) in 222/837, and the dedicatee of the highest number of odes (twenty-nine) by Abū Tammām; his son, General Abū Saʿīd Yūsuf, was sent by al-Mutawakkil on a campaign in Armenia and killed there in 237/852, was a patron of al-Buḥturī.

Abū Ṣāliḥ see *Ibn Yazdād.*

Abū Ṣaqr see *Ismāʿīl ibn Bulbul.*

Abū l-Shīṣ Muḥammad (ibn ʿAbd Allāh) ibn Razīn al-Khuzāʿī, Abū Jaʿfar (d. ca. 196/812) minor Abbasid poet of Shiʿi persuasion and part of Abū Nuwās's circle (q.v.).

Abū l-Ṭamaḥān Ḥanẓalah ibn al-Sharqī l-Qaynī (d. ca. 30/650) poet of questionable Muslim faith who straddled both the pre-Islamic and Islamic eras; for a while the companion of the Prophet's uncle al-Zubayr ibn ʿAbd al-Muṭṭalib.

Abū Tawbah al-Shaybānī perhaps identical with Abū Tawbah Maymūn ibn Ḥafṣ (or ibn Jaʿfar) the Grammarian (d. ca. 215/830), who was a student of al-Kisāʾī and active as lexicographer and tutor in Baghdad.

Abū l-Ṭayyib Muḥammad ibn Isḥāq al-Naḥwī l-Lughawī (d. 351/962) originally from ʿAskar Mukram in southwest Iran (Khuzistan), he was active as a lexicographer in Baghdad and composed the earliest extant biographical dictionary of grammarians.

Abū ʿUbaydah Maʿmar ibn al-Muthannā (d. 210/825) a client of non-Arab background, he became one of the most important early Arabic philologists and scholars of pre-Islamic Arab history and among the first to record his scholarship in book form.

Abū ʿUyaynah see *Ibn Abī ʿUyaynah.*

Abū l-Wazīr Aḥmad ibn Khālid (fl. first half of the third/ninth century) secretary under al-Wāthiq, he served the vizier Ibn al-Zayyāt (q.v.) as secretary and succeeded him briefly under al-Mutawakkil before falling into disgrace.

Abū Yazīd see *Khālid ibn Yazīd al-Shaybānī.*

accounts (Ar. akhbār, sg. khabar) short prose texts provided with a chain of transmitters and containing historical or literary information; much early prose consists of collections of such texts.

ʿĀd ancient Arabian people to whom the prophet Hūd was sent.

adab education, or culture, as understood in the Abbasid period, i.e., the repertoire of general literary knowledge and social etiquette necessary for an educated individual to succeed in society and government service (as opposed to specialized knowledge in a scholarly discipline).

ʿAdī (ibn Zayd ibn Mālik) ibn al-Riqāʿ, Abū Duʾād (or Dāwūd) (d. ca. 99–101/717–20) Umayyad praise poet.

adīb (pl. udabāʾ) a person possessing *adab* (q.v.).

admonition (Ar. ʿitāb) a poem reprimanding a patron for his behavior (usually for withheld or delayed remuneration) but respectful in tone and tempered with praise.

al-Afshīn, Khaydhār ibn Kāwūs (d. 226/841) a descendent of the princes of the Ushrusāna region east of Samarkand and a general of al-Muʿtaṣim (q.v.) who quelled the Khurramite revolt led by Bābak (q.v.); later he encouraged the revolt of Māziyār, was tried, found guilty of apostasy, and killed.

al-Afwah al-Awdī, Abū Rabīʿah Ṣalāʾah ibn ʿAmr (d. ca. AD 570) pre-Islamic poet, chief of the tribe of Awd, and a respected arbiter who coined gnomic sayings.

Aḥmad ibn Abī Duʾād see *Ibn Abī Duʾād.*

Aḥmad ibn Abī Fanan, Abū ʿAbd Allāh (d. ca. 260–70/874–83) a client of African origin, he was active in Baghdad as poet and secretary and patronized by the Ṭāhirids (q.v.).

Aḥmad ibn Abī Ṭāhir see *Ibn Abī Ṭāhir.*

Aḥmad ibn Ismāʿīl see *Ibn al-Khaṣīb.*

Aḥmad ibn Isrāʾīl (fl. second half third/ninth century) secretary of Nestorian Christian origin, he suffered extortion under al-Wāthiq, then became head of estates under al-Mutawakkil and vizier for al-Muʿtazz (q.v.).

Aḥmad ibn al-Khaṣīb see *Ibn al-Khaṣīb.*

Aḥmad ibn Muḥammad al-Muʿtaṣim (r. 248–52/862–66) Abbasid prince and later Caliph al-Mustaʿīn.

Aḥmad ibn Yaḥyā see *Thaʿlab.*

Aḥmad ibn Yaḥyā see *al-Balādhurī.*

Aḥmad ibn Yazīd see *al-Muhallabī.*

Aḥnaf ibn Qays al-Tamīmī (d. 72/691) famous governor, general, and chief of the Tamīm in Basra; his astute advice made him a byword for political shrewdness.

Ahwāz city in Khuzistan, southwest Iran.

al-ʿAkawwak see *ʿAlī ibn Jabalah.*

akhbār see *accounts.*

al-Akhṭal, Ghiyāth ibn Ghawth ibn al-Ṣalt (d. ca. 92/710) a Christian of the tribe of Taghlib who together with Jarīr and al-Farazdaq formed the famous poetic triad of the Umayyad period; in the poetic jousts between Jarīr and al-Farazdaq he sided with the latter.

ʿAlī ibn al-ʿAbbās ibn Jurayj al-Rūmī see *Ibn al-Rūmī*.

ʿAlī ibn Abī Ṭālib (d. 40/660) cousin and son-in-law of the Prophet, and fourth caliph, considered by the Shiʿa to be the first imam.

ʿAlī ibn Ismāʿīl al-Nawbakhtī, Abū l-Ḥasan (fl. second half of the third/ninth century) member of the Shiʿi Nawbakht family (q.v.) and a transmitter of the grammarian Thaʿlab (q.v.).

ʿAlī ibn Jabalah al-ʿAkawwak (d. 213/828) a praise poet of Khurasani descent; al-Maʾmūn is said to have had him executed because of his semi-blasphemous praise for Abū Dulaf (q.v.). He was nicknamed "Chunky" because he was short and fat.

ʿAlī ibn al-Jahm (d. 249/863) early Abbasid poet of orthodox, proto-Sunni tendencies, loyal to the Abbasids, and favored in particular by Caliph al-Mutawakkil.

ʿAlī ibn Yaḥyā ibn Abī Manṣūr al-Munajjim, Abū l-Ḥasan (d. 275/888) poet and literary historian; he lived in Samarra and composed a book on ancient and modern poets.

al-Āmidī, Abū l-Qāsim al-Ḥasan ibn Bishr (d. 371/981–82) employed as a secretary in Basra and Baghdad, he wrote about poets and poetry; notable for *The Weighing* (*al-Muwāzanah*), his comparative evaluation of Abū Tammām's artificial style versus al-Buḥturī's natural style, which he favors.

Amorium (Ar. ʿAmmūriyyah) Byzantine border fortress southwest of Ankara, conquered by al-Muʿtaṣim (q.v.) in 223/838 after it had resisted sieges mounted by ʿAbd al-Malik, al-Mahdī, and al-Rashīd.

ʿAmr ibn Hind (r. AD 554–70) ruler of al-Ḥīrah (q.v.), member of the Lakhmid dynasty who served as vassals to the Sasanians.

ʿAmr ibn Kulthūm (fl. sixth century AD) pre-Islamic poet and author of a great ode (*muʿallaqah*).

ʿAmr ibn Maʿdīkarib (Abū Thawr) (d. after 16/637) a poet and leading figure of the Yemeni Zubayd tribe, famous for his exploits in the

Muslims' victory over the Sasanians in al-Qādisiyyah near Kufa between 14/635 and 16/637.

Ancients (Ar. mutaqaddimūn) the poets who lived before Islam and in the early Islamic period; their language served as linguistic proof for the codification of classical Arabic (*ʿarabiyyah*) (q.v.).

anecdote see *nawādir*.

ʿarabiyyah see *classical Arabic*.

Arṭāh ibn Suhayyah al-Murrī (Arṭāh ibn Zufar ibn ʿAbd Allāh) (d. 86/705 or later) early Islamic poet of satire and praise, the latter dedicated to Muʿāwiyah (q.v.).

Asad ibn ʿAbd Allāh al-Qasrī (d. 120/738) Umayyad governor of Khurasan (r. 106–9/724–27 and 117–20/735–38) under Caliph Hishām (q.v.).

al-Aʿshā, Maymūn ibn Qays (d. ca. 7/629) a Christian of the tribe of Bakr and one of the great poets of pre-Islamic times; though he lived to see Islam, he never converted.

Ashjaʿ al-Sulamī, Abū l-Walīd (d. ca. 195/811) minor Abbasid poet of Alid sentiment and panegyrist of al-Rashīd.

al-Aṣmaʿī, Abū Saʿīd ʿAbd al-Malik ibn Qurayb (d. 213/828) lexicographer and narrator of anecdotes, connected to the Barmakids and al-Rashīd (qq.v.); his teachings, mostly on the lexicon of specific themes, were put into book form by subsequent generations of students.

al-ʿAttābī, Kulthūm ibn ʿAmr (d. 208/823 or 220/835) praise poet, secretary, and courtier, associated with the Barmakids and the caliphs al-Rashīd and al-Maʾmūn; a famed prose stylist, he read Persian, and composed several books on *adab* and lexicography.

awāʾil those persons who were the "first" to do all sorts of things and the title of books dedicated to them; also: ancient poets (q.v.).

ʿAwānah ibn al-Ḥakam al-Kalbī (d. 147/764 or 153/770) early historian of disputed origin whose works only survive in later citations, such as those by al-Haytham ibn ʿAdī (q.v.).

ʿAwn ibn Muḥammad al-Kindī, Abū Mālik (fl. first half of the third/ninth century) transmitter of historical and literary accounts contemporary with Abū Tammām and the source for Abū Bakr al-Ṣūlī's recension of the poet's collected works and many of his accounts.

Aws ibn Ḥajar (d. shortly before the Hijra, AD 622) one of the great poets of the Muḍar group of tribes prior to al-Nābighah and Zuhayr (qq.v.), he described wine, weapons, and manly virtue in his poetry and composed famous laments.

ʿAyyāsh ibn Lahīʿah al-Ḥaḍramī (fl. first half of the third/ninth century) head of poll-tax (*jizyah*) collection and police in Egypt, and Abū Tammām's first patron.

Ayyūb (fl. first half of the second/eighth century) Umayyad prince and son of Caliph Sulaymān ibn ʿAbd al-Malik (q.v.).

ʿAzzah bint Ḥumayl al-Ḥājibiyyah the beloved of the Umayyad poet Kuthayyir (q.v.).

Bābak (d. 223–24/838) head of the Khurramī sect, he started a rebellion in Azerbaijan in 201/816–17; he was finally vanquished in 222/837 by al-Muʿtaṣim's general al-Afshīn (q.v.).

badīʿ see *New Style*.

Badr town near Medina, site of a battle in 2/624 in which the Muslims and their Medinese allies fought the Meccans and in which the Muslims achieved their first victory.

Badr servant of Mukhallad ibn Bakkār al-Mawṣilī (q.v.).

al-Baʿīth, Khidāsh ibn Bishr al-Mujāshiʿī (fl. first quarter of the second/eighth century) of Persian background, he was a poet and orator of the Tamīm tribe drawn into the poetic joust between Jarīr and al-Farazdaq, taking the side of the latter.

Bajkam al-Rāʾiqī (d. 329/941) a Turkish commander who became chief lieutenant under the regent (*amīr al-umarāʾ*) Ibn Rāʾiq, appointed by Caliph al-Rāḍī in 324/936; he replaced Ibn Rāʾiq in 326/938.

Bakr ibn Wāʾil ancient confederacy of tribes in central, east, and (later) northern Arabia, belonging to the tribal group of Rabīʿah ibn Nizār of the northern Arabs (ʿAdnān); famous for their long feud with their brother tribe, the Taghlib, lasting to the mid-sixth century AD.

al-Balādhurī, Abū Jaʿfar Aḥmad ibn Yaḥyā (d. 279/892) leading Iraqi historian who composed among other books two major histories, one on the early conquests, the other on famous early Islamic personalities arranged by tribe.

al-Bandanījī, Ibrāhīm ibn al-Faraj (fl. mid-third/ninth century) minor poet whose name derives from the town of Bandanijān near Baghdad; not identical with the lexicographer al-Yaman ibn Abī l-Yaman (d. 284/897), who has the same *nisbah*.

Banū (sons of) precedes and indicates the name of a tribe or dynasty.

Baradān town north of Baghdad on the main road to Samarra.

Barmakids celebrated family of high officials and viziers of Iranian background in the early Abbasid period, they were also fabulously generous patrons of the arts and sciences; their downfall in 187/803 became a symbolic event in historiography. Their name derives from the title of the family's ancestor, Barmak (Sanskrit *parmak*), high priest of a Buddhist temple near Balkh.

Barqaʿīd town on the outskirts of Mosul whose inhabitants were proverbial for thievery.

Bashshār ibn Burd, Abū Muʿādh (d. 167/783–84) of Persian descent, he was a pioneer in the modern style (q.v.), famous for his courtly love poems and feared for his satire; his heretical, Manichean beliefs may have led to his execution by Caliph al-Mahdī.

boast (Ar. fakhr) a poem extolling one's own virtues, ancestry, and/or merits.

borrowing see *sariqah*.

al-Buḥturī, Abū ʿUbādah (or Abū l-Ḥasan) al-Walīd ibn ʿUbayd (d. 284/897) a prominent modern poet and disciple of Abū Tammām, though his style was smoother and more idiomatic; politically savvy, he praised the Abbasid caliphs from al-Mutawakkil to al-Muʿtaḍid (qq.v.).

Buzurgmihr (fl. sixth century AD) a minister of the Sasanian king Chosroes (Ar. Kisrā Anūshirwān), his wisdom and virtue were legendary and he is credited for many wise precepts in Middle Persian (Pahlavi) and Arabic literature.

caliph (Ar. khalīfah) head of the Muslim community.

Capella (Ar. al-ʿAyyūq) a fixed star in the Auriga constellation.

case endings (Ar. iʿrāb) the (mostly) unwritten markers of case and mood at the ends of Arabic words, which require study of grammar to be pronounced correctly (except for linguistically skilled Arab Bedouins in early Islamic times).

chain of transmitters (Ar. isnād) reference placed at the beginning of a hadith report (q.v.) or other account (*khabar*) for the purpose of authentication.

Chosroes (Ar. Kisrā) The name of several Sasanian kings and their dynastic title in the Arabic sources.

classical Arabic (Ar. ʿarabiyyah) the written and formal spoken language of Abbasid and later times, as opposed to colloquial Arabic, which lacked case endings, and a mixed form (Middle Arabic) used in private correspondence and popular literature.

collected works (Ar. dīwān) the poetic works of a poet or a tribe; from the second/eighth century on, collected works edited by Arabic philologists formed (together with Bedouin speech and the Qurʾan) the basis for codifying classical Arabic (q.v.).

Commander of the Faithful one of the titles of the caliph (q.v.).

compilation (Ar. taṣnīf, muṣannaf) a work compiled of pre-existing material selected and presented in thematic order; as opposed to composition (*taʾlīf*), a work written from scratch.

continuation (Ar. ijāzah) to continue or compose a repartee to another's verse in the same rhyme and meter.

critics see *poetry critics.*

Daghfal a genealogist proverbial for his erudition.

Dāwūd ibn al-Jarrāḥ, Abū Sulaymān (fl. mid-third/ninth century) member of a family of high officials of Iranian origin from Dayr Qunnā, he headed government offices under al-Mutawakkil (assisting Ibrāhīm ibn al-ʿAbbās) (q.v.) and al-Mustaʿīn and authored (no longer extant) books on scribes and epistles. He was the father of Muḥammad ibn Dāwūd (q.v.).

Deneb literally "tail," Alpha Cygni, the brightest star in the Cygnus constellation. The name also denotes other stars that represent the tails of animals in constellations.

description, poem of (Ar. waṣf, pl. awṣāf) a new poetic genre in the Abbasid period, referring to a poem describing an object, situation, or mood.

Dhū Qār site of a battle between Arab tribes (ca. AD 604–11), in which the confederacy of Bakr ibn Wāʾil (belonging to the Rabīʿah branch of the northern, or ʿAdnānī, Arabs) vanquished an alliance of the Arab

Taghlib and the Sasanians. The battle was the first Arab defeat of the Persians and ranked close in importance to the Muslims' first victory against the Meccan pagans at Badr (q.v.).

Dhū l-Rummah, Ghaylān ibn ʿUqbah (d. 117/735) Umayyad poet, famous for desert descriptions in archaic style; he devoted many poems to his beloved Mayyah.

Diʿbil ibn ʿAlī l-Khuzāʿī (d. 244/859 or 246/860) a naturally talented poet from Qirqīsiyāʾ (q.v.) and author of a book about poets; of pro-Alid sentiment, he praised ʿAlī and fearlessly satirized high officials and caliphs.

dinar (Ar. dīnār, from Latin denarius*)* gold coin, originally weighing 4.25 grams; in the third/ninth century one dinar equaled twenty to twenty-five silver dirhams.

dirham (from Greek *drachmē*) silver coin, until the mid-third/ninth century weighing 2.91 and 2.96 grams; in the third/ninth century twenty to twenty-five dirhams equaled one gold dinar.

Dissidents (Ar. Khawārij) sectarians who refused to support ʿAlī after his agreement to arbitration with Muʿāwiyah (q.v.) at Ṣiffīn, a process which they condemned.

dīwān see *collected works.*

al-Faḍl ibn al-Ḥubāb al-Jumaḥī l-Baṣrī, Abū Khalīfah (d. 305/917) Basran judge, Hadith scholar, transmitter of literary accounts, and editor of the biographical dictionary of poets by his uncle (Ibn Sallām) al-Jumaḥī (q.v.).

al-Faḍl ibn Marwān (fl. first half of the third/ninth century) secretary who supervised all government offices under al-Muʿtaṣim until he fell into disgrace in 220/835.

Faḍl ibn Muḥammad ibn Abī Muḥammad al-Yazīdī, Abū l-ʿAbbās (d. 278/891) a litterateur, transmitter, and poet belonging to the literary Yazīdī family.

al-Faḍl ibn al-Rabīʿ ibn Yūnus, Abū l-ʿAbbās (d. 207/822–23 or 208/823–24) son of the chamberlain of al-Manṣūr and al-Mahdī, he became chamberlain then vizier to al-Rashīd and after him, al-Amīn.

fakhr see *boast.*

al-Farazdaq, Abū Firās Hammām ibn Ghālib (d. ca. 110/728) with Jarīr and al-Akhṭal he formed the famous poetic triad of the Umayyad period; he praised caliphs and others, but is best known for his lifelong poetic jousts with Jarīr.

farsakh (from Persian *parasang*) a unit of distance of about four miles, or six kilometers.

Flytings (Ar. Naqā'iḍ) satires between al-Farazdaq and Jarīr (qq.v.); its edition is ascribed to the early philologist Abū 'Ubaydah and its commentary contains much Arab tribal lore.

format (Ar. rasm) structure, or plan, of a book; a new and quickly embraced medium in the third/ninth century.

freed slave (Ar. mawlā) a person bound to a social superior (patron) either contractually or through former ties of servitude. A *mawlā* had usually converted to Islam at the hands of his patron.

al-Gharīḍ, Abū Yazīd 'Abd al-Malik (d. ca. 98/716–17) a famous Meccan singer of the Umayyad period.

Ghassanids (or Jafnids) an Arabian dynasty used by the Romans as vassals against the Sasanians; their kings were given the title of phylarch.

al-Ghawr the lowlands around Damascus.

ghazal see *love lyric*.

great ode (Ar. mu'allaqah, pl. mu'allaqāt) one of most celebrated (seven or ten) pre-Islamic odes which belong to the classics of Arabic literature; collected perhaps by Ḥammād al-Rāwiyah (q.v.).

al-Habā'ah, Battle of named after the well of al-Habā'ah where it took place, this battle was part of the long war between the tribes of 'Abs and Dhubyān.

Ḥabīb ibn 'Abd Allāh ibn al-Zubayr member of a clan that suffered a long history of violent deaths, namely each individual in the following genealogical chain: 'Umārah ibn Ḥamzah ibn 'Abd Allāh ibn al-Zubayr ibn al-'Awwām ibn Khuwaylid. 'Umārah and his father Ḥamzah were killed in the Battle of Qudayd by the Ibāḍiyyah; 'Abd Allāh ibn al-Zubayr (q.v.) was killed in Mecca by al-Ḥajjāj ibn Yūsuf; al-Zubayr was killed in the Valley of Sibā' by Abū Jurmūz al-Sa'dī; al-'Awwām was killed by Kinānah; and Khuwaylid was killed by the tribe of Ka'b ibn 'Amr ibn Khuzā'ah.

hadith (Ar. ḥadīth) short narrative introduced by a chain of transmitters usually conveying the words or depicting the behavior of the Prophet Muḥammad; a principal source of law alongside the Qur'an.

Hadith the body of hadiths.

Hagar (Ar. Hājar) concubine or, according to Islamic tradition, wife of Abraham (Ibrāhīm) and the mother of Ishmael (Ismā'īl), the legendary ancestor of the Arabs.

Ḥājibī girl see *'Azzah.*

al-Ḥajjāj ibn Yūsuf (d. 95/714) famous Umayyad governor of Iraq whose harsh but effective government restored internal stability.

Ḥamdawayh al-Aḥwal the Scribe perhaps identical with Abū 'Amr Shamir ibn Ḥamdawayh al-Harawī (d. 255/869), a Herati who came to Baghdad to study with leading scholars of the Basran-Baghdadian school and upon his return home composed a comprehensive dictionary arranged in alphabetical order, which is no longer extant because he allegedly refused to have it copied.

al-Ḥāmiḍ, Abū Mūsā Sulaymān ibn Muḥammad (or Muḥammad ibn Sulaymān) ibn Aḥmad (d. 305/917) lexicographer of the Kufan school; assistant and successor to Tha'lab, he authored several thematic dictionaries which he copied with great precision but withheld from colleagues at his death. His unpleasant character earned him the nickname "Sourpuss."

Ḥammād 'Ajrad (d. ca. 155–68/772–84) poet and famed satirist of the late Umayyad and early Abbasid period, notorious for his dissolute life, and suspected of heresy (Manicheism).

Ḥammād ibn Isḥāq al-Mawṣilī (fl. first half of the third/ninth century) courtier and transmitter mainly of the books and songs of his father, Isḥāq al-Mawṣilī (q.v.).

Ḥammād al-Rāwiyah (d. 155/772) one of the first collectors and transmitters of early poetry, but accused of forgery by some; he is perhaps the collector of the great odes (q.v.). His student was Khalaf al-Aḥmar (q.v.).

al-Ḥārith ibn Muḍāḍ (al-Jurhumī) (fl. first/sixth century) chief of the Jurhum tribe of the southern Arabs (Qaḥṭān), who migrated north and settled in Mecca until, according to Islamic legend, they were driven out by the Khuzāʿah tribe.

Hārūn ibn Muḥammad ibn ʿAbd al-Malik (al-Zayyāt, Abū Mūsā) (fl. first half of the third/ninth century) transmitter and secretary; his father was Ibn al-Zayyāt (q.v.).

Hārūn al-Rashīd see *al-Rashīd.*

al-Ḥasan ibn Rajāʾ (fl. first half of the third/ninth century) governor of Shiraz under al-Maʾmūn and al-Muʿtaṣim and a patron of Abū Tammām.

al-Ḥasan ibn ʿUlayl al-ʿAnazī (d. 290/903) an expert transmitter of historical and literary accounts active in Samarra.

al-Ḥasan ibn Wahb al-Ḥārithī, Abū ʿAlī (d. ca. 248/862) an elegant poet and prose stylist from a family of secretaries of Christian origin (as was his brother Sulayman) (q.v.); he assisted Ibrāhīm ibn al-ʿAbbās al-Ṣūlī and headed the chancellery office under al-Muʿtaṣim and al-Wāthiq during the vizierate of Ibn al-Zayyāt (q.v.); a patron and fervent supporter of Abū Tammām.

Hāshim, Banū clan within the tribe of Quraysh to which the Prophet and the ancestors of the subsequent Abbasid dynasty belonged.

Ḥātim al-Ṭāʾī (fl. the sixth century AD) pre-Islamic knight and poet who became proverbial for his generosity and his embodiment of Bedouin virtues.

Ḥayr (from Arabic *ḥāʾir,* "enclosure, pleasure garden") a castle in Samarra, built by al-Mutawakkil and surrounded by spacious gardens.

al-Haythamibn ʿAdīibn ʿAbdal-Raḥmānal-Ṭāʾī, Abū ʿAbdal-Raḥmān (d. 207/822) genealogist and transmitter of historical accounts, frequently cited by later historians.

al-Ḥazanbal, Abū ʿAbd Allāh Muḥammad ibn ʿAbd Allāh ibn ʿĀṣim al-Tamīmī l-Iṣbahānī (fl. second half of the third/ninth century) knowledgable transmitter of historical and literary accounts.

heretic see *zindīq.*

hijāʾ see *lampoon.*

Ḥimyar pre-Islamic tribe who established a kingdom in Yemen overthrown by the Christian Ethiopians in the sixth century AD.

al-Ḥīrah city near Kufa on the lower Mesopotamia and pre-Islamic capital of the Arab Lakhmid kings.

Hishām ibn ʿAbd al-Malik (r. 105–25/724–43) Umayyad caliph.

Ḥudhāq a clan of the Iyād tribe (q.v.) of the northern Arabs (ʿAdnān).

Ḥumayd ibn ʿAbd al-Ḥamīd al-Ṭūsī, Abū Ghānim (d. 210/825) general of al-Maʾmūn and instrumental in his victory over the counter-caliph Ibrāhīm ibn al-Mahdī; he was also a celebrated patron of poets.

al-Ḥusayn ibn al-Ḍaḥḥāk see *al-Khalīʿ*.

al-Ḥuṣayn ibn al-Ḥumām ibn Rabīʿah al-Murrī (fl. sixth century AD) wise leader of the Murrah tribe who may have lived into the time of Islam.

al-Ḥuṣrī, Abū Isḥāq Ibrāhīm ibn ʿAlī (d. 413/1022) poet and man of letters active in Qayrawān, he exerted a profound influence on the flowering of literature in the Muslim West; his anthologies assemble excerpts from the finest contemporary poets and prose stylists.

al-Ḥuṭayʾah, Jarwal ibn Aws al-ʿAbsī (d. ca. mid-first/seventh century) poet of the Qays tribe who lived both before and during Islam, an itinerant panegyrist and much-feared satirist.

Ibn ʿAbbād, Abū Jaʿfar Muḥammad, the Scribe (fl. second half of the third/ninth century) client of the Makhzūm tribe and son of a secretary, he was one of the greatest Meccan singers under the Abbasids.

Ibn ʿAbd Kān, Abū Jaʿfar Muḥammad (d. 278/891–92) first head of the chancery of the state in Egypt founded by the semi-independent governor Aḥmad ibn Ṭūlūn.

Ibn Abī Duʾād, Abū ʿAbd Allāh Aḥmad (d. 240/854) chief judge, head of the judiciary, and adviser to the caliphs al-Maʾmūn, al-Muʿtaṣim, and al-Wāthiq (qq.v.).

Ibn Abī Khaythamah (Abū Bakr Aḥmad al-Nasāʾī) (d. 279/892) Baghdadi hadith transmitter, man of letters, historian, and author of a book on poets; he harbored Qadari sympathies, i.e., support for the concept of free will.

Ibn Abī Rabīʿah see *ʿUmar ibn Abī Rabīʿah*.

Ibn Abī Ṭāhir Ṭayfūr, Abū l-Faḍl Aḥmad (d. 280/893) Baghdadi historian, *adīb*, and bookseller-copyist who was involved in the writerly milieu of Baghdad; among his many works are the *Book of Baghdad, Prose and Poetry*, and *Women's Eloquence*.

Ibn Abī ʿUyaynah the Younger, Abū l-Minhāl Abū ʿUyaynah ibn Muḥammad (fl. early second/eighth century) Basran poet who composed love poetry, satire, and descriptive poetry.

Ibn al-Aʿrābī, Abū ʿAbd Allāh Muḥammad ibn Ziyād (d. 231/846) genealogist, transmitter of poetry, and lexicographer of the Kufan school who authored many thematic dictionaries.

Ibn Dāwūd see *Muḥammad ibn Dāwūd*.

Ibn Jabalah see *ʿAlī ibn Jabalah*.

Ibn al-Jahm see *ʿAlī ibn al-Jahm*.

Ibn al-Jarrāḥ see *Muḥammad ibn Dāwūd*.

Ibn al-Kalbī, Abū l-Mundhir Hishām ibn Muḥammad (d. 204/819) Iraqi polymath who authored over one hundred books on history, genealogy, and poetry, notably a compendium on tribes that arranged them into rosters, and a work on pre-Islamic idols.

Ibn al-Khaṣīb, Aḥmad ibn Ismāʿīl ibn Ibrāhīm al-Jarjarāʾī (d. 265/879) he held several secretarial positions under al-Wāthiq and al-Mutawakkil (and suffered torture), then became vizier under al-Muntaṣir and briefly under al-Mustaʿīn before being exiled to Crete.

Ibn al-Khayyāṭ al-Madīnī l-Makkī, ʿAbd Allāh (ibn Muḥammad, or ibn Yūnus) ibn Sālim (d. ca. 158–69/775–85) poet of satire and bawdy verse whose life spanned the Umayyad and Abbasid dynasties and was attached to the family of ʿAbd Allāh ibn Zubayr.

Ibn Lajaʾ al-Taymī, ʿUmar (or ʿAmr) ibn al-Ashʿath (alive until the early first/seventh century) a *rajaz* poet of the Taym, a friend of al-Farazdaq who traded satires with Jarīr.

Ibn Lisān al-Ḥummarah, Rabīʿah ibn Ḥiṣn (fl. first/seventh century) Bedouin of the tribe of Taym al-Lāt, knowledgeable in genealogy and well known for his wisdom and lively repartee.

Ibn al-Mahdī see *Ibrāhīm ibn al-Mahdī*.

Ibn Mayyādah, Abū Shuraḥbīl (or Abū Sharāḥīl) al-Rammāḥ ibn al-Abrad (d. 136/754 or 149/766) Umayyad poet who composed panegyrics, love lyrics, and occasional satire in a pure Arabic diction.

Ibn Mihrawayh, Abū ʿAbd Allāh Muḥammad ibn al-Qāsim al-Dīnawarī (d. 275/888) important early collector and transmitter of poetry and poets' accounts and author of a book about poets; he is one of the main sources of al-Iṣbahānī's (q.v.) *Book of Songs*.

Ibn al-Muʿadhdhal, ʿAbd al-Ṣamad (d. ca. 240/854) eloquent Basran poet and satirist of Arab descent, renowned for his foul tongue.

Ibn al-Mudabbir, Ibrāhīm ibn Muḥammad ibn ʿAbd Allāh (d. 279/892–93) Abbasid litterateur, poet, prose stylist, and courtier from a family of secretaries of Persian origin; he served as head of a government office and briefly as vizier under al-Muʿtamid (q.v.).

Ibn al-Muʿtazz, Abū l-ʿAbbās ʿAbd Allāh (d. 296/908) Abbasid prince and poet in the modern style, he wrote the first study of modern poetics and a biographical dictionary of modern poets; he was killed after he had been caliph for one day.

Ibn Qanbar (or Ibn Qunbur), al-Ḥakam ibn Muḥammad al-Māzinī (fl. early third/ninth century) a Basran poet of the Tamīm tribe, he composed love lyrics and was vanquished by Muslim ibn al-Walīd (q.v.) in a satirical context.

Ibn Qays ibn Shurayḥ al-Ruqayyāt, ʿUbayd Allāh ibn Qays (d. 80/699) Qurayshi poet who supported the counter-caliphate of ʿAbd Allāh ibn al-Zubayr (q.v.) and composed mainly love lyrics (q.v.) in the erotic Ḥijāzī style.

Ibn al-Rūmī, Abū l-Ḥasan ʿAlī ibn al-ʿAbbās ibn Jurayj (d. 283/896) versatile, inventive, and prolific poet of Greek-Persian background who excelled equally in panegyrics and vitriolic satire.

Ibn Sallām see *al-Jumaḥī*.

Ibn Sīdah, Abū l-Ḥasan ʿAlī ibn Ismāʿīl (d. 458/1066) prolific Andalusian philologist and lexicographer best known for two comprehensive dictionaries, one in alphabetical and the other in thematic order.

Ibn al-Ṭathriyyah, Abū Makshūḥ (or Abū l-Ṣimma) Yazīd ibn al-Muntashir (d. 126/744) love poet of the late Umayyad period.

Ibn Ṭawq see *Mālik ibn Ṭawq*.

Ibn Thawābah, Abū l-ʿAbbās Aḥmad ibn Muḥammad (d. 277/890) rose from a poor Christian family to serve in different secretarial functions under the Abbasid caliphs from al-Muhtadī to al-Muʿtaḍid (qq.v.); a talented stylist and poet, he hosted a poetic circle and patronized poets but was disliked for his affected behavior as a social upstart.

Ibn Yazdād, Abū Ṣāliḥ ʿAbd Allāh ibn Muḥammad (d. 265/878–79) secretary who headed the office of domains under al-Mutawakkil and shortly served as vizier to al-Mustaʿīn in 249/863. His father Muḥammad, a man of letters and an elegant stylist, had served as secretary under al-Maʾmūn.

Ibn al-Zayyāt, Muḥammad ibn ʿAbd al-Malik (r. 221–33/833–47) vizier serving under al-Muʿtaṣim and al-Wāthiq (qq.v.).

Ibn al-Zubayr see *ʿAbd Allāh ibn al-Zubayr.*

Ibrāhīm ibn al-ʿAbbās al-Ṣūlī (d. 243/857 or later) of Turkish descent, he was the great-uncle of the compiler of *The Life and Times of Abū Tammām*, Abū Bakr al-Ṣūlī, and the most famous Abbasid secretary-poet, heading government offices under Ibn al-Zayyāt and later viziers of al-Mutawakkil (qq.v.).

Ibrāhīm ibn Ismāʿīl ibn Ibrāhīm al-Jarjarāʾī (fl. mid-third/ninth century) brother of Ibn al-Khaṣīb (q.v.).

Ibrahīm ibn al-Mahdī (d. 224/839) Abbasid prince and, briefly, counter-caliph (r. 201–3/817–19), and a gifted composer and musician.

Ibrāhīm ibn al-Mudabbir see *Ibn al-Mudabbir.*

Ibrāhīm ibn al-Rabāḥ (fl. first half of third/ninth century) secretary who headed the Office of Expenses under al-Maʾmūn and the office of estates under al-Wāthiq (qq.v.).

ʿIlāf ibn Hulwān of Quḍāʿah reputedly the first person to construct a type of camel saddle, which was named after him.

ʿilm al-shiʿr (knowledge, field, or discipline of poetry) the professional expertise of the poetry critic, as opposed to a scholar of language (or philologist).

Imruʾ al-Qays (fl. mid-sixth century AD) son of a prince from the tribal federation of Kindah; the most famous pre-Islamic poet and author of the best-known great ode (*muʿallaqah*); credited with the invention of the abandoned campsite motif (*aṭlāl*) in the *nasīb* (q.v.).

iʿrāb see *case endings.*

ʿIṣābah al-Jarjarāʾī, Abū Isḥāq Ismāʿīl ibn Muḥammad (or Ibrāhīm ibn Bādhām) (fl. first half of the third/ninth century) minor Abbasid poet.

al-Iṣbahānī, Abū l-Faraj ʿAlī ibn al-Ḥusayn (d. 356/967) born in Isfahan and of Umayyad descent, he was a historian, man of letters, and musicologist; he authored the famous *Book of Songs* (*Kitāb al-Aghānī*), which contains portraits of poets, musicians, and personalities from pre-Islamic to Abbasid times.

Isḥāq ibn Ibrāhīm ibn Ḥusayn al-Muṣʿabī (r. 207–35/822–49) military governor of Baghdad and Iraq, belonging to the virtually autonomous line of Ṭāhirid governors of Khurasan and prefects of Baghdad, and a long-term patron of Abū Tammām.

Isḥāq ibn Ibrāhīm al-Mawṣilī (d. 235/850) of Persian origin, he was the greatest musician of his time, as well as a poet, courtier, man of letters, and author of books on music; his father was the musician, composer, and courtier Ibrāhīm al-Mawṣilī (d. 188/804).

Ismāʿīl ibn Bulbul, Abū l-Ṣaqr (r. 265–78/878–91) of Iranian origin but claiming Arab ancestry (Banū Shaybān), and holding Shiʿi sympathies, he served as vizier to al-Muʿtamid.

Iyād a northern Arab tribe (ʿAdnān).

Iyās ibn Muʿāwiyah ibn Qurrah al-Muzanī (d. 121/739) judge of Basra who became proverbial for his shrewdness and sagacity.

al-Jabal (or al-Jibāl) mountainous region in northwest Iran.

Jarīr ibn ʿAṭiyyah ibn Khaṭafā (d. 111/729) he formed, with al-Akhṭal and al-Farazdaq, the famous poetic triad of the Umayyad period; acclaimed for his love poetry, mostly in the form of *nasīb* (q.v.), he is best known for his lifelong poetic jousts with al-Farazdaq.

Jāsim town southwest of Damascus and birthplace of Abū Tammām; according to legend it was founded by Noah's great-grandson Jāsim after the destruction of the tower of Babel.

al-Jumaḥī, Abū ʿAbd Allāh Muḥammad ibn Sallām (d. 232/846–47) Basran philologist, poetry critic, and author of an important early anthology and classification of pre- and early Islamic poets.

al-Junayd ibn ʿAbd al-Raḥmān al-Murrī (d. first quarter of the second/eighth century) governor of Khurasan and Sind under Caliph Hishām during whose reign he died.

Kaʿb ibn Zuhayr (d. ca. 50/670) son of Zuhayr (q.v.) and a poet who straddled both the pre-Islamic and Islamic eras; he first rejected Islam, but after being outlawed by Muḥammad, he delivered an ode, known as the "Mantle Ode," (Ar. "*al-Burdah*"), to Muḥammad and was granted protection.

Kalb Arab tribal group of Yemeni descent which for political reasons sometimes claimed to belong to the northern Arabs (ʿAdnān).

Kayyis a genealogist proverbial for his erudition.

khabar see *accounts*.

Khalaf al-Aḥmar (d. ca. 180/796) poet and transmitter of early poetry and student of Ḥammād al-Rāwiyah (q.v.).

al-Khalīʿ, Abū ʿAlī l-Ḥusayn ibn al-Ḍaḥḥāk al-Ashqar al-Baṣrī (d. 250/864) originally from Khurasan, he was a friend of Abū Nuwās, a poet at the Abbasid court, and companion of several caliphs.

Khālid ibn Yazīd ibn Ḥātim (fl. mid-second/eighth century) from the Muhallabī family, governor of Jurjān under al-Mahdī and al-Hādī; lampooned by his cousin, the poet Ibn Abī ʿUyaynah (q.v.), whom he mistreated.

Khālid ibn Yazīd ibn Mazyad al-Shaybānī, Abū Yazīd (d. 230/844–45) from 227/842 until his death, governor of Armenia under Caliph al-Wāthiq and patron of Abū Tammām.

Khālid al-Qasrī (d. 126/743–44) Umayyad governor of Mecca and then Iraq under Hishām; his great power and wealth eventually led to his downfall and execution.

al-Khalīl ibn Aḥmad al-Farāhīdī l-Azdī (d. 175/791) Basran founder of the disciplines of phonetics and prosody and author of the earliest preserved dictionary, for which he devised his own system of organization (bundles of word roots in all permutations, arranged according to place of articulation in the mouth).

al-Khansāʾ, Tumāḍir bint ʿAmr (d. after 23/644) the greatest female poet in Arabic, famous for her laments of her brothers, Ṣakhr and Muʿāwiyah.

al-Khathʿamī, Abū ʿAbd Allāh Aḥmad ibn Muḥammad al-Kūfī (fl. third/ninth century) poet and author of a lost book on poets, contemporary of Abū Tammām.

Khawārij see *Dissidents*.

Khiyār the Scribe perhaps identical with a certain Khiyār ibn Najāḥ lampooned by Abū Nuwās for plagiarizing him.

Khuld palace with spacious gardens built in 157/773 by al-Manṣūr on the bank of the Tigris and the quarter surrounding it in the northeastern periphery of Baghdad, south of the Tigris.

Khurasan (Ar. Khurāsān) province in northeast Iran, sometimes including Transoxania (modern Uzbekistan).

al-Khuraymī, Abū Yaʿqūb Isḥāq ibn Ḥassān ibn Qūhī (d. 214/829) poet of Sogdian origin and client of the Khuraym tribe, he composed a lament describing the destruction of Baghdad during the civil war between the brothers al-Amīn and al-Maʾmūn.

al-Kindī, Abū Yūsuf Yaʿqūb ibn Isḥāq (d. after 255/869) philosopher and polymath who entertained a circle of translators of Greek and Syriac, connected with the Abbasid court and tutor of prince Aḥmad ibn al-Muʿtaṣim (q.v.).

Kisrā see *Chosroes*.

al-Kudaymī, Abū l-ʿAbbās Muḥammad ibn Yūnus al-Qurashī (d. 286/899) hadith collector who traveled in the Hijaz and Yemen and then settled in Baghdad.

al-Kumayt ibn Zayd al-Asadī (d. 126/743) of Kufan origin, his poetry in Bedouin-like diction celebrated the Prophet, ʿAlī ibn Abī Ṭālib, and other members of the Prophet's family and put him in conflict with the Umayyad authorities.

Kuthayyir (d. 105/723) poet famous for ʿUdhri-style love lyrics (q.v.) to his beloved ʿAzzah.

Labīd ibn Rabīʿah al-ʿĀmirī (d. ca. 41/661) famous pre-Islamic poet who converted to Islam and author of a great ode.

Lakhmids ethnically Arab dynasty with their capital at al-Ḥīrah (q.v.), they served the Sasanians of Persia as vassals against the Romans.

lament (Ar. rithāʾ or marthiyah, pl. marāthī) poem eulogizing a male (or more rarely female) deceased, occasionally with a call for revenge.

lampoon (Ar. hijāʾ) a poem chastising and insulting an adversary in eloquent (occasionally humorous) language; its tone ranges from the tempered to the vitriolic and obscene; lampoons often had serious consequences, such as the addressee's (and his clan's) shame and the poet's imprisonment, exile, or execution.

Laqīṭ ibn Yaʿmar al-Iyādī (fl. sixth century AD) pre-Islamic orator-poet of the Iyād tribe living near al-Ḥīrah (q.v.).

al-Lāt pre-Islamic Arabian deity.

league see *farsakh.*

love lyric (Ar. ghazal) independent love poem as opposed to the amatory prelude of the ode (*nasīb*) (q.v.); major styles are the flirtatious Ḥijāzī lyric, the Umayyad ʿUdhrī lyric celebrating faithful love until death, both of the Umayyad period, and the courtly lyric of the Abbasid period.

Maʿarrat al-Nuʿmān town in northern Syria midway between Ḥamāh and Aleppo.

Maʿbad ibn Wahb (d. ca. 125/743) singer and prolific composer who performed in Mecca and at the Umayyad court.

Mabhūtah al-Hāshimī is otherwise unknown, being mentioned only in *The Life and Times of Abū Tammām.*

al-Madāʾinī, Abū l-Ḥasan ʿAlī ibn Muḥammad (d. 228/842–43) prolific early historian and methodical Hadith scholar who settled in Baghdad; his many works survive only in later citations by al-Ṭabarī and al-Balādhurī (qq.v.).

Madhḥij a South Arabian tribal group attested in pre-Islamic times.

madīḥ see *panegyric.*

al-Mahdī (r. 158–69/775–85) Abbasid caliph.

Maḥmūd ibn al-Ḥasan al-Warrāq (d. ca. 230/845) Baghdadi poet of ascetic and gnomic verse who was also a bookseller and a sometime slave merchant.

Mālik ibn Abī l-Samḥ of Ṭayy (d. ca. 136/754) leading singer of Medina, who was trained by Maʿbad (q.v.) and who sang before the Umayyad caliph al-Walīd II and Sulaymān ibn ʿAlī, uncle of Abbasid caliphs.

Mālik ibn Ṭawq ibn ʿAttāb al-Taghlibī (d. 260/873–74) general and governor of western Mesopotamia under al-Maʾmūn and a long-term patron of Abū Tammām.

al-Maʾmūn (r. 197–218/813–33) Abbasid caliph; his rule was interrupted by the counter-caliphate of his uncle Ibrahīm ibn al-Mahdī (q.v.).

maʿnā (pl. maʿānī) stands variously for the meaning of a passage of prose or poetry, as opposed to its wording (*lafẓ*) (q.v.); the theme of a poem or verse; or the particular way, or motif, in which this theme is formulated.

Manṣūr ibn Bādhān al-Iṣbahānī (fl. end of second/eighth and beginning of third/ninth century) minor satirical poet who lived in Persia.

Manṣūr ibn Salamah ibn al-Zibriqān al-Namarī (Abū l-Faḍl, or Abū l-Qāsim) (d. 190/805) poet from upper Mesopotamia and disciple of the poet al-ʿAttābī (q.v.) and later court poet of the Barmakids and Abbasids; he had pro-Alid sympathies, which he did not express in his poetry.

marthiyah see *lament.*

Marwān (ibn Sulaymān ibn Yaḥyā) ibn Abī Ḥafṣah, Abū l-Simṭ (d. ca. 182/797) poet whose material success might have been owed to his accessible pro-Abbasid odes.

al-Marzubānī, Abū ʿUbayd Allāh Muḥammad ibn ʿImrān (d. 384/994) descended from a wealthy family in Khurasan, he was one of the most versatile and prolific *adab* scholars of the fourth/tenth century, and his literary gatherings were also famous as social events.

al-Maṣṣīṣah (Byzantine Mopsuestia) town on the Byzantine frontier near modern-day Adana in Turkey, fortified by the Abbasids and the site of repeated Byzantine raids.

mathal variously means example, analog, pithy saying, or parable.

mawlā see *freed slave.*

Mithqāl, Abū Jaʿfar Muḥammad ibn Yaʿqūb al-Wāsiṭī (fl. second half of the third/ninth century) satirical poet and transmitter of Ibn al-Rūmī (q.v.), whose works he collected.

Moderns (Ar. muḥdathūn, sg. muḥdath) the poets of the early Abbasid period who used the New Style (*badīʿ*) (q.v.); the singular form stands for the style of their poetry.

Mosul (Ar. al-Mawṣil) city in upper Mesopotamia.

muʿallaqah see *great ode.*

Muʿāwiyah ibn Abī Sufyān, Abū ʿAbd al-Raḥmān (Muʿāwiyah I) (r. 41–60/661–80) governor of Syria and a shrewd statesman, he adopted the cause of vengeance for the assassinated caliph ʿUthmān (both belonged to ʿAbd Shams) and established the Sufyānid branch of the Umayyads as a hereditary dynasty.

al-Mubarrad, Abū l-ʿAbbās Muḥammad ibn Yazīd ibn ʿAbd al-Akbar al-Azdī (d. 285/898) famous grammarian of the Basran-Baghdadi school and a rival of Thaʿlab (q.v.).

Muḍar a major tribal group of the northern Arabs (ʿAdnān).

al-Muhallab ibn Abī Ṣufrah, Abū Saʿīd al-Azdī (d. 82/702) member of the Azd tribe, a general under the earliest Righteous Caliphs, governor of Khurasan under the Umayyads, and the founder of the influential Muhallabī family.

al-Muhallabī, Abū Jaʿfar Aḥmad ibn Yazīd (fl. mid-third/ninth century) transmitter of the works of his father Yazīd al-Muhallabī (q.v).

al-Muhallabī, Abū Khālid Yazīd ibn Muḥammad (d. after 248/862) man of letters, transmitter, and poet from the Muhallabī family of governors and literati, whose chronicle he wrote; a companion of Caliph al-Mutawakkil (q.v.).

Muḥammad ibn ʿAbbād see *Ibn ʿAbbād.*

Muḥammad ibn ʿAbd Allāh ibn ʿĀṣim al-Tamīmī see *al-Ḥazanbal.*

Muḥammad ibn ʿAbd al-Malik al-Zayyāt see *Ibn al-Zayyāt.*

Muḥammad ibn ʿAlī ibn ʿĪsā l-Qummī, Abū Jaʿfar (fl. mid-third/ninth century) a notable of Qumm and patron of Abū Tammām and al-Buḥturī.

Muḥammad ibn Dāwūd ibn al-Jarrāḥ, Abū ʿAbd Allāh (d. 296/908) descended from an Iranian family of officials from Dayr Qunnā in southern Iraq which had converted to Christianity and then embraced Islam, he was a capable administrator, serving several Abbasid caliphs, and vizier of Ibn al-Muʿtazz (q.v.) for one day before being executed; an esteemed man of letters, he composed several books, especially on contemporary poets, two of which are preserved.

Muḥammad ibn al-Haytham ibn Shabābah al-Khurāsānī governor of Jabal province and patron of Abū Tammām.

Muḥammad ibn al-Ḥāzim al-Bāhilī, Abū Jaʿfar (fl. end of the second/eighth and the beginning of the third/ninth century) a naturally talented Basran poet who composed much satire, even of caliphs, and praised only Caliph al-Maʾmūn.

Muḥammad ibn Ḥumayd al-Ṭūsī, Abū Muslim (d. 214/829) general of al-Maʾmūn, who fell fighting the rebel Bābak (q.v.); his father, general Ḥumayd (d. 210/825), had assured al-Maʾmūn's victory in the civil war with his brother al-Amīn.

Muḥammad ibn Isḥāq al-Naḥwī see *Abū l-Ṭayyib al-Lughawī.*

Muḥammad ibn Manṣūr ibn Ziyād, known as "the Army Man" (Fatā l-ʿAskar) (fl. first half of the third/ninth century) of Iranian origin and a client of the Barmakids (whose downfall he survived); headed the Land Tax Office under al-Rashīd.

Muḥammad ibn Mūsā ibn Ḥammād al-Barbarī, Abū Aḥmad (d. 294/906–7 or 289/902) prolific Baghdadi historian and author of literary compilations frequently cited by al-Ṣūlī and al-Iṣbahānī (qq.v.).

Muḥammad ibn al-Qāsim ibn Khallād see *Abū l-ʿAynāʾ.*

Muḥammad ibn al-Qāsim ibn Mihrawayh see *Ibn Mihrawayh.*

Muḥammad ibn Sallām see *al-Jumaḥī.*

Muḥammad ibn Ṭāhir II, Abū ʿAbd Allāh (r. 248–59/862–73) governor of Khurasan, prefect of Baghdad, and Iraq (not to be confused with his kinsman Muḥammad ibn ʿAbd Allāh ibn Ṭāhir I, who ruled Baghdad and Iraq from 237/851 to 253/867 as military governor).

Muḥammad ibn Yaḥyā ibn al-Jahm al-Barmakī (fl. first half of the third/ninth century) governor of northern Mesopotamia under al-Maʾmūn and connected with the Muʿtazilī intelligentsia (and possibly affiliated with the Barmakids); he was also a philosopher, scientist, and a famous wit.

Muḥammad ibn Yazīd see *al-Mubarrad.*

Muhammad ibn Yūsuf see *Abū Saʿīd al-Thaghrī.*

Muḥammad ibn Zakariyyā ibn Dīnār al-Ghalābī l-Baṣrī l-Ṣaḥḥāf, Abū ʿAbd al-Raḥmān (d. 298/911) respected Basran historian of Shiʿi leanings who wrote many books on early Alid history.

muḥdath see *Moderns*.

al-Muhtadī (r. 255–56/869–70) Abbasid caliph.

al-Mukhabbal, Abū Yazīd Rabīʿah ibn Mālik al-Saʿdī (d. ca. 13–35/634–56) poet of the early Islamic period from central Arabia.

Mukhallad ibn Bakkār al-Mawṣilī (fl. first half of the third/ninth century) minor Abbasid poet who satirized Abū Tammām and imitated the poet al-ʿAbbās ibn Aḥnaf (d. 188/803 or later).

Muknif, Abū Sulmā l-Madanī (fl. late second/eighth or early third/ninth century) a minor Abbasid poet and descendent of Zuhayr ibn Abī Sulmā (q.v.).

al-Muktafī (r. 289–95/902–8) Abbasid caliph.

al-Muntaṣir (r. 247–48/861–62) Abbasid caliph.

al-Muqtadir (r. 295–317/908–29) Abbasid caliph.

Muṣʿab ibn al-Zubayr, Abū ʿAbd Allāh (or Abū ʿĪsā) (d. 72/691) governor of Iraq under the Umayyads and instrumental in the defeat of the pro-Alid rebel al-Mukhtār (d. 67/687), later fought in defense of the counter-caliphate of his brother ʿAbd Allāh ibn al-Zubayr (q.v.).

Muslim ibn al-Walīd, known as Ṣarīʿ al-Ghawānī (d. 208/823) Kufan poet who praised al-Rashīd, the Barmakids, and other high officials; a forerunner of the modern style combined with natural diction, he stopped composing late in life and destroyed part of his work. He was one of the very few modern poets Abū Tammām borrowed from.

al-Mustaʿīn (r. 248–52/862–66) Abbasid caliph.

al-Muʿtaḍid (r. 279–89/892–902) Abbasid caliph.

al-Muʿtamid (r. 256–79/870–92) Abbasid caliph.

al-Mutanabbī (d. 354/965) a self-declared "prophet" and a difficult character, he was an eminently successful panegyrist of various rulers and high dignitaries. His skill at expressing complex images in pithy language and his creative reuse of the poetic tradition made him the most famous poet in the Arabic language.

al-Muʿtaṣim, Abū Isḥāq (r. 218–27/833–42) Abbasid caliph.

al-Muʿtazz (r. 252–55/866–69) Abbasid caliph.

al-Muttaqī (r. 333–34/944–46) Abbasid caliph.

Muzāḥim ibn Fātik al-Muʿtaḍidī (or al-Muqtadirī), Abū l-Layth (or Abū Fātik) (fl. mid-forth/tenth century) dedicatee of *The Life and Times of Abū Tammām*, addressed and praised in the preface, and recipient of al-Ḥāmid's (q.v.) bequest of his books. He is otherwise unknown.

Nabatean (Nabaṭī) Aramaic-speaking inhabitants of the Syrian and Iraqi countryside.

al-Nābighah al-Dhubyānī, Ziyād ibn Muʿāwiyah (fl. sixth century AD) active at the court of the Lakhmid kings of al-Ḥīrah and the Ghassanid rulers (qq.v.) in Syria, he is considered one of the greatest Arabic poets.

al-Nābighah al-Jaʿdī, Ḥibbān ibn Qays (d. ca. 63/683) a poet who straddled both the pre-Islamic and Islamic eras, and a supporter of ʿAlī ibn Abī Ṭālib (q.v.), was banished in old age to Isfahan by ʿAlī's rival and successor, Muʿāwiyah (q.v.).

Nafnaf servant of the poet Diʿbil (q.v.).

Najāḥ ibn Salamah (fl. mid-third/ninth century) secretary who headed the office of domains under al-Wāthiq (and suffered extortion) and the Office of Financial Inspection under al-Mutawakkil, who was in turn placed in charge of extorting funds from ʿUmar ibn Faraj (q.v.).

al-Najāshī, Qays (or Ṣimʿān) ibn ʿAmr (d. shortly after 49/669) a poet of Abyssinian descent who straddled both the pre-Islamic and Islamic eras, and whose satire was feared.

Najd desert plateau in the center of the Arabian Peninsula and home of several tribes, such as Tamīm, famous for their poetry, and of Ṭayy (q.v.) after their migration north.

al-Namarī see *Manṣūr al-Namarī*.

Naqāʾiḍ see *Flytings*.

naql (copying, transposing) a term denoting various forms of borrowing, such as the borrowing of meaning and/or wording, the transfer of a motif to a different poetic genre, or a transposition of prose into poetry.

nasīb the amatory prelude of an ode (q.v.), as opposed to the independent love lyric (*ghazal*) (q.v.).

Naṣr ibn Manṣūr ibn Bassām, Abū l-ʿAbbās (d. 227/842) head of several government offices under al-Muʿtaṣim and minor patron of Abū Tammām.

Naṣr ibn Sayyār al-Laythī l-Kinānī (d. 131/748) the last Umayyad governor of Khurasan, appointed by Hishām after the death of Asad ibn ʿAbd Allāh al-Qasrī (q.v.) in 120/738.

nawādir (sg. nādirah) stands variously for snippets on grammar and lexicon assembled into compilations and, secondly, choice anecdotes.

Nawbakht (or Naybakht) an Iranian family (whose name means "new fortune") remarkable for its influence on the advancement of learning and on the political legitimization of the Imāmī Shiʿah during the first two Abbasid centuries.

New Style (Ar. badīʿ) the poetic style of the Moderns (*muḥdathūn*) (q.v.), rich in tropes and creative borrowings from older poetry. It arose at the end of the second/eighth century. The debate over its merits accelerated the development of poetics.

Nishapur (Ar. Nīshābūr, Persian Abrashahr) capital of the Ṭāhirids (q.v.) in northeast Iran (Khurasan).

Nizār see *Rabīʿah.*

Nūḥ (Noah) Qurʾanic prophet.

Nūḥ ibn ʿAmr al-Saksakī l-Ḥimṣī (fl. first half of the third/ninth century) a minor patron of Abū Tammām.

al-Nuʿmān III ibn al-Mundhir (r. ca. AD 580–602) Lakhmid king of al-Ḥīrah, vassal of the Sasanians of Persia, and patron of several Arab poets, among them al-Nābighah and Labīd (qq.v.).

Nuṣayb ibn Rabāḥ (d. ca. 111/729) born of a black slave woman, he became a great poet, favored by Umayyad caliphs and princes, for whom he composed panegyrics.

ode (Ar. qaṣīdah) a long (usually panegyric) poem comprising several themes and composed in classical Arabic with a caesura and a continuous rhyme (*qāfiyah*) (q.v.); in the classical sources, it denotes any long poem irrespective of genre.

Palmyra (Ar. Tadmur) city-state in central Syria situated on the caravan trade route and inhabited in late antiquity by ethnic Arabs who left inscriptions in Palmyrenian, a late Aramaic dialect with its own script.

panegyric (Ar. madīḥ) ode celebrating an often high-standing person's virtues, ancestry, and/or merits; the praise is usually introduced by other themes, such as the amatory prelude (*nasīb*) (q.v.) and the camel section (*raḥīl*), and is followed by a dedication and occasionally a request of the poet.

pint see *raṭl.*

plagiarism see *sariqah.*

poetry critics (Ar. al-nuqqād li-l-shiʿr) experts in the field of poetry (*ʿilm al-shiʿr*) (q.v.) as opposed to scholars of language (or philologists).

qāfiyah see *rhyme word.*

al-Qāhir (r. 322–29/934–40) Abbasid caliph.

qaṣīdah see *ode.*

al-Qāsim ibn Ismāʿīl see *Abū Dhakwān.*

Qaṭarī ibn Fujāʾah (d. 78/697 or 79/698) poet and one of the leading Dissidents (q.v.) who refused to support either ʿAlī or Muʿāwiyah in the battle for the caliphate and who believed themselves to be the only true Muslims.

Qays ʿAylān one of the two branches of Muḍar, which along with Rabīʿah constituted the northern Arabs (ʿAdnān).

Qays ibn Zuhayr ibn Jadhīmah al-ʿAbsī (fl. second half of the sixth century) chief of the ʿAbs tribe, which was driven into exile by their sister tribe of Dhubyān (both members of Ghaṭafān) during their long feud, named the War of Dāḥis after the stallion Dāḥis over which the quarrel arose.

Qirqīsiyāʾ town in northwest Mesopotamia, situated on the Khabur River where it flows into the Euphrates.

Qūmis (Greek Komisené) a region southeast of the Caspian Sea between Rayy (modern Tehran) and Khurasan.

Quraysh the tribe of Muḥammad, the Prophet of Islam.

Quṭrabull (or Qaṭrabull) village between Baghdad and ʿUkbarā famous for its wine production and taverns and the site of many jovial outings.

Rabīʿah ibn Nizār a major tribal group of the northern Arabs (ʿAdnān).

al-Rāḍī (r. 322–29/934–40) Abbasid caliph.

rajaz a flexible meter and the type of poetry composed in it, consisting of rhyming half-verses and often devoted to lighter subjects but containing much rare and difficult vocabulary.

Raqabah ibn Maṣqalah al-ʿAbdī (fl. mid-second/eighth century) author of witty sayings and anecdotes.

al-Rashīd, Hārūn (r. 170–93/786–809) Abbasid caliph.

raṭl a measure of volume roughly corresponding to a pint, i.e., 473 milliliters.

reprimand see *admonition.*

rhyme word (Ar. qāfiyah) in classical Arabic poems the continuous end rhyme of a poem, by which poems can be referred to and according to which many poets' collected works (q.v.) are arranged.

rithāʾ see *lament.*

al-Ruḥbah town in western Mesopotamia between Kufa and al-Qādisiyyah.

saga see *sīrah.*

Sahm brother of Abū Tammām.

Sahm ibn Ḥanẓalah ibn Khuwaylid al-Ghanawī (d. ca. 65–86/685–705) a poet and warrior who lived in Syria and who straddled both the pre-Islamic and Islamic eras.

Ṣāliḥ Abū Tammām's assistant and reciter.

Salm ibn ʿAmr al-Khāsir (d. 186/802) a Basran poet and student of Bashshār (q.v.), he composed panegyrics, laments, and poems about his lost fortune (which he later recovered).

al-Samawʾal ibn Gharīḍ ibn ʿĀdiyāʾ (fl. sixth century AD) born to a Ghassanid mother and into a Jewish tribe, he was a poet and the ruler of Taymāʾ and became proverbial for his loyalty.

sariqah (theft) and akhdh (borrowing) the (whole or partial) taking over of the wording and/or meaning of an existing verse, which is judged variously depending on the new verse's quality and whether it was contemporary with or later than its model.

satire see *lampoon.*

Shaʿban (Ar. Shaʿbān) eighth month of the Muslim calendar, which in the earlier Arab solar year fell in the summer.

Sharā, Mount a region proverbial for its lions.

Shawwal (Ar. Shawwāl) tenth month of the Muslim calendar.

al-Sijistānī, Abū Ḥātim Sahl ibn Muḥammad (d. ca. 255/868–69) Basran grammarian specializing in morphology, he formed the link between the generation of his teachers al-Aṣmaʿī (q.v.) and Abū Zayd al-Anṣārī, and that of his student al-Mubarrad (q.v.).

sīrah ancient saga or narrative centered around a historical or pseudo-historical person or also, in the plural, the assembled vitae of such persons; later the term is appropriated for the biography of one individual, beginning with the Prophet.

siyar see *sīrah*.

Sulaymān ibn ʿAbd al-Malik, Abū Ayyūb (r. 96–99/715–17) Umayyad caliph.

Sulaymān ibn ʿAlī ibn ʿAbd Allāh (d. 142/759) early Abbasid prince and uncle of the first Abbasid caliphs al-Ṣaffāh and al-Manṣūr, he served as governor of Basra.

Sulaymān ibn Wahb, Abū Ayyūb (d. 272/885) from a family of secretaries of Christian origin, he served as secretary to al-Maʾmūn, then as vizier for al-Mahdī, and again for al-Muhtadī and al-Muʿtamid (qq.v.); brother of al-Ḥasan ibn Wahb (q.v.).

Taʾabbaṭa Sharran, Thābit ibn Jābir (fl. first half of the sixth century AD) one of the legendary pre-Islamic outcast brigand-poets.

al-Ṭabarī, Abū Jaʿfar Muḥammad ibn Jarīr (d. 310/923) descended from an affluent family in the Caspian province of Ṭabaristān, he settled in Baghdad and became a preeminent historian, jurist, and Qurʾan commentator.

Tadmur see *Palmyra*.

Ṭāhirids (r. 205–78/821–91) semi-independent dynasty in the early Abbasid period established by general Ṭāhir ibn al-Ḥusayn; one branch governed Khurasan in northeast Iran, and the other branch supplied the prefects of Baghdad.

Ṭarafah ibn al-ʿAbd (fl. mid-sixth century AD) important early pre-Islamic poet of the Qays ʿAylān clan whose fame rests on his great ode (q.v.), he is said to have unwittingly delivered his own death warrant.

taṣnīf see *compilation*.

al-Tawwajī, Abū Muḥammad ʿAbd Allāh ibn Muḥammad (d. 230/845 or shortly after) a Qurashī client, he transmitted lexicography and poetry mainly from the philologist Abū ʿUbaydah (d. 210/825) of the Basran school and was connected to the court of al-Wāthiq (q.v.).

Taym al-Lāt ibn Thaʿlabah (changed after Islam to Taym Allāh) tribe belonging, with the ʿAbd Qays and the Bakr ibn Wāʾil, to the tribal group of Rabīʿah ibn Nizār of the northern Arabs (ʿAdnān).

Ṭayy, Ṭayyiʾ a South Arabian tribe that emigrated to the north, where they played an important role in pre-Islamic times, interacting with Arab vassals of the Romans and the Sasanians; in Syriac sources the name became generic for all Arabs (*Ṭayyāyē, Ṭayôyē*).

Thābit Quṭnah, Abū l-ʿAlāʾ Thābit ibn Kaʿb (d. 110/728) minor Umayyad poet of archaic Bedouin style and of Murjiʾī persuasion, i.e., identifying faith with belief to the exclusion of acts. He participated in the campaigns in Transoxania and became a friend of Governor Yazīd ibn al-Muhallab (q.v.); he earned his nickname "Cotton pad" thanks to the bandage he wore over his eye wounded in battle.

Thaʿlab, Abū l-ʿAbbās Aḥmad ibn Yaḥyā l-Shaybānī (d. 291/904) leading grammarian of the Kufan school at the time when its representatives had moved to Baghdad, and rival of al-Mubarrad (q.v.).

theft, literary see *sariqah*.

Theophilos (r. AD 829–42) Byzantine king of the Amorian dynasty.

Tihāmah region comprising the southern half of the west coast of the Arabian Peninsula.

al-Ṭirimmāḥ, al-Ḥakam ibn Ḥakīm, Abū Nafar (or Abū Ḍabībah) (d. 110/728) eloquent poet of the Umayyad middle period who resided in Kufa and was famous for his desert descriptions.

Ṭufayl ibn ʿAwf al-Ghanawī, Abū Qurrān (d. after AD 608) one of the oldest poets of Qays and famous for his horse descriptions, for which he was nicknamed Ṭufayl al-Khayl.

ʿUbayd ibn Ayyūb al-ʿAnbarī, Abū l-Miṭrāb (or Abū l-Miṭrād) al-Liṣṣ ("the Thief") (fl. between mid-second/eighth and mid-third/ninth century) an Umayyad outcast and brigand-poet who described the wild animals and demons of the desert.

ʿUbayd Allāh ibn ʿAbd Allāh ibn Ṭāhir, Abū Aḥmad (d. 300/913) member of the semi-independent dynasty of the Ṭāhirids (q.v.) who ruled Khurasan in northeast Iran, he served three times as prefect of Baghdad (253–55/867–69, 266–71/879–84, and 276–78/890–91) and was also a gifted poet, poetry critic, and composer, who was interested in the sciences as well as a patron of the arts.

Udad an ancestor tribe of the Ṭayy (q.v.), belonging to the southern Arabs (Qaḥṭān).

ʿUmar ibn Abī Rabīʿah (d. 93/712 or 103/721) Meccan poet who later settled in Medina and the most prominent representative of the light-hearted, flirtatious Ḥijāzī style of love lyric (q.v.).

ʿUmar ibn Faraj al-Rukhkhajī (fl. mid-third/ninth century) son of Faraj ibn Ziyād (head of the Office of Private Domains under al-Maʾmūn during the vizierate of al-Ḥasan ibn Sahl), he was high secretary under al-Mutawakkil, when he became a victim of extortion.

ʿUmar ibn Shabbah ibn ʿAbīdah al-Numayrī, Abū Zayd (d. 262/875–76 or a year earlier) Basran Hadith scholar and expert on history as well as poets and poetry, compiled many collections of accounts and is an important source for major works of Arabic literature.

ʿUmar ibn al-Walīd ibn ʿAbd al-Malik (fl. end of first/seventh or beginning of second/eighth century) Umayyad prince, son of al-Walīd I (q.v.).

ʿUmārah ibn ʿAqīl ibn Bilāl ibn Jarīr (d. ca. 232–47/847–61) early Abbasid poet who composed in an archaic style and one of the last poets whose language was regarded as pure and acceptable as linguistic proof; he was a great-grandson of Jarīr (q.v.).

Umayyads (r. 41–132/661–750) the first Islamic dynasty, which ruled from the capital Damascus.

al-ʿUtbī, Abū ʿAbd al-Raḥmān Muḥammad ibn Ubayd al-Umawī (d. 228/842) Basran poet, *adīb*, genealogist, and historian of the Umayyads who authored several books.

Uways ibn ʿĀmir al-Murādī l-Qaranī (d. 37/657) legendary early renunciant who wore only coarse garments and lived in solitude.

al-ʿUzzā pre-Islamic Arabian deity.

Wāʾil see *Bakr ibn Wāʾil.*

al-Walīd ibn ʿAbd al-Malik (Walīd I) (r. 86–96/705–15) Umayyad caliph.

al-Walīd ibn Yazīd (Walīd II) (r. 125–26/743–44) Umayyad caliph whose assassination by rebels led to the break up of the Umayyad caliphate;

as a prince he entertained poets and musicians in his various Syrian residences, and was a gifted poet himself.

waṣf see *description.*

al-Wāthiq (r. 227–32/842–47) Abbasid caliph.

wording (lafẓ) the verbal expression of *maʿnā* (poetic meaning) (q.v.), both being evaluated separately in early Abbasid poetic criticism.

Yaḥyā ibn ʿAlī ibn Yaḥyā l-Munajjim, Abū Aḥmad (d. 300/913) descended from a Zoroastrian Persian family, an *adīb* and companion of several caliphs, he also hosted a rationalist theological circle and expanded his father's (ʿAlī ibn Yaḥyā) (q.v.) book on poets to include those of the early Abbasid period.

Yaḥyā ibn Ḥamzah al-Ḥaḍramī, Abū ʿAbd al-Raḥmān (d. 183/799) respected Hadith scholar and judge of Damascus for three decades.

Yaʿqūb ibn Isḥāq see *al-Kindī.*

Yazīd ibn Ḥātim ibn Qabīṣah ibn al-Muhallab ibn Abī Ṣufrah (d. ca. 170–93/786–809) member of the Muhallabī family, he was governor of Azerbaijan and then Egypt and North Africa (Ifrīqiyah) under the early Abbasids.

Yazīd ibn al-Muhallab ibn Abī Ṣufrah (d. 102/720) son of the general al-Muhallab (q.v.) and his successor to the governorship of Khurasan under the Umayyads; deposed and arrested by al-Ḥajjāj (q.v.), who feared his tribal power base, he sought refuge with prince Sulaymān (q.v.), who reinstated him upon his own accession to the caliphate; arrested for a second time, Yazīd started a revolt in Syria during which he was killed.

Yazīd ibn Muḥammad see *al-Muhallabī.*

Yazīd ibn al-Ṭathriyyah see *Ibn al-Ṭathriyyah.*

Yazīd ibn Walīd (Yazīd III) (r. 126/744) the last Umayyad caliph, he ruled for six months; his nickname "The Reducer" (al-Nāqiṣ) is owed to the fact that he cut the pay of his troops.

Yūnus ibn Ḥabīb, Abū Abd al-Raḥmān (d. 182/798) major Basran grammarian who studied with Bedouins and developed his own grammatical method that included the use of analogy.

al-Zajjāj, Abū Isḥāq Ibrāhīm ibn al-Sarī (d. 311/923) best grammarian of his time and follower of the Basran-Baghdadi method but using Kufan elements; he had left the Kufan grammarian Thaʿlab to become the master pupil of the Basran al-Mubarrad (qq.v.).

zindīq, pl. zanādiq used generally to mean heretic, originally a Manichean dualist and later anyone suspected of unorthodox creed; also frequently used as a label for free-thinking scientists and literati.

Zufar see *Arṭāh ibn Suhayyah.*

Zuhayr ibn Abū Sulmā (d. AD 609) celebrated pre-Islamic poet, known for his gnomic sayings and the meticulous composition of his odes, and author of a great ode (q.v.).

Zuhr a clan of the Iyād tribe (q.v.) of the northern Arabs (ʿAdnān).

Bibliography

‘Abbās, Iḥsān. *Ta’rīkh al-naqd al-adabī ‘inda l-‘arab min al-qarn al-thānī ḥattā l-qarn al-thāmin al-hijrī*. Amman: Dār al-Shurūq li-l-Nashr wa-l-Tawzī‘, 1986.

Abū Ḥanīfah al-Dīnawarī. *The Book of Plants of Abū Ḥanīfa al-Dīnawarī: Part of the Alphabetical Section* (ا - ز). Edited by Bernhard Lewin. Uppsala Universitets Årsskrift 10. Uppsala: Lundequistska; Wiesbaden: Harrassowitz, 1953.

———. *Le dictionnaire botanique d’Abū Ḥanīfa ad-Dīnawarī (Kitāb an-Nabāt, de* س - ي*)*. Edited by Muhammad Hamidullah. Cairo: Institut Français d’Archéologie Orientale du Caire, 1973.

Abū Nuwās, al-Ḥasan ibn Hāni’. *Dīwān*. Edited by Ewald Wagner and Gregor Schoeler (vol. 4). 5 vols. and 2 vols. index. Wiesbaden: Franz Steiner; Berlin: Klaus Schwarz, 1958–2006.

Abū Tammām, Ḥabīb ibn Aws al-Ṭā’ī. *Dīwān bi-sharḥ al-Khaṭīb al-Tibrīzī*. Edited by Muḥammad ‘Abduh ‘Azzām. 4 vols. Cairo: Dār al-Ma‘ārif, 1951–65.

———. *Al-Ḥamāsah*. *See* al-Marzūqī.

———. *Sharḥ al-Ṣūlī li-Dīwān Abī Tammām*. Edited by Khalaf Rashīd Nu‘mān. 3 vols. Baghdad: Wizārat al-A‘lām, 1977.

———. *Al-Waḥshiyyāt wa-huwa l-Ḥamāsah al-ṣughrā*. Edited by ‘Abd al-‘Azīz al-Maymanī l-Rājkūtī and Maḥmūd Muḥammad Shākir. Cairo: Dār al-Ma‘ārif, 1963.

Abū ‘Ubaydah. *Kitāb al-Dībāj*. Edited by ‘Abd Allāh ibn Sulaymān al-Jarbū‘ and ‘Abd al-Raḥmān ibn Sulaymān al-‘Aythamayn. Cairo: Maktabat al-Khānjī, 1991.

———. *Naqāʾiḍ Jarīr wa-l-Farazdaq*. Edited by Anthony Ashley Bevan. 3 vols. Leiden: Brill, 1905–12.

Ahlwardt, Wilhelm. *The Divans of the Six Ancient Poets*. Greifswald, 1869. Reprint, Osnabrück: Biblio Verlag, 1972.

ʿAlī ibn al-Jahm. *Dīwān*. Edited by Khalīl Mardam Bak. Beirut: Lajnat al-Turāth al-ʿArabī, 1949.

Āmidī, Abū l-Qāsim al-Ḥasan ibn Bishr al-. *Al-Muwāzanah bayn shiʿr Abī Tammām wa-l-Buḥturī*. Edited by al-Sayyid Aḥmad Ṣaqr. 2 vols. Cairo: Dār al-Maʿārif, 1960.

Arberry, A. J. *The Koran Interpreted*. London: Allen and Unwin, 1955.

Ashtor, Eliyahu. "Essai sur les prix et les salaires dans l'empire califien." *Rivista degli studi orientali* 36 (1961): 16–69.

ʿAskarī, Abū Hilāl al-Ḥasan ibn ʿAbd Allāh al-. *Dīwān al-maʿānī*. Edited by Muḥammad Salīm Ghānim. 2 vols. Beirut: Dār al-Gharb al-Islāmī, 2003.

———. *Kitāb al-Ṣināʿatayn al-kitābah wa-l-shiʿr*. Edited by ʿAlī Muḥammad al-Bijāwī and Muḥammad Abū l-Faḍl Ibrāhīm. Cairo: ʿĪsā l-Bābī l-Ḥalabī, 1952. Reprint, Cairo: Dār al-Fikr al-ʿArabī, 1971.

Badawi, M.M. "The Function of Rhetoric: Abū Tammām's Ode on Amorium." *Journal of Arabic Literature* 9 (1978): 43–56.

Bashshār ibn Burd. *Dīwān*. Edited by Muḥammad al-Ṭāhir ibn ʿĀshūr. 4 vols. Algiers: al-Sharikah al-Waṭaniyyah li-l-Nashr wa-l-Tawzīʿ, 1976.

Bergsträsser, Gotthelf. *Uṣūl naqd al-nuṣūṣ wa-nashr al-kutub (1931–32)*. Edited by Muḥammad Ḥamdī l-Bakrī. Cairo: Dār al-Kutub, 1969.

Boustany, Said. *Ibn al-Rūmī: Sa vie et son oeuvre*. Beirut: Publications de l'Université Libanaise, 1967.

Bray, Julia. "Third and Fourth Century Bleeding Poetry." *Arabic and Middle Eastern Literature*, 2 (1999): 75–92.

Buḥturī, al-Walīd ibn ʿUbayd al-. *Dīwān*. Edited by Ḥasan Kāmil al-Ṣayrafī. 5 vols. Cairo: Dār al-Maʿārif, 1972–78.

Diʿbil ibn ʿAlī l-Khuzāʿī. *Dīwān*. Edited by ʿAbd al-Ṣāḥib al-Dujaylī. Najaf: Maṭbaʿat al-Aʿrāb, 1962. Reprint, Beirut: Dār al-Kitāb al-Lubnānī, 1972.

EAL Encyclopedia of Arabic Literature. 2 vols. Edited by Julie Scott Meisami and Paul Starkey. London: Routledge, 1998.

EI2 The Encyclopeadia of Islam, second ed. 11 vols. with supplement vol. and index vol. Edited by P. Bearman, Th. Bianquis, C.E. Bosworth, E. van Donzel, and W.P. Heinrichs. Leiden: Brill, 1960–2009.

EI3 Encyclopaedia of Islam, third ed. Edited by Kate Fleet, Gudrun Krämer, Denis Matringe, John Nawas, and Everett Rowson. Leiden: Brill, 2007–.

Gruendler, Beatrice. "Abstract Aesthetics and Practical Criticism in Ninth-Century Baghdad." In *Takhyīl: The Imaginary in Classical Arabic Poetics*, edited by Marlé Hammond and Geert J. van Gelder, 196–220. Oxford: Gibb Memorial Trust, 2008.

———. "Abū Tammām." *EI3*. Accessed February 27, 2014.

———. "Arabic Philology through the Ages." In *World Philology*, edited by Kevin Chang, Benjamin Elman, and Sheldon Pollock, 92–113. Cambridge, MA: Harvard University Press, 2015.

———. "Ibn Abī Ḥajalah." In *Essays in Arabic Literary Biography*, edited by Joseph Lowry and Devin Stewart, 118–25. Wiesbaden: Harrassowitz, 2009.

———. "Leaving Home: *Al-ḥanīn ilā l-awṭān* and its Alternatives in Classical Arabic Literature." In *Visions and Representations of Homeland in Modern Arabic Poetry and Prose Literature*, edited by Sebastian Günther and Stefan Milich. Hildesheim, Zurich, and New York: Georg Olms Publishers, 2015.

———. *Medieval Arabic Praise Poetry: Ibn al-Rūmī and the Patron's Redemption*. London and New York: RoutledgeCurzon, 2003.

———. "Meeting the Patron: An *Akhbār* Type and Its Implications for Muhdath Poetry." In *Ideas, Images, Methods of Portrayal: Insights into Arabic Literature and Islam*, edited by Sebastian Günther, 51–77. Wiesbaden: Harrassowitz, 2005.

———. "Motif vs. Genre: Reflections on the *Dīwān al-Maʿānī* of Abū Hilāl al-ʿAskarī." In *Ghazal as World Literature I: Transformations of a Literary Genre*, edited by Thomas Bauer and Angelika Neuwirth, 57–85. Beirut-Stuttgart: Ergon, 2005.

———. "*Qaṣīda*: Its Reconstruction in Performance and Reception." In *Classical Arabic Humanities in Its Own Terms: Festschrift for Wolfhart*

Heinrichs on His 65th Birthday, edited by Beatrice Gruendler with the assistance of Michael Cooperson, 325–89. Leiden and New York: Brill, 2007.

———. "Verse and Taxes: The Function of Poetry in Selected Literary *Akhbār* of the 3rd/9th Century." In *On Fiction and Adab in Medieval Arabic Literature*, edited by Philip Kennedy, 85–124. Wiesbaden: Harrassowitz, 2005.

Heinrichs, Wolfhart. "An Evaluation of Sariqa." *Quaderni di Studi Arabi* 5–6 (1987–88): 357–68.

———. "Muslim b. al-Walīd und *badīʿ*." In *Festschrift Ewald Wagner zum 65. Geburtstag. Bd. 2: Studien zur arabischen Dichtung*, edited by Wolfhart Heinrichs and Gregor Schoeler, 211–45. Beirut and Wiesbaden: Steiner, 1994.

———. "Paired Metaphors in *Muḥdath* Poetry." *Occasional Papers of the School of Abbasid Studies* 1 (1986): 1–22.

———. "Sariqa." In *EI2*, 12:706–10.

Hindī, Naẓīr al-Islam [Naẓīrul-Islam] al-. "Die *Akhbār* von Abū Tammām von aṣ-Ṣūlī." Ph.D. dissertation, University of Breslau [Wrocław], Poland, 1940.

Hoyland, Robert G. *Arabia and the Arabs: From the Bronze Age to the Coming of Islam*. London and New York: Routledge, 2001.

Ḥuṣrī, Abū Isḥāq Ibrāhīm ibn ʿAlī l-. *Zahr al-ādāb*. Edited by ʿAlī Muḥammad al-Bijāwī. 2 vols. Cairo: ʿĪsā l-Bābī l-Ḥalabī, 1953.

Ḥuṭayʾah, al-. *Dīwān al-Ḥuṭayʾah bi-riwāyat wa-sharḥ Ibn al-Sikkīt*. Edited by Nuʿmān Muḥammad Amīn Ṭāhā. Cairo: Maktabat al-Khānjī, 1987.

Ibn ʿAbd al-Barr, Abū ʿUmar Yūsuf ibn ʿAbd Allāh. *Bahjat al-majālis wa-uns al-mujālis*. Edited by Muḥammad Mursī l-Khūlī. 2 vols. Cairo: al-Dār al-Miṣrī li-l-Taʾlīf wa-l-Tarjamah, 1962. Reprint, 1967–69.

Ibn ʿAbd Rabbih. *Al-ʿIqd al-farīd*. Edited by Muḥammad Saʿīd al-ʿAryān. 8 pts. in 4 vols. Cairo: Dār al-Fikr, 1940.

Ibn al-Anbārī, Abū Bakr Muḥammad ibn al-Qāsim. *Sharḥ al-qaṣāʾid al-sabʿ al-ṭiwāl*. Edited by ʿAbd al-Salām Hārūn. Cairo: Dār al-Maʿārif, 1963. Reprint, 1980.

Ibn al-Jawzī, Abū l-Faraj ʿAbd al-Raḥmān. *Dhamm al-hawā*. Edited by Muṣtafā ʿAbd al-Wāḥid and Muhammad al-Ghazālī. Cairo: Dār al-Kutub al-Ḥadīthah, 1962.

Ibn Khallikān, Abū l-ʿAbbās Shams al-Dīn ibn Muḥammad. *Wafayāt al-aʿyān*. Edited by Iḥsān ʿAbbās. 8 vols. Beirut: 1968–72. Reprint, Beirut: Dār al-Thaqāfah, 1997.

Ibn al-Marzubān al-Karkhī l-Baghdādī, Muḥammad ibn Sahl. *Al-Ḥanīn ilā l-awṭān*. Edited by Jalīl al-ʿAṭiyyah. Beirut: ʿĀlam al-Kutub, 1986–87.

Ibn al-Nadīm. *Al-Fihrist*. Edited by Ayman Fuʾād al-Sayyid. 4 vols. London: al-Furqan Islamic Heritage Foundation, 2009.

Ibn Qutaybah, Abū Muḥammad ʿAbd Allāh ibn Muslim. *Al-Shiʿr wa-l-shuʿarāʾ*. Edited by M. J. de Goeje. Leiden: Brill, 1902.

———. *ʿUyūn al-akhbār*. Edited by Yūsuf ʿAlī Ṭawīl. 2 vols. Beirut: Dār al-Kutub al-ʿIlmiyyah, 1985.

Ibn al-Rūmī, Abū l-Ḥasan ʿAli ibn al-ʿAbbās. *Dīwān*. Edited by Ḥusayn Naṣṣār. 6 vols. Cairo: al-Hayʾah al-Miṣriyyah al-ʿĀmmah li-l-Kitāb, 1973–81.

Iṣbahānī, Abū l-Faraj al-. *Al-Aghānī*. Beirut: Dār al-Thaqāfah, 1955. Reprint, 1981.

Isḥāq ibn Ibrāhīm ibn Wahb al-Kātib, Abū l-Ḥusayn. *Al-Burhān fī wujūh al-bayān*. Edited by Ḥifnī Muḥammad Sharaf. Cairo: Maṭbaʿat al-Risālah, 1969.

Jāḥiẓ, al-, attributed. *See* al-Kisrawī.

Jarīr. *Dīwān*. Edited by Karam al-Bustānī. Beirut: Dār Bayrūt li-l-Ṭibāʿah wa-l-Nashr, n.d.

Jumaḥī, Muḥammad ibn Sallām al-. *Ṭabaqāt fuḥūl al-shuʿarāʾ*. Edited by Maḥmūd Muḥammad Shākir. 2 vols. Cairo: Matbaʿat al-Madanī, 1974.

Khansāʾ, al-. *Dīwān*. Edited by Ibrāhīm Shams al-Dīn. Beirut: Muʾassasat al-Aʿlamī li-l-Maṭbūʿāt, 2001.

Khoury, Raif G. *Wahb b. Munabbih*. 2 vols. Wiesbaden: Harrassowitz, 1972.

Kisrawī, Mūsā ibn ʿĪsā [attributed to al-Jāḥiẓ] al-. *Al-Ḥanīn ilā l-awṭān*. In *Rasāʾil al-Jaḥiẓ*. Edited by ʿAbd al-Salām Hārūn. 4 vols. Cairo: Maktabat al-Khānjī, 1964–79. Reprint, Beirut: Dār al-Jīl, 1991, 2:378–412.

Larkin, Margaret. "Abu Tammām." In *Arabic Literary Culture: 500–925*, edited by Shawkat Toorawa and Michael Cooperson, 33–52. Detroit: Thomson and Gale, 2005.

Leder, Stefan. "Al-Ṣūlī." In *EI2*, 9:846–48.

Marzubānī, Abū ʿUbayd Muḥammad ibn ʿImrān al-. *Muʿjam al-shuʿarāʾ*. Edited by ʿAbd al-Saṭṭār Aḥmad Farrāj. Baghdad: Dār Iḥyāʾ al-Kutub al-ʿArabiyyah, 1960.

———. *Al-Muwashshaḥ fī maʾākhidh al-ʿulamāʾ ʿalā l-shuʿarāʾ*. Edited by Muḥammad Ḥasan Shams al-Dīn. Beirut: Dār al-Kutub al-ʿIlmiyyah, 1995.

Marzūqī, Abū ʿAlī Aḥmad ibn Muhammad al-. *Sharḥ Dīwān al-Ḥamāsah*. Edited by Aḥmad Amīn and ʿAbd al-Salām Hārūn. 2 vols. Cairo: 1951. Reprint, Beirut: Dār al-Jīl, 1991.

Massé, Henri. "Buzurgmihr." In *EI2*, 1:1358–59.

Masʿūdī, al-. *Murūj al-dhahab wa-maʿādin al-jawhar*. Edited by Barbier de Meynard and Pavet de Courteille, revised and corrected by Charles Pellat. 7 vols. Beirut: Lebanese University, 1966–79.

Maydānī, Abū l-Faḍl Ahmad ibn Muḥammad al-. *Majmaʿ al-amthāl*. Edited by Muḥammad Muḥyī l-Dīn ʿAbd al-Ḥamīd. 2 vols. n. pl., n.d.

Meisami, Julie Scott. "Abū Tammām." In *Encyclopedia of Arabic Literature*, 1:47–49.

———. Review of *Abū Tammām and the Poetics of the ʿAbbāsid Age* by Suzanne Stetkevych. *Journal of Arabic Literature*, 25 (1994): 66–76.

Miskawayh. *Al-Ḥikmah al-khālidah, Jāvīdān khirad*. Edited by ʿAbd al-Salām Hārūn. Cairo: Maktabat al-Nahḍah al-ʿArabiyyah, 1952.

Motlagh, Djalal Khaleghi. "Bozorgmehr-e Boktagān." In *Encyclopaedia Iranica*, edited by Ehsan Yarshater, 4:427–29. London and Boston: Routledge and Kegan Paul, 1983.

Mubarrad, Abū l-ʿAbbās Muḥammad ibn Yazīd al-. *Al-Kāmil fī l-lughah wa-l-adab*. Beirut: Maktabat al-Maʿārif, 1 vol. n.d.

Muslim ibn al-Walīd. *Sharḥ Diwān Ṣarīʿ al-Ghawānī Muslim ibn al-Walīd al-Anṣārī*. Edited by Sāmī l-Dahhān. Cairo: Dār al-Maʿārif, 1957.

Nābighah al-Dhubyānī, al-. *Dīwān*. Edited by Muḥammad al-Ṭāhir ibn ʿĀshūr. Algiers: al-Shirkah al-Waṭaniyyah li-l-Tawzīʿ, 1976.

Naqāʾiḍ Jarīr wa-l-Farazdaq. *See* Abū ʿUbaydah.

Osti, Letizia. "Authors, Subjects and Fame in the *Kitāb al-Fihrist* by Ibn al-Nadim: The Case of al-Ṭabarī and al-Ṣūlī." *Annali di Ca' Foscari, Serie Orientale* 38 (1999): 155–70.

———. "In Defence of the Caliph: Abū Bakr al-Ṣūlī and the Virtues of al-Muqtadir." In *'Abbāsid Studies II. Occasional Papers of the School of Abbasid Studies. Leuven, 28 June - 1 July, 2004*, edited by John Nawas, 283–301. Leuven: Peeters, 2010.

———. "Notes on a Private Library in Fourth/Tenth-Century Baghdad." *Journal of Arabic and Islamic Studies* 12 (2012): 215–23.

———. "The Remuneration of a Court Companion in Theory and Practice." *Journal of Abbasid Studies* 1, no. 2 (2014): 85–107.

———. "Al-Ṣūlī and the Caliph: Norms, Practices and Frames." In *Le dialogue dans la culture arabe: Structures, fonctions, significations (VIIIe-XIIIe siècles)*, edited by Mirella Cassarino and Antonella Ghersetti. Soveria Mannelli, Italy: Il Rubbettino, 2015.

———. "Tailors of Stories: Biographers and the Lives of the *Khabar*." *Synergies monde arabe*, 6 (2009): 283–91.

———. "The Wisdom of Youth: Legitimising the Caliph al-Muqtadir." *Al-Masāq* 19 (2007): 17–27.

Ouyang, Wen-chin. *Literary Criticism in Medieval Arabic Islamic Culture.* Edinburgh: Edinburgh University Press, 1997.

Qāḍī l-Quḍā'ī, al-. *A Treasury of Virtues: Sayings, Sermons, and Teachings of 'Alī with the One Hundred Proverbs Attributed to al-Jāḥiẓ.* Edited and translated by Tahera Qutbuddin. New York: New York University Press, 2013.

Qifṭī, Jamāl al-Dīn Abū l-Ḥasan 'Alī ibn Yūsuf (Ibn) al-. *Inbāh al-ruwāh 'alā anbā' al-nuḥāh.* Edited by Muḥammad Abū l-Faḍl Ibrāhīm. 4 vols. Cairo: Maṭba'at Dar al-Kutub al-Miṣriyyah, 1950–74.

Ritter, Hellmut. "Abū Tammām." In *EI2*, 1:153–55.

Seidensticker, Tilman. "Al-Ṣūlī." In *Encyclopedia of Arabic Literature*, 2:744–45.

Sezgin, Fuat. *Geschichte des arabischen Schrifttums. Band I: Qur'ānwissenschaften, Ḥadīth, Geschichte, Fiqh, Dogmatik, Mystik bis ca. 430 H.* Leiden: Brill, 1975.

———. *Geschichte des arabischen Schrifttums. Band II: Poesie bis ca. 430 H.* Leiden: Brill, 1975.

———. *Geschichte des arabischen Schrifttums. Band VIII: Lexikographie bis ca. 430 H.* Leiden: Brill, 1982.

———. *Geschichte des arabischen Schrifttums. Band IX: Grammatik bis ca. 430 H.* Leiden: Brill, 1984.

Sharīf al-Murtaḍā, ʿAlī ibn al-Ḥusayn al-. *Āmālī l-Murtaḍā.* Edited by Muḥammad Abū l-Faḍl Ibrāhīm. 2 vols. Cairo: Dār Iḥyāʾ al-Kutub al-ʿArabiyyah, 1954.

Sourdel, Dominique. *Le Vizirat ʿabbāside de 749 à 936 (132 à 324 de l'hégire).* 2 vols. Damascus: Institut français de Damas, 1959–60.

Stetkevych, Suzanne P. "The Abbasid Poet Interprets History: Three Qaṣīdahs by Abū Tammām." *Journal of Arabic Literature* 10 (1979): 49–64.

———. *Abū Tammām and the Poetics of the ʿAbbāsid Age.* Leiden: Brill, 1991.

Ṣūlī, Abū Bakr Muḥammad ibn Yaḥyā l-. *Akhbār Abī Tammām.* Edited by Khalīl Muḥammad ʿAsākir, Muḥammad ʿAbduh ʿAzzām, and Naẓīr al-Islām al-Hindī. Cairo: Lajnat al-Taʾlīf wa-l-Tarjamah wa-l-Nashr, 1937. Reprint, Beirut: al-Maktab al-Tijārī li-l-Ṭibāʿah wa-l-Tawzīʿ wa-l-Nashr, [1956].

———. *Akhbār al-Buḥturī.* Edited by Ṣāliḥ al-Ashtar. Damascus: al-Majmā l-ʿIlmī l-ʿArabī, 1958.

Ṭabarī, Muḥammad ibn Jarīr al-. *Taʾrīkh al-rusul wa-l-mulūk.* Edited by Muḥammad Abū l-Faḍl Ibrāhīm. 10 vols. Cairo: Dār al-Maʿārif, 1960–69.

Tibrīzī, al-Khaṭīb al-. *See* Abū Tammām.

Ullmann, Manfred. *Wörterbuch der klassischen arabischen Sprache.* 2 vols., Wiesbaden: Harrassowitz, 1970–2000.

Yāqūt, Shihāb al-Dīn Abū ʿAbd Allāh al-Ḥamawī. *Muʿjam al-buldān.* Edited by Muḥammad ʿAbd al-Raḥmān al-Marʿashlī. 4 vols. Beirut: Dār al-Iḥyāʾ al-Turāth al-ʿArabī, n.d.

Zakeri, Mohsen. *Persian Wisdom in Arabic Garb: ʿAlī b. ʿUbayda al-Rayḥānī (d. 219/834) and his Jawāhir al-kilam wa-farāʾid al-ḥikam.* 2 vols. Leiden: Brill, 2007.

Further Reading

Further Works by al-Ṣūlī

Ṣūlī, Abū Bakr Muḥammad ibn Yaḥyā l-. *Adab al-kuttāb*. Edited by Ahmad Ḥasan Basaj. Beirut: Dār al-Kutub al-ʿIlmiyyah, 1994.

———. *Al-Awrāq (ashʿār awlād al-khulafāʾ wa-akhbāruhum)*. Edited by J. Heyworth Dunne. London: Luzac, 1936.

———. *Al-Awrāq (qism akhbār al-shuʿarāʾ)*. Edited by J. Heyworth Dunne. London: Luzac, 1934.

———. *Al-Awrāq (akhbār al-Rāḍī bi-llāh wa-l-Muttaqī li-llāh)*. Edited by J. Heyworth Dunne. London: Luzac, 1935.

———. *Mā lam yunshar min Awrāq al-Ṣūlī (akhbār al-sanawāt 295–315)*. Edited by Hilāl Nājī. Beirut: ʿĀlam al-Kutub, 2000.

Khalidov, Anas B. "An Unpublished Portion of *Kitāb al-Awrāq* by aṣ-Ṣūlī in a Unique Petersburg Manuscript (Russian)." In *Ibn al-Nadīm und die mittelalterliche Literatur. Beiträge zum 1. Johann Wilhelm Fück-Kolloquium (Halle 1987)*. Wiesbaden: Harrassowitz, 73–77.

General Works on Classical Arabic Literature

Allen, Roger. *The Arabic Literary Heritage: The Development of Its Genres and Criticism*. Cambridge: Cambridge University Press, 1998.

———. *An Introduction to Arabic Literature*. Cambridge: Cambridge University Press, 2000.

Ashtiany [Bray], Julia, T.M. Johnstone, J.D. Latham, and R.B. Serjeant, eds. *ʿAbbasid Belles-Lettres*. The Cambridge History of Arabic Literature. Cambridge: Cambridge University Press, 1990.

Bray, Julia. "Arabic Literature." In *Islamic Cultures and Societies to the End of the Eighteenth Century*, edited by Robert Irwin, 383–413. The New Cambridge History of Islam. Cambridge: Cambridge University Press, 2010.

Beeston, A. F. L., T.M. Johnstone, R.B. Sergjeant, and G.R. Smith, eds. *Arabic Literature to the End of the Umayyad Period*. The Cambridge History of Arabic Literature. Cambridge: Cambridge University Press, 1983.

Gätje, Helmut, ed. *Grundriss der arabischen Philologie, vol. 2: Literaturwissenschaft*. Wiesbaden: Reichert, 1987.

Gruendler, Beatrice, Verena Klemm, and Barbara Winkler. "Literatur." In *Einführung in den Islam*, edited by Rainer Brunner. Stuttgart: Kohlhammer Verlag, 2015.

Heinrichs, Wolfhart, ed. *Orientalisches Mittelalter*. Neues Handbuch der Literaturwissenschaft. Wiesbaden: Aula, 1990.

Kilito, Abdelfattah. *The Author and His Doubles: Essays on Classical Arabic Culture*. Translated by Michael Cooperson. Syracuse, New York: Syracuse University Press, 2001. Originally published as *L'auteur et ses doubles. Essai sur la culture arabe classique* (Paris: Éditions du Seuil, 1985).

Toelle, Heidi, and Katia Zakharia. *A la découverte de la littérature arabe du VIe siècle à nos jours*. Paris: Flammarion, 2003.

Classical Arabic Poetry and Poetics

Antoon, Sinan. *The Poetics of the Obscene in Premodern Arabic Poetry: Ibn al-Ḥajjāj and Sukhf*. New York: Palgrave Macmillan, 2014.

Gruendler, Beatrice. *Medieval Arabic Praise Poetry: Ibn al-Rūmī and the Patron's Redemption*. London and New York: RoutledgeCurzon, 2003.

Jacobi, Renate. *Studien zur Poetik der altarabischen Qaside*. Wiesbaden: Steiner, 1971.

Meisami, Julie S. *Structure and Meaning in Medieval Arabic and Persian Poetry*. London: RoutledgeCurzon, 2003.

Schoeler, Gregor. "The Genres of Classical Arabic Poetry: Classifications of Poetic Themes and Poems by Pre-Modern Critics and Redactors of *Dīwāns*." *Qaderni di studi arabi N.S.* 5–6 (2010–11): 1–48.

Stetkevych, Suzanne P., ed. *Early Islamic Poetry and Poetics*. Farnham, Surrey: Ashgate Variorum, 2009.

———. *The Poetics of Islamic Legitimacy: Myth, Gender and Ceremony in the Classical Arabic Ode*. Bloomington: Indiana University Press, 2002.

Szombathy, Zoltan. *Mujūn: Libertinism in Mediaeval Muslim Society and Literature*. Warminster: Gibb Memorial Trust, 2013.

Van Gelder, Geert Jan. "Muḥdathūn." In *EI2*, 12:637–40.

———. *Sound and Sense in Classical Arabic Poetry*. Wiesbaden: Harrassowitz, 2012.

Wagner, Ewald. *Grundzüge der klassischen arabischen Dichtung*. 2 vols. Darmstadt: Wissenschaftliche Buchgesellschaft, 1987–88.

Abbasid Court Culture, Patronage, and the Emergence of the Book

Ali, Samer. *Arabic Literary Salons in the Islamic Middle Ages: Poetry, Performance and the Presentation of the Past*. Notre Dame, IN: University of Notre Dame Press, 2010.

Gruendler, Beatrice. "*Tawqīʿ* (Apostille): Verbal Economy in Verdicts of Tort Redress." In *The Weaving of Words: Approaches to Classical Arabic Literature*, edited by Lale Behzadi and Vahid Behmardi, 101–29. Beirut and Wiesbaden: Ergon, 2009.

Gruendler, Beatrice, and Louise Marlow, eds. *Writers and Rulers: Perspectives on Their Relationship from Abbasid to Safavid Times*. Wiesbaden: Reichert, 2004.

Günther, Sebastian. "Assessing the Sources of Classical Arabic Compilations: The Issue of Categories and Methodologies." *British Journal of Middle Eastern Studies* 32 (2005): 75–98.

Kilpatrick, Hilary. *Making the Great Book of Songs: Compilation and the Author's Craft in Abū l-Faraj al-Iṣbahānī's Kitāb al-Aghānī*. London: RoutledgeCurzon, 2003.

Schoeler, Gregor. *The Genesis of Literature in Islam: From the Aural to the Read*. Translated by Shawkat Toorawa. Edinburgh: Edinburgh University Press, 2009. Expanded from the original version, *Écrire et transmettre dans les débuts de l'Islam* (Paris: Presses Universitaires de France, 2002.)

———. *The Oral and the Written in Early Islam*. Translated by Uwe Vagelpohl and edited by James E. Montgomery. Oxford and New York: Routledge, 2006.

Sharlet, Jocelyn. *Patronage and Poetry in the Islamic World: Social Mobility and Status in the Medieval Middle East and Central Asia*. London and New York: I. B. Tauris, 2011.

Toorawa, Shawkat. *Ibn Abī Ṭāhir Ṭayfūr and Arabic Writerly Culture: A Ninth-Century Bookman in Baghdad*. London and New York: RoutledgeCurzon, 2005.

Toorawa, Shawkat, and Michael Cooperson, eds. *Arabic Literary Culture: 500–925*. Detroit: Thomson and Gale, 2005.

Translations

Farrin, Raymond. *Abundance from the Desert: Classical Arabic Poetry*. Syracuse, NY: Syracuse University Press, 2011.

Irwin, Robert, ed. *Night and Horses and the Desert: An Anthology of Classical Arabic Literature*. New York: Anchor Books, 1999.

Van Gelder, Geert Jan. *Classical Arabic Literature: A Library of Arabic Literature Anthology*. New York: New York University Press, 2013.

Index

Aḥmad ibn Yazīd. *See* al-Muhallabī
Aḥnaf ibn Qays al-Tamīmī, §77, §110.1
Ahwāz, §120, §177
al-ʿAkawwak. *See* ʿAlī ibn Jabalah
akhbār, khabar. See accounts
akhdh. See borrowing
al-Akhṭal, Ghiyāth ibn Ghawth ibn al-Ṣalt, §7.3, §13.6, §22.1, §§86.5–7
ʿAlī ibn al-ʿAbbās ibn Jurayj al-Rūmī. *See* Ibn al-Rūmī
ʿAlī ibn Abī Ṭālib, §69.10, §87.4
ʿAlī ibn al-Ḥasan the Scribe (transmitter), §164
ʿAlī ibn al-Ḥusayn ibn Yaḥyā the Scribe (transmitter), §74
ʿAlī ibn Ismāʿīl al-Nawbakhtī, Abū l-Ḥasan, §59, §85
ʿAlī ibn Jabalah al-ʿAkawwak, §§13.4–5, §62
ʿAlī ibn al-Jahm, xxxiii, §§31–33, §69.2, §91.2, §179, 189n92, 214n475
ʿAlī ibn Muḥammad al-Anbārī, Abū l-Ḥasan (transmitter), §40.1
ʿAlī ibn Yaḥyā ibn Abī Manṣūr al-Munajjim, Abū l-Ḥasan, §24.2, §24.7
allusion, §78.5, 207n378, 208n393; Qurʾanic, 199n246, 200n263
al-Āmidī, Abū l-Qāsim al-Ḥasan ibn Bishr, xxvi, 190n100, 197n215, 197n216, 209n415
Amorium (Ar. ʿAmmūriyyah), xii xvi–xviii, xxiii, xxxiv, §20.2, §20.5, §§61.2–3, §73, 187n54, 194n178, 199n245
ʿAmr ibn Abī Qaṭīfah, (transmitter), §163
ʿAmr ibn Ḥafṣ al-Minqarī (transmitter), §92.5
ʿAmr ibn Hāshim al-Sarawī (transmitter), §152
ʿAmr ibn Hind, §69.15
ʿAmr ibn Kulthūm, 198n220
ʿAmr ibn Maʿdīkarib (Abū Thawr), §§106.1–2, §110.1, 207n379, 208n382, 208n387
analogy (*tamthīl*), §110.1, 210n425
ancestry, §23.1, §24.4, §§59–60, §83, §89.8, §115, 208n395, 208n398, 210n419, 214n472, 214n473
Ancients (*mutaqaddimūn*), xvii, xxvi, xxxii, xxxvi, §9.1–2, §11.1–2, §14.1, §18, §20.6, §23.1, §24.15, §35, §51.1, §61.1, §61.3, §69.9, §103, §109
anecdote. *See nādirah*
anthology, anthologies, 185n12, 185n14; about Abū Tammām, §10.1; by Abū Tammām, xxiv, xxxii, 186n26, 197n216, 198n225, 198n226, 201n278, 206n367, 210n422, 210n426, 210n430, 213n465
antithesis, antitheses, xxiv
apology (*iʿtidhār*), xxxvi, §§13.1–2, §25.1, §69.13, §76, §§78.2–3, §78.5, §95.2, §143, 199n238
Aquila (constellation), §8, 184n8
ʿarabiyyah. See classical Arabic
Armenia, §79.1, 201n274
Arṭāh ibn Suhayyah al-Murrī (Arṭāh ibn Zufar ibn ʿAbd Allāh), §149
Asad ibn ʿAbd Allāh al-Qasrī, §143
al-Aʿshā, Maymūn ibn Qays, §22.8, §86.5
Ashjaʿ al-Sulamī, Abū l-Walīd, §33
al-Aṣmaʿī, Abū Saʿīd ʿAbd al-Malik ibn Qurayb, §17.1, §19.4, §§51.1–2, §69.8, §71.6, §127.2

Hārūn ibn Muḥammad ibn ʿAbd al-Malik (al-Zayyāt, Abū Mūsā), §173
Hārūn al-Rashīd. *See* al-Rashīd.
al-Ḥasan ibn Rajāʾ, §65.1, §§82–84, §86.1, §90, §92.2
al-Ḥasan ibn ʿUlayl al-ʿAnazī, §132
al-Ḥasan ibn Wahb al-Ḥārithī, Abū ʿAlī, xxxiii, §61.1, §§61.3–4, §66.1, §91.1, §92.1, §§93.1–2, §93.4, §94.2, §95.1, §98, §167, §169, §174, §178, §181, 192n138, 192n143, 195n182, 205n338
Hāshim, Banū, §7.3, §61.1
Ḥātim al-Ṭāʾī, §77, §110.1
Ḥayr (castle), §78.1
al-Haytham ibn ʿAdī ibn ʿAbd al-Raḥmān al-Ṭāʾī, Abū ʿAbd al-Raḥmān, §95.3
al-Ḥazanbal, Abū ʿAbd Allāh Muḥammad ibn ʿAbd Allāh ibn ʿĀṣim al-Tamīmī l-Iṣbahānī, §22.7, §69.1
heretic. *See zindīq*
hijāʾ. *See* lampoon
Ḥimyar, §116.1, §152
al-Ḥīrah, 195n195
Hishām ibn ʿAbd al-Malik, §140.2, §143, §151
honor (in poetry), §24.1–2, §24.6, §24.10, §24.21, §§47.7–8, §52.5, §60, §116.1, §183, 214n476
hope (*rajāʾ*) (expressed in poetry), §34.1, §43.1, §47.11, §61.2, §78.2, §80.1, §82, §93.4, §94.1, §96, §104, §106.1, §111, §168, §180, §183, 201n285
horse. *See* description
Ḥudhāq, §78.5
Ḥujr ibn Aḥmad §20.5
Ḥumayd, Banū, §91.5, 203n319
Ḥumayd ibn ʿAbd al-Ḥamīd al-Ṭūsī, Abū Ghānim, §13.4, §107
al-Ḥusayn ibn ʿAlī, Abū ʿAbd Allāh (transmitter), §38
al-Ḥusayn ibn al-Ḍaḥḥāk. *See* al-Khalīʿ
al-Ḥuṣayn ibn al-Ḥumām ibn Rabīʿah al-Murrī, §147
al-Ḥusayn ibn Wadāʾ (transmitter), §92.2
al-Ḥuṣrī, Abū Isḥāq Ibrāhīm ibn ʿAlī, xxvi
al-Ḥuṭayʾah, Jarwal ibn Aws al-ʿAbsī, §24.9, §24.15, §168
hyperbole, exaggeration, §72.2, 189n96, 204n326, 208n395
hyrax, §116.1

Ibn ʿAbbād, Abū Jaʿfar Muḥammad, the Scribe, §24.13
Ibn ʿAbd Kān, Abū Jaʿfar Muḥammad, §67
Ibn Abī Duʾād, Abū ʿAbd Allāh Aḥmad, §72.1, §73–§77, §§78.2–5, §80.2, §104, §167, 200n257
Ibn Abī Khaythamah (Abū Bakr Aḥmad al-Nasāʾī), §122.2
Ibn Abī Rabīʿah. *See* ʿUmar ibn Abī Rabīʿah
Ibn Abī Saʿd (transmitter), §81.2
Ibn Abī Ṭāhir Ṭayfūr, Abū l-Faḍl Aḥmad, xxxvii, §24.18, §53, §86.3, §100.6, §133, §§134.1–2, §§135–138, §140.1, §141, §§142–154, 210n429
Ibn Abī ʿUyaynah the Younger, Abū l-Minhāl Abū ʿUyaynah ibn Muḥammad, §65.2

imitation, xv–xvi, xxxiv–xxxv, xln21, xlin24, §§40.2–3, §43.3, §69.24, §93.4, 209n400. *See also* emulation
improvisation (*ijāzah*), xiii, xxxv, §83, §98, 200n252, 202n289. *See also* continuation (of improvisation) (*ijāzah*)
Imru' al-Qays, §12.1, §20.6, §69.22, §86.5, 198n221
insult, §69.10, §87.6, §99.2; of Abū Tammām, §9.2, §69.6, §94.1, §95.1, §110.1, §118; of al-Ṣūlī, §6.2; used in poetry, xvii, §§24.10–11, §24.19, §24.21, §§24.25–26, §121, §168, 208n392. *See also* lampoon (*hijā'*)
innovation, innovativeness (poetic), xvi, xxx, xxxiii–xxxiv, xxxvii, §11.1, §23.2, §61.3, 196n198. *See also* Moderns, New Style
intercessor, intercession, §34.1, §78.5, §78.7, §80.2, §87.1
invention, inventiveness (poetic), xvi, xxiv, xxxii, xxxv, §11.1, §26.1, §52.8, §72.1. *See also* Moderns, New Style
i'rāb. *See* case endings
'Iṣābah al-Jarjarā'ī, Abū Isḥāq Ismā'īl ibn Muḥammad (or Ibrāhīm ibn Bādhām), §90
al-Iṣbahānī, Abū l-Faraj 'Alī ibn al-Ḥusayn, xxvi, 213n462
Isḥāq ibn Ibrāhīm ibn Ḥusayn al-Muṣ'abī, §73, §§102–104
Isḥāq ibn Ibrāhīm al-Mawṣilī, §103, 202n298
Ismā'īl ibn 'Abd Allāh (transmitter), §154
Ismā'īl ibn Bulbul, Abū l-Ṣaqr, §43.5
Ismā'īl ibn Muhājir (transmitter), §81.2
isnād (chain of transmission), xxvii, §78.2, 200n254, 201n288, 210n429. *See also* transmission, transmitter
Iyād (tribe), §78.3, §78.5, 200n257
Iyās ibn Mu'āwiyah ibn Qurrah al-Muzanī, §110.1

al-Jabal (or al-Jibāl) (province), §92.2
Jarīr ibn 'Aṭiyyah ibn Khaṭafā, xxxvii, §7.3, §24.24, §69.19, §§86.5–6, §§89.2–4, §§89.6–7, §101.3, §161.4, 202n300, 203n306, 212n448
Jāsim, §29, §114
Jesus, §119
Joseph (Yūsuf), 206n359, 212n451
judge, xxxiii, §41.2, §49.2, §74, §78.2, §89.7, §91.2, §93.1, §101.2, §106.1, §133
al-Jumaḥī, Abū 'Abd Allāh Muḥammad ibn Sallām, §§89.3–89.4, §§89.6–89.7
al-Junayd ibn 'Abd al-Raḥmān al-Murrī, §172

Ka'b, Banū, §69.12
Ka'b ibn Zuhayr, §71.3, §74
Kalb (tribe), §116.1, §138
Karbalā', battle of, §97
Kayyis, §77
khabar. *See* accounts
Khalaf al-Aḥmar, §86.6, 199n236
al-Khalī', Abū 'Alī l-Ḥusayn ibn al-Ḍaḥḥāk al-Ashqar al-Baṣrī, §100.2, §114
Khālid al-Ḥadhdhā (poet), §114
Khālid ibn Yazīd ibn Ḥātim, §60

matching (of style) (*taqdīr*), xlin24, §48.1, §83, 190n100
mathal, tamaththul. See pithy saying
mawlā. See freed slave
Maymūn ibn Hārūn (transmitter), §170
meaning, xxxiv–xxxv, xlin24, §22.8, §26.1, §47.1, §47.6, §69.19, §100.2, 190n100, 190n117, 191n121, 192n140, 194n171, 196n206, 200n266. *See also maʿnā*
men of letters, literati, §46.1, §72.2, §83. *See also* culture, men of merchandise (in poetry), §66.2, §99.1
metaphor(s) (*istiʿārah*), xxxii, xxxiv, 194n171, 195n193, 197n213, 198n223, 200n264, 203n322, 205n348; combination of (formal unity), 186n30; of city as woman, 194n177; of commerce, 202n291; of fever for generosity, §§21.1–21.6; of travel, 187331n46; of water, xxxvi, §§22.1–10, 186n27, 186n29, 192n146; of wing of humility, §22.8
Miṣmaʿ, Banū, §24.10
Mithqāl, Abū Jaʿfar Muḥammad ibn Yaʿqūb al-Wāsiṭī, §63
Modern(s) (muḥdath(ūn), xxv–xxvi, xxix, xxxi–xxxii, xxxvi, §4.6, §9.2, §11.1–2, §20.6, §23.1, §33, §35, §61.1, §72, §88.2, 184n2. *See also* motif(s) (of poetry), Modern
money, xxix, §36.1, §49.2, §74, §79.1, §93.2, §138, 192n138
moon (in poetry), xxxiv, §4.5, §8, §12.3, §24.14, §24.18, §30, §48.4, §50.2, §52.7, §60, §§69.4–6, §69.11, §69.15, §§69.17–21, §78.5, §92.3, §93.1, §94.1, §101.1, §150, §172, 196n208, 297n213, 197n216
Mosul (Ar. al-Mawṣil), xxiii, xxvii, §92.1, §113, §§174–175, §§177–178
motif(s) (of poetry), borrowed, taken, reused, §6.1, §13.4, §15.2, §25.2, §26.1, §37, §40.3, §43.1, §47.3, §§69.14–20, 187n47, 187n60, 188n85, 193n158, 196n198, 196n201, 206n362; common, shared, §§43.3–6, §52.8, 190n100; criticized, found fault with, xxxiv, §20.2, §40.3, §124, 196n208, 197n216, 199n245, 205n344; entitlement to, §26.1, §§34.1–2, §81.5; evaluation of, §69.6; expanded, development of, xxxii, xxxv, xln20, §11.1, §13.4, §30, §40.3, §46.5, §51.1, §65.2; falling short in, §37, §47.8; lifted, stolen, plagiarized, xxxiv, §§34.1–2; Modern, xxxii, §11.1, §24.15, §§65.1–2, §109, 184n5, 186n30, 193n165, 194n173, 197n213; novel, innovative, coined, xxiv, xxxv, §11.1, §26.1, §43.7, §51.1, §61.1, §§72.1–2, §78.4, §96, §100.3, §103, §177, 198n229; of abandoned campsite, §11.1, §92.4, 188n85, 198n219, 198n222; of dignity as a gift, §§34.1–2; of dog barking at stars, §§24.14–16; of eagles following army, §81.2–3, §§81.5–6; of fallen moon, xxxiv, §69.5, §§69.10–28, §94.1; of falling in love through sound, §70.3, 198n229; of fate defeating virtue, §25.5, §47.5; of figs and grapes, xxxiv, §§20.1–6; of friendship outweighing kinship, §§41.1–2; of impossible escape, §§13.1–4; of insanity, §§21.1–6; of love for death, §45, §71.8; of people not worth a lampoon, §§24.1–9,

al-Namarī. *See* Manṣūr al-Namarī
naql (copying, transposing) (of poetry), xln21, xlin24, 190n100, 197n212. *See also* borrowing, *sariqah*
nasīb (amatory prelude), 189n213
Naṣr ibn Manṣūr ibn Bassām, Abū l-ʿAbbās, §165
Naṣr ibn Sayyār al-Laythī l-Kinānī, §143, 189n93
Nawbakht (or Naybakht), Banū, §§10.1–2
New Style (*badīʿ*), xxiv, 329n2. *See also* Moderns
Nishapur. *See* Abrashahr
Nizār. *See* Rabīʿah
novelty (in poetry), xxxv, §26.1, §52.8, §66.1, §177
Nūḥ (Noah), §116.3, 209n402
Nūḥ ibn ʿAmr al-Saksakī l-Ḥimṣī, §47.5
al-Nuʿmān III ibn al-Mundhir, §13.1, §69.13, §78.4, §78.8, 200n261
Nuṣayb ibn Rabāḥ, §69.20

ode (*qaṣīdah*), xii, xvi–xviii, xxiii, xxxiii–xxxiv, §13.1, §44.2, §81.2, §83, §§94.1–2, §96, §103, §105, §110.1, §125, §135, §168, 195n23, 187n52, 188n66, 189n96, 191n124, 191n132, 193n162, 194n170, 194n173, 195n182, 196n198, 196n203, 199n245, 206n354, 207n379, 208n389, 210n416; abridgment of, xxiv, xxxiv, xxxvi, xxxviii, 193n152, 194n173, 194n182, 196n198, 205n349; selection from, §61.4, 195n182. *See also* great ode
originality (*ibdāʿ*), xxxv, xln20, §2.1, 184n2. *See also* New Style, self-reliance, innovation, invention

page (*ghulām*), §93.1–4, §98, §170
Palmyra (Ar. Tadmur), §40.1
panegyric, praise poem (*madīḥ*), xxii–xxiii, xxx, xxxvi, §8, §13.4, §§40.2–3, §§43.3–7, §59, §62, §§66.1–2, §68, §§69.1–5, §§69.13–15, §71.3, §§72.1–2, §73, §78.2, §§78.4–5, §79.2, §§81.1–2, §§82–83, §89.1, §90, §92.1, §92.4, §93.3, §96, §103, §105, §107, §110.1, §118, §120, §125, §129, §135, §143, §150, §160, §165, 186n26, 188n66, 188n79, 188n83, 189n96, 193n162, 193n164, 194n170, 199n244, 199n249, 204n332, 206n362, 208n387, 211n436
panegyrist, praise poet, xxii, §74
paronomasia, 187n53, 204n329, 205n345, 205n347, 207n376, 214n477, 214n478. *See also* pun
patron(s), xiv, xxiii–xxiv, xxvii, xxix–xxx, xxxii–xxxiii, 188n72, 199n249, 201n271, 206n358, 207n370, 209n411, 211n436. *See also* gift(s) (of patron)
performance context, xxiii, §3
Persian, xxiv–xxv, §69.1, §100.2, §116.2, 203n310; language, xxv, §100.1
personification, xxiv, 193n156, 207n368, 211n440
petitioner(s), §46.5, §48.3, §52.3, §83, §99.1, §104
philosopher(s), §69.9
physiomancy (*firāsah*), 208n393
pint. *See raṭl*

pithy saying (*mathal*), xxv, §2.2, §7.3, §11.2, §172
plagiary. *See* borrowing, *sariqah*
praise poem. *See* panegyric
praise poet. *See* panegyrist, poet laureate
poem of praise. *See* panegyric
poet, professional, xxiii, xxxiv
poet laureate, §99.2, §106.1. *See also* panegyrist
poetry, apprentice, apprenticeship in, xxiii, §87.1; classical Arabic, xiv, xvi, xxii; discipline of *see* knowledge, literary; income from, xxiii, xxv; payment, reward for, xxiii–xxv, xxix, xxxiv, §34.2, §41.1, §43.3, §64.3, §§69.3–4, §71.3, §74, §79.2, §§81.1–6, §§82–83, §87.1, §101.4, §105, §106.2, §§107–109, §116.3, §160, 188n72, 196n199, 199n242, 207n374, 207n378, 211n441; recipient(s) of, xxiii, §74, §108, 208n386, 211n436
poetry critics (*al-nuqqād li-l-shiʿr*), xxiv–xxv, xxx–xxxii, xxxvi, §7.2, §10.2, §20.4, §21.1, §23.1, §23.7, §24.6, §52.8, §69.21, §70.1, §71.1, §71.3, §86.4, 196n208
Potiphar, 212n451
prose, xvi, xviii, §2.1, §23.3, §57, §61.1, §69.15, §87.1, §93.1, §122.2, 204n336
pun, word play, 186n37, 187n54, 192n144, 194n181, 196n200, 196n206, 199n245, 201n274, 201n283, 201n285, 202n290, 203n321, 205n343, 207n380, 207n381, 209n402, 209n406, 209n412, 211n446, 212n446, 214n469. *See also* paronomasia
qāfiyah. *See* rhyme word
al-Qāhir (Abbasid caliph), xxvii
al-Qaʿqāʿ, Banū, §94.1
qaṣīdah. *See* ode
al-Qāsim ibn Ismāʿīl. *See* Abū Dhakwān
Qaṭarī ibn Fujā'ah, §95.3
Qays ʿAylān (tribe), §94.1, §116.1
Qays ibn Zuhayr ibn Jadhīmah al-ʿAbsī, §166
Qilābah al-Jarmī (transmitter), §147
Qirqīsiyā', §40.3
Qūmis (Greek Komisené), §99.2
Quraysh, §4.1, §43.7, §44.6, §71.3
Quṭrabull (or Qaṭrabull), §40.2, 188n73

Rabīʿah ibn Nizār (tribe), §60, §69.3, §80.1
al-Rāḍī, xxvii
rajā'. *See* hope
rajaz, §43.7, §87.2, §129
Raqabah ibn Maṣqalah al-ʿAbdī, §144
al-Rashīd, Hārūn, §52.6, §74
raṭl, §91.4
al-Rāzī, Abū Sahl (transmitter), §72.1, §160
reception (literary), xxv, xxx, xxxixn6
recite, recitation, xvi–xvii, xxxvi, §2.2, §7.2, §9.1, §10.2, §14.1, §20.4, §22.7, §23.6, §§23.8–9, §24.15, §25.3, §25.5, §30, §36.1, §40.1, §40.3, §50.1, §52.3, §55.2, §56, §§59–60, §61.1, §64.1, §66.1, §69.1, §69.8, §69.11, §69.15, §69.18, §71.2, §§72.1–2, §73, §75, §77, §81.2, §§82–83, §87.2, §§89.2–3, §89.8, §90, §91.2, §92.2, §92.5, §93.3, §94.2, §97, §98, §100.2, §101.1, §103, §106.1,

§§110.1–2, §111, §115, §116.1, §§123–125, §129, §135, §160, §161.4, §165, §172, §177, §180, 185n23, 187n46, 187n52, 187n54, 191n124, 191n132, 199n245, 206n354, 207n378, 208n389, 211n442, 212n450; repetition of, §167, 213n457
reprimand. *See* admonition
reward. *See* poetry
rhyme word/letter (*qāfiyah*), xvi, §96, 185n20, 190n117, 191n118, 203n306, 205n343
rhymed prose (*saj'*), 204n336
rithā'. *See* lament
robe of honor, xxix, §§92.1–2, §93.4, §99.2, §165
al-Ruḥbah, §113

Ṣafiyyah al-Bāhiliyya, §69.18, 197n217
saga. *See sīrah*
Sahm, §158, §159
Sahm ibn Ḥanẓalah ibn Khuwaylid al-Ghanawī, §71.7
Ṣāliḥ, §98, §170
Salm ibn 'Amr al-Khāsir, §§13.2–3, §13.6
Samarra, xxx, §49.1, §73, §78.1
al-Samaw'al ibn Gharīḍ ibn 'Ādiyā', §71.8
Ṣamṣām (sword), §106.1, 207n379
sariqah (theft, plagiary), xxxv, xln21, xlin23, §4.7, §47.1, §78.4, §52.8, 190n100, 196n205, 197n212. *See also* borrowing (*akhdh*)
satire. *See* lampoon
scholar(s), xiv, xxv–xxvi, xxix–xxx, xxxii, xxxvii, xxxixn7, §§2.1–2, §2.4, §3, §4.1, §4.3, §§5.1–2, §7.3, §§9.1–2, §20.6, §23.3, §26.1, §32, §42.2, §§69.7–8, §86.5, §87.1, §87.3, §89.9, §95.2, §101.3, 196n206
scribe, xiii, xxiii, xxv, xxix–xxx, xxxiii–xxxiv, xlin24, §10.1, §20.5, §24.13, §24.28, §61.1, §69.8, §69.15, §74, §82, §91.1, §92.2, §93.4, 95.2, §116.3, §127.1, §157, §174, 189n100, 209n402, 212n452. *See also* clerk and secretary, secretaryship
secretary, secretaryship, xxvi, xxix, xxxiv, §67, §93.4, §164, 192n138. *See also* clerk and scribe
selection. *See* ode
self-reliance (literary), xxxv, §52.8, 55.1. *See also* New Style, originality
Sha'ban (Ar. Sha'bān), §91.5, 203n322
Sharā, Mount, §20.2
Shawwal (Ar. Shawwāl), §165
al-Sijistānī, Abū Ḥātim Sahl ibn Muḥammad, xxxiii, §19.4, §71.4, §124
singer, §§100.1–2, §100.4
sīrah, pl. *siyar* (saga), §4.1
slave(s), §23.8, §§24.9–10, §24.29, §95.3, §98, §101.5, §116.1; as a metaphor, §71.3, §79.1, §93.4. *See also* freed slaves
song(s), §4.4, §§46.4–5, §69.18, §§100.1–4, 198n220, 206n366, 210n422
star(s) (in poetry), §4.5, §8, §§12.2–4, §13.5, §§24.15–16, §47.4, §48.1, §69.1, §§69.4–5, §69.11, §§69.13–15, §§69.18–20, §69.25, §69.27, §§91.1–2, §94.1, §101.1, §117, §150, §183, 184n8, 198n230, 198n231, 203n316, 209n406
stipend(s), xxv, §34.2, §36.1. *See also* poetry, payment for

al-ʿUtbī, Abū ʿAbd al-Raḥmān Muḥammad ibn Ubayd al-Umawī, §23.6, §46.2
Uways ibn ʿĀmir al-Murādī l-Qaranī, §92.1, 204n325
al-ʿUzzā, §86.3, 202n292

Wā'il. *See* Bakr ibn Wā'il
al-Walīd ibn ʿAbd al-Malik (Walīd I), §69.19, §78.5, §78.7
al-Walīd ibn Yazīd (Walīd II), §133, 185n13
waṣf. See description
al-Wāthiq, §§49.1–2, §50.1, §74, §93.4, §96, §171, §173, 188n66, 192n138, 199n244, 199n245
water. *See* metaphors
wine, xii, xxii–xxiii, §4.5, §40.2, §79.1, §§91.1–5, §93.4, §94.1, 203n317, 203n319, 203n322
wine song (*khamriyyah*), 198n220, 210n422
wording (*lafẓ*), xlin24, §30, §43.1, §47.1, §47.6, §52.8, §61.1, §69.18, 187n47, 189n100, 190n109, 190n117, 191n118, 191n121

Yaḥyā ibn ʿAlī ibn Yaḥyā l-Munajjim, Abū Aḥmad, §14.1, §23.9, §24.8, §103
Yaḥyā ibn Ḥamzah al-Ḥaḍramī, Abū ʿAbd al-Raḥmān, §133
Yaḥyā ibn Ismāʿīl al-Umawī (transmitter), §154
Yaʿqūb ibn Jaʿfar (transmitter), §116.3
Yaʿqūb ibn Isḥāq. *See* al-Kindī
Yazīd ibn Ḥātim ibn Qabīṣah ibn al-Muhallab ibn Abī Ṣufrah, §138
Yazīd ibn al-Muhallab ibn Abī Ṣufra, xxvi, §§78.5–6, §§147–148
Yazīd ibn Muḥammad. *See* al-Muhallabī
Yazīd ibn al-Ṭathriyyah. *See* Ibn al-Ṭathriyyah
Yazīd ibn Walīd (Yazīd III), §22.8, §133
Yemen, §17.1, §75, §78.1, §80.2, §172, 213n460
Yūnus ibn Ḥabīb, Abū Abd al-Raḥmān, §22.1

al-Zajjāj, Abū Isḥāq Ibrāhīm ibn al-Sarī, §23.9
zindīq (heretic), §49.1
Zufar. *See* Arṭāh ibn Suhayyah
Zuhayr ibn Abū Sulmā, §46.5, §86.5, §94.1
Zuhr, §78.5

About the NYU Abu Dhabi Institute

The Library of Arabic Literature is supported by a grant from the NYU Abu Dhabi Institute, a major hub of intellectual and creative activity and advanced research. The Institute hosts academic conferences, workshops, lectures, film series, performances, and other public programs directed both to audiences within the UAE and to the worldwide academic and research community. It is a center of the scholarly community for Abu Dhabi, bringing together faculty and researchers from institutions of higher learning throughout the region.

NYU Abu Dhabi, through the NYU Abu Dhabi Institute, is a world-class center of cutting-edge research, scholarship, and cultural activity. The Institute creates singular opportunities for leading researchers from across the arts, humanities, social sciences, sciences, engineering, and the professions to carry out creative scholarship and conduct research on issues of major disciplinary, multidisciplinary, and global significance.

About the Translator

Beatrice Gruendler (PhD Harvard University, 1995) has been Professor of Arabic at the Freie Universität Berlin since 2014. She has also taught at Yale University (1996–2014) and Dartmouth College (1995–96). Her main areas of research are the development of the Arabic script, classical Arabic poetry and its social context, the integration of modern literary theory into the study of Near Eastern literatures, and early Islamic book-culture (ninth century AD) viewed from the perspective of media history. Besides numerous articles, her major publications include: *The Development of the Arabic Scripts: From the Nabatean Era to the First Islamic Century* (1993, Arabic trans. 2004); *Medieval Arabic Praise Poetry: Ibn al-Rūmī and the Patron's Redemption* (2003); as contributing co-editor, *Understanding Near Eastern Literatures: A Spectrum of Interdisciplinary Approaches* (2000) and *Writers and Rulers: Perspectives from Abbasid to Safavid Times* (2004); and, as contributing editor, *Classical Arabic Humanities in Their Own Terms* (2007).

The Library of Arabic Literature

For more details on individual titles, visit www.libraryofarabicliterature.org

Classical Arabic Literature: A Library of Arabic Literature Anthology
Selected and translated by Geert Jan van Gelder (2012)

A Treasury of Virtues: Sayings, Sermons, and Teachings of ʿAlī, by al-Qāḍī al-Quḍāʿī, with the *One Hundred Proverbs* attributed to al-Jāḥiẓ
Edited and translated by Tahera Qutbuddin (2013)

The Epistle on Legal Theory, by al-Shāfiʿī
Edited and translated by Joseph E. Lowry (2013)

Leg over Leg, by Aḥmad Fāris al-Shidyāq
Edited and translated by Humphrey Davies (4 volumes; 2013–14)

Virtues of the Imām Aḥmad ibn Ḥanbal, by Ibn al-Jawzī
Edited and translated by Michael Cooperson (2 volumes; 2013–15)

The Epistle of Forgiveness, by Abū l-ʿAlāʾ al-Maʿarrī
Edited and translated by Geert Jan van Gelder and Gregor Schoeler (2 volumes; 2013–14)

The Principles of Sufism, by ʿĀʾishah al-Bāʿūniyyah
Edited and translated by Th. Emil Homerin (2014)

The Expeditions: An Early Biography of Muḥammad, by Maʿmar ibn Rāshid
Edited and translated by Sean W. Anthony (2014)

Two Arabic Travel Books

Accounts of China and India, by Abū Zayd al-Sīrāfī
Edited and translated by Tim Mackintosh-Smith (2014)

Mission to the Volga, by Aḥmad ibn Faḍlān
Edited and translated by James Montgomery (2014)

Disagreements of the Jurists: A Manual of Islamic Legal Theory, by al-Qāḍī al-Nuʿmān
Edited and translated by Devin J. Stewart (2015)

Consorts of the Caliphs: Women and the Court of Baghdad, by Ibn al-Sāʿī
Edited by Shawkat M. Toorawa and translated by the Editors of the Library of Arabic Literature (2015)

What ʿĪsā ibn Hishām Told Us, by Muḥammad al-Muwayliḥī
Edited and translated by Roger Allen (2 volumes; 2015)

The Life and Times of Abū Tammām, by Abū Bakr Muḥammad ibn Yaḥyā al-Ṣūlī
Edited and translated by Beatrice Gruendler (2015)

The Sword of Ambition: Bureaucratic Rivalry in Medieval Egypt, by ʿUthmān ibn Ibrāhīm al-Nābulusī
Edited and translated by Luke Yarbrough (2016)

Brains Confounded by the Ode of Abū Shādūf Expounded, by Yūsuf al-Shirbīnī
Edited and translated by Humphrey Davies (2 volumes; 2016)

Light in the Heavens: Sayings of the Prophet Muḥammad, by al-Qāḍī al-Quḍāʿī
Edited and translated by Tahera Qutbuddin (2016)

Risible Rhymes, by Muḥammad ibn Maḥfūẓ al-Sanhūrī
Edited and translated by Humphrey Davies (2016)

A Hundred and One Nights
Edited and translated by Bruce Fudge (2016)

The Excellence of the Arabs, by Ibn Qutaybah
Edited by James E. Montgomery and Peter Webb
Translated by Sarah Bowen Savant and Peter Webb (2017)

Scents and Flavors: A Syrian Cookbook
Edited and translated by Charles Perry (2017)

Arabian Satire: Poetry from 18th-Century Najd, by Ḥmēdān al-Shwēʿir
Edited and translated by Marcel Kurpershoek (2017)

In Darfur: An Account of the Sultanate and Its People, by Muḥammad ibn ʿUmar al-Tūnisī
Edited and translated by Humphrey Davies (2 volumes; 2018)

War Songs, by ʿAntarah ibn Shaddād
Edited by James E. Montgomery
Translated by James E. Montgomery with Richard Sieburth (2018)

Arabian Romantic: Poems on Bedouin Life and Love, by ʿAbdallah ibn Sbayyil
Edited and translated by Marcel Kurpershoek (2018)

Dīwān ʿAntarah ibn Shaddād: A Literary-Historical Study, by James E. Montgomery (2018)

English-only Paperbacks

Leg over Leg, by Aḥmad Fāris al-Shidyāq (2 volumes; 2015)

The Expeditions: An Early Biography of Muḥammad, by Maʿmar ibn Rāshid (2015)

The Epistle on Legal Theory: A Translation of al-Shāfiʿī's Risālah, by al-Shāfiʿī (2015)

The Epistle of Forgiveness, by Abū l-ʿAlāʾ al-Maʿarrī (2016)

The Principles of Sufism, by ʿĀʾishah al-Bāʿūniyyah (2016)

A Treasury of Virtues: Sayings, Sermons, and Teachings of ʿAlī, by al-Qāḍī al-Quḍāʿī with the *One Hundred Proverbs* attributed to al-Jāḥiẓ (2016)

The Life of Ibn Ḥanbal, by Ibn al-Jawzī (2016)

Mission to the Volga, by Ibn Faḍlān (2017)

Accounts of China and India, by Abū Zayd al-Sīrāfī (2017)

A Hundred and One Nights (2017)

Disagreements of the Jurists: A Manual of Islamic Legal Theory, by al-Qāḍī al-Nuʿmān (2017)

What ʿĪsā ibn Hishām Told Us, by Muḥammad al-Muwayliḥī (2018)

War Songs, by ʿAntarah ibn Shaddād (2018)

The Life and Times of Abū Tammām, by Abū Bakr Muḥammad ibn Yaḥyā al-Ṣūlī (2018)